RACE, LABOR, AND VIOLENCE IN THE DELTA

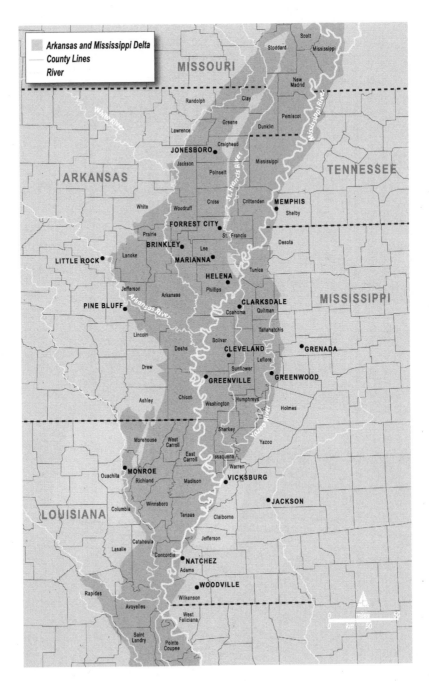

Cartography by Jack Critser.

RACE, LABOR, AND VIOLENCE IN THE DELTA

ESSAYS TO MARK THE CENTENNIAL OF THE ELAINE MASSACRE

EDITED BY
MICHAEL PIERCE AND CALVIN WHITE JR.

The University of Arkansas Press
Fayetteville • 2022

ISBN: 978-1-68226-205-4 (cloth)
ISBN: 978-1-68226-206-1 (paper)
eISBN: 978-1-61075-775-1

26 25 24 23 22   5 4 3 2 1

Manufactured in the United States of America

Designed by Liz Lester

∞ The paper used in this publication meets the minimum requirements of the American National Standard for Permanence of Paper for Printed Library Materials Z39.48–1984.

Library of Congress Cataloging-in-Publication Data
Names: Pierce, Michael C. (Michael Cain), editor. | White, Calvin, 1973– editor.
Title: Race, labor, and violence in the Delta: essays to mark the centennial of the Elaine Massacre / edited by Michael Pierce and Calvin White Jr.
Other titles: Essays to mark the centennial of the Elaine Massacre
Description: Fayetteville: University of Arkansas Press, 2022. | Includes bibliographical references and index. | Summary: "This essay collection grew out of a conference marking the hundredth anniversary of one of the nation's deadliest labor conflicts—the 1919 Elaine Massacre, during which white mobs ruthlessly slaughtered over two hundred African Americans across Phillips County, Arkansas, in response to a meeting of unionized Black sharecroppers. The essays here demonstrate that the brutality that unfolded in Phillips County was characteristic of the culture of race- and labor-based violence that prevailed in the century after the Civil War"—Provided by publisher.
Identifiers: LCCN 2021060183 (print) | LCCN 2021060184 (ebook) | ISBN 9781682262054 (cloth; alkaline paper) | ISBN 9781682262061 (paperback) | ISBN 9781610757751 (ebook)
Subjects: LCSH: African Americans—Violence against—Arkansas—Arkansas Delta—History—19th century—Congresses. | African Americans—Violence against—Arkansas—Arkansas Delta—History—20th century—Congresses. | African Americans—Arkansas—Arkansas Delta—Economic conditions—19th century—Congresses. | African Americans—Arkansas—Arkansas Delta—Economic conditions—20th century—Congresses. | Labor unions—Organizing—Arkansas—Arkansas Delta—Congresses. | Night riding (Racial violence)—Arkansas—Arkansas Delta—Congresses. | Elaine Massacre, Elaine, Ark., 1919—Congresses. | Arkansas Delta (Ark.)—Race relations—Congresses. | Mississippi River Delta (La.)—Race relations—Congresses.
Classification: LCC E185.93.A8 R335 2022 (print) | LCC E185.93.A8 (ebook) | DDC 976.700496073—dc23/eng/20211222
LC record available at https://lccn.loc.gov/2021060183
LC ebook record available at https://lccn.loc.gov/2021060184

COVER IMAGE: Joe Jones, *The Struggle in the South*, 1935 Commonwealth College Mural, oil on Masonite. *Courtesy of the Joe Jones Family; University of Arkansas at Little Rock (Center for Arkansas History and Culture and Department of Art and Design).*
COVER DESIGN: Erin Kirk

This project was supported by the Blair Legacy Series, a conference series of the University of Arkansas Diane D. Blair Center of Southern Politics & Society.

*To the men and women who fought against economic
and racial oppression in order to live what they believed
to be their true versions of freedom. May we never forget.*

*And to Trish, Ben, Sam, Shatara,
and Monroe, as inspirations always.*

CONTENTS

Acknowledgments ix

Introduction 3

CHAPTER 1

Black Agricultural Labor Activism and
White Oppression in the Arkansas Delta:
The Cotton Pickers' Strike of 1891
Matthew Hild 13

CHAPTER 2

"Night Riding Must Not Be Tolerated in Arkansas":
One State's Uneven War against Economic Vigilantism
Guy Lancaster 29

CHAPTER 3

Black Workers, White Nightriders, and the Supreme
Court's Changing View of the Thirteenth Amendment
William H. Pruden III 49

CHAPTER 4

Henry Lowery Lynching: A Legacy of the Elaine
Massacre?
Jeannie Whayne 65

CHAPTER 5

Black Women, Violence, and Criminality in Post–
World War I Arkansas, 1919–1922
Cherisse Jones-Branch 81

CHAPTER 6

Steadily Holding Our Heads above Water: The Flood
of 1927, White Violence, and Black Resistance to Labor
Exploitation in the Mississippi Delta
Michael Vinson Williams 95

CHAPTER 7

"Boss Man Tell Us to Get North": Mexican Labor
and Black Migration in Lincoln County, Arkansas,
1948–1955
Michael Pierce   *115*

CHAPTER 8

Sweet Willie Wine's 1969 Walk against Fear: Black
Activism and White Response in East Arkansas
Fifty Years after the Elaine Massacre
John A. Kirk   *133*

CHAPTER 9

"Sick and Sinister": Intersections of Violence and
the Struggle for Economic Justice in the Late
Twentieth Century
Greta de Jong   *151*

EPILOGUE

Evil in the Delta
Michael Honey   *167*

Notes   181

Contributors   223

Index   227

ACKNOWLEDGMENTS

The conference marking the centennial of the Elaine Massacre and this volume were both made possible by the financial and administrative support of the University of Arkansas's Diane D. Blair Center of Southern Politics & Society and Fulbright College of Arts and Sciences. Special thanks go to Angie Maxwell, Todd Shields, Kim Gillow, and Melinda Adams. The University of Arkansas Humanities Center and the University of Arkansas Department of History provided additional help. Our colleagues at Philander Smith College and the Mosaic Templars Cultural Center in Little Rock generously hosted the conference, showing scholars from across the nation the rare combination of professionalism and warmth that has long characterized both institutions. The efforts of Christina Schutt and Tamika Edwards are especially appreciated.

The contributions of other participants at the conference have improved this volume. These very fine scholars include Dianna Freelon Foster, Alison Greene, Karlos Hill, Story Matkin-Rawn, Brian Mitchell, Susan O'Donovan, Adolph Reed Jr., Touré Reed, Jarod Roll, Kenneth W. Warren, Patrick G. Williams, and Nan Woodruff.

At the University of Arkansas Press, Mike Bieker, David Scott Cunningham, James Fraleigh, Melissa King, Liz Lester, Charlie Shields, and Jenny Vos deserve praise for their expertise and professionalism. They have supported this project from the get-go and made the publication process as painless as possible.

Last but not least, thanks go to the University of Arkansas at Little Rock's (UALR's) Center for Arkansas History and Culture (CAHC) for restoring Joe Jones's *The Struggle in the South* and allowing us to use a portion of it on the cover. Jones painted the mural in 1935 for installation at Commonwealth College, a left-wing institution that was located near Mena, Arkansas. Abandoned when the college closed in 1940, the mural deteriorated until rescued by the folks at UALR. The beautifully restored mural is now on public display at UA Little Rock Downtown in the River Market District. CAHC director Deborah Baldwin and gallery director Brad Cushman deserve special gratitude for leading the conservation and preservation efforts and giving us permission to use the work.

RACE, LABOR, AND VIOLENCE IN THE DELTA

In late September 2019, seventeen historians from across the country traveled to the Mosaic Templars Cultural Center in Little Rock, Arkansas, to participate in an academic conference that marked the hundredth-year anniversary of the Elaine Massacre. Sponsored by the Diane D. Blair Center for the Study of Southern Politics & Society at the University of Arkansas, Fayetteville, the two-day conference ultimately resulted in the publication of this edited collection of essays.

The Elaine Massacre ranks among the deadliest episodes of both racial violence and labor suppression in the nation's history. It began on September 30, 1919, when a planter-directed posse of whites disrupted a meeting of the Progressive Farmers and Household Union of America near the tiny town of Elaine in southern Phillips County, Arkansas. Members of the posse shot into the church, in which nearly a hundred Black union members—mostly tenants, sharecroppers, and agricultural laborers—were meeting to coordinate collective action to prevent the worst abuses of the plantation system, especially the dishonest accounting that cheated the workers out of their promised shares, impoverished them, and perpetuated the peonage that kept them unfree. After those assembled in the church returned fire, possibly killing a posse member, white gangs flooded the area and began four days of indiscriminate killing of those African Americans suspected of being union members.[1]

The exact number of African Americans murdered that fall in the cotton fields near Elaine will never be known. White authorities probably never believed that the Black victims were worth counting and had reason to minimize the official numbers. Estimates of the number of deaths run into the hundreds. But some things are certain. The victims were not killed solely because of their race, nor were they killed just for joining a labor union (white people could join unions with little threat of death). They were killed because they were African Americans who refused to submit to the planters and organized to fight for economic justice.

The conference program and papers did not focus on the horrific events at Elaine—those have been carefully explored by several historians, including most recently Grif Stockley, Brian Mitchell, and Guy Lancaster—but instead looked more broadly at the intersections of race, labor, and violence in the Delta regions along the Mississippi River from Reconstruction into the post–Civil Rights Movement era. The broad focus was not intended to divert attention from the Elaine Massacre but to highlight the fact that the massacre was not an isolated episode. The underlying causes—sharecropping and tenancy, white supremacy, peonage, Jim Crow, disfranchisement—arose from the chaos of the Civil War as the planter class tried to reassert the types of hegemony it enjoyed before emancipation and freedpeople attempted to realize the nation's promise that "all men are created equal." Perhaps more importantly, the papers also make clear that many of the conditions that gave rise to the massacre continued through the twentieth century and reckon with the persistence of racial and economic inequality in one of the nation's most impoverished regions. The nation's promise has yet to be redeemed.

During the two-day event, historians presented research that examined the delicate dance that occurred between Black laborers and white landowners and how their interactions profoundly shaped the region's history, economy, and culture. Delta landowners continued to depend upon cheap labor after the Civil War and, like those in other cotton-growing regions, devised methods designed to keep vestiges of slavery in place. The result was a system of peonage that continued to exploit Blacks and often poor whites for their labor. Keenly aware of their exploitation, laborers developed their own methods of garnering what they felt to be a more equitable share of the profits. They employed strikes, union formation, and the ultimate display of agency—the physical movement of their bodies—to fight their exploitation. The struggle against Jim Crow and racial exploitation in the Delta was necessarily a fight for better working conditions, fair labor practices, and economic justice. Such brazen acts of resistance, though, often resulted in racial violence at the hands of "nightriders"—armed mobs aided by state and local officials. Therefore, the ultimate purpose of this three-part essay collection is to highlight the violence that occurred at the intersection of labor and race in the Arkansas, Mississippi, and Louisiana Deltas. Essays touch on themes of migration, nightriding, the federal government's increasing unwillingness to protect the labor rights of freedpeople, lynching, the criminalization of Black bodies, the Great Flood of 1927, the bracero program, the violence of the economic marketplace, and the 1969 "march against fear."

The Elaine Massacre and the effort to reexamine the racial violence that occurred throughout the Delta formed our central reason for assembling, but this volume has a larger purpose: to remember the people who lost their lives and property struggling for racial and economic justice in the region. That makes this volume personal, a way of honoring William Woods, my maternal great-great-grandfather, who like many others was violently pushed off his land in the late 1920s. William Woods homesteaded 177 acres in Calhoun County, Arkansas, just south of the town of Harrell in 1903. He lived on this land for more than twenty years before whites burned his home and threatened to kill him if he returned to his farm. Tenacious in his efforts, he returned only to be arrested and held in jail for nine days. Upon release, my great-great-grandfather was told in no uncertain terms that, if he ever returned to his property, he and his family would be killed. This act of economic violence plunged his family into destitute poverty. However, Grandpa Will never gave up on his farm, and some twenty years later he was still writing to state officials seeking justice. In a letter to Gov. Homer Adkins, he pleaded for help to get his farm back. Astonishingly, he received a reply from Adkins's executive secretary simply stating that "I would suggest that you employ a competent lawyer to look after your interest." Like thousands of other African Americans who were pushed off their land, my great-great-grandfather's story is yet another example of the state's failure to protect its Black citizens as they were exploited for their land, labor, and economic wellbeing.[2]

Essays in part 1 of the collection illuminate Arkansas's history of reacting violently to labor activists and their activities after Reconstruction and through the World War I era. Matthew Hild's examination of the 1891 cotton pickers' strike in eastern Arkansas argues that the rise of Jim Crow and racial segregation in the state made it easier for planters to employ mass violence to defeat the efforts of Black workers to attain economic justice. Hild highlights attempts in the 1880s to bring Black and white workers together in organizations such as the Agricultural Wheel, the Knights of Labor, and the Union Labor Party. The biracial nature of these labor groups seemed to offer some protection for Black strikers, with Hild using a cotton pickers' strike in 1886 at the Tate Plantation in Pulaski County to show how such disputes did not have to end with mass killings. But the threat that these biracial groups in league with the Republican Party posed to the Democratic Party's hegemony led the ruling party to fan the flames of racial hatred, pass laws mandating the segregation of races in public life, and take steps to disfranchise African Americans and many poor whites. The subsequent collapse of biracial organizing left Black workers more vulnerable to violent attack by landowners and employers. This was most clearly illustrated during the 1891 cotton pickers' strike in Lee County that saw white posses execute or jail twenty-one Black strikers. Hild suggests that the segregation of labor organizations made it easier for planters to employ mass violence against Black strikers, which was certainly the case at Elaine.

Guy Lancaster's essay takes a deep look into the practice of nightriding in Arkansas. Revealing that it had become commonplace after the arrival of Jim Crow in the 1890s, Lancaster explains the difference between lynching and nightriding, two modes of inflicting terror that are often confused as the same. Whereas the brutal practice of lynching usually played out mostly in towns and served as grotesque communal events that brought members of the white community together, nightriding was a rural phenomenon that revealed deep cleavages within the white community. Nightriding typically stemmed from lower-class whites' economic grievances with either African Americans as a result of competing for work and wages in local markets or white landowners who preferred cheaper Black labor. Unlike lynching, nightriding disturbed white merchants and planters, who suffered property loss and often found themselves on the receiving end of intimidation and violent acts for employing Black workers. As a result of whites' victimization, the General Assembly sought to increase punishments for the perpetrators, resulting in the passage of Act 112 in 1909. Lancaster makes clear that the passage of this measure was more about protecting the economic interests of white employers than halting violence against Black laborers. He notes that some of the Black men arrested during the Elaine Massacre were charged with nightriding.

William H. Pruden III's essay expands the examination of the practice of nightriding in Arkansas to show the federal government's increasing unwillingness after the turn of the twentieth century to use the Reconstruction Amendments to protect Black workers from violent assaults. Pruden's research centers on two cases, *United States v. Morris* (1903) and *Hodges v. United States* (1906), that involved groups of white men who intimidated Black sharecroppers and sawmill laborers in Cross and Poinsett Counties. Sawmill owner Jim Davis petitioned local authorities to protect his property and Black workers from threats made by nightriders who wanted jobs at the sawmill to be reserved for whites, but the powers that be in the county sympathized with the night marauders and rejected Davis's pleas. The nightriders' efforts to prevent Black men from working at Davis's sawmill caught the attention of William G. Whipple, the U.S. attorney for the Eastern District of Arkansas, who ultimately brought charges against several men for violating the Civil Rights Act of 1866. The lower court ruled that the Thirteenth Amendment empowered Congress to pass the measure and protect the employment rights of freedpeople and their descendants. The Supreme Court, though, disagreed, ruling in *Hodges v. United States* that the Thirteenth Amendment no longer gave Congress such power. Pruden argues that the Supreme Court's decision was not only part of the Court's long retreat from using the Reconstruction Amendments to protect African Americans but also a manifestation of laissez-faire constitutionalism, the idea that the Constitution requires governments to remain neutral concerning labor relations so as to allow the natural working of the free market. Pruden concludes by noting that the Supreme Court only began to dismantle the legal underpinnings of Jim Crow and disfranchisement after New Deal constitutionalism replaced laissez-faire constitutionalism.

Jeannie Whayne's essay focuses on the horrific and highly publicized 1921 lynching of Henry Lowery in Mississippi County, Arkansas, to highlight the continued brutality the plantation system meted out to Black laborers who dared challenge the economic status quo to gain more control over their lives. Whayne shows that Lowery's resistance, in the form of a request for a written statement of his sharecropper's account, and subsequent lynching were not a consequence of the Elaine Massacre but rather "business as usual" on Delta plantations locked in the grip of a global cotton economy that made no room for conscience or heart. Much like the Elaine Massacre, Lowery's lynching prompted negative press nationally and became a potent symbol in the National Association for the Advancement of Colored People's (NAACP's) campaign to end racial terror.

Essays in part 2 of the collection examine the continued violence upon Black bodies in the post–World War I period in Arkansas and Mississippi. Cherisse Jones-Branch's essay focuses on labor and its impact on Black Arkansan women in this era, arguing that they were victimized by their employers as well as the state. Arkansas presented little economic opportunity for Black women after the Great War. By criminalizing their poverty through vague statues like "disturbing the peace," or forcing many of them into lives of petty crime such as bootlegging, the state increasingly sought to control Black women's bodies through the courts and prison system. The justice system then denied these women their femininity and the social protections provided to white women. Jones-Branch shows that once incarcerated, Black women were forced to work as domestics in the homes of corrections officials as the state subjected their bodies to sexual and physical abuse. She painstakingly concludes that Black women's participation in "criminal" enterprises were forms of resistance to being shut out of lawful enterprises and that the carceral state sought to extinguish this resistance by degrading their bodies.

Michael Vinson Williams's essay continues the theme of Black resistance through an examination of the Great Flood of 1927's effects on African American labor in the Mississippi Delta. Williams highlights that not only did people and institutions create situations that allowed for the exploitation of labor, but so did nature. Rains started to fall throughout the Mississippi Valley in August of 1926, and by April of the following year, floodwaters had devastated 170 counties in seven states, with the Delta, especially in Arkansas, Mississippi, and Louisiana, getting the worst of it. Williams, focusing on the Greenville, Mississippi, area, notes that African Americans saw the flood as an opportunity to escape their plantation existence, while their white counterparts viewed it as another threat to their ongoing efforts to control their Black labor force. To keep Black people bound to the land, whites in the region employed several tactics. Among those were compelling railroad agents to refuse to sell tickets to Black men and women, conscripting Black citizens into work camps where they were economically and physically brutalized, and, when necessary, committing overt violence. Most troubling, officials referred to African American citizens as "refugees," restricting their movement to such an extent that outsiders wondered if the Civil War had been fought and the Emancipation Proclamation ever written and signed. As Williams shows, whites demanded their labor to fortify Delta towns, reinforce levees, and repair damage to plantation lands. As this dynamic played out, Black men and women, as they had always done, resisted, which resulted in several violent episodes throughout Mississippi and Arkansas.

As the waters receded and the Federal government funded the rebuilding of the levee system, exploitation of Black workers worsened. Williams reveals that the NAACP ultimately brought national attention to the conditions Black southerners were facing. NAACP officials Walter White and Roy Wilkins took up the mantle of resistance for those who could not fight for themselves. Publicly lambasting President Hoover as well as the War Department (which managed flood control), White and Wilkins made the exploitation and squalor Black people faced in the flood camps part of the national conversation. They met with success in 1933, when New Deal officials acceded to many of the NAACP's demands by increasing pay and reducing working hours. In this way, the flood contributed to focusing Civil Rights organizations' attention upon extracting change from the Democratic Party leadership.

Essays in part 3 of the collection evaluate violence and resistance in post–World War II Arkansas, Mississippi, and Louisiana. Michael Pierce's essay offers a critical examination of the bracero program and its consequences for Black labor in Lincoln County, Arkansas, in the 1950s. Challenging the widely accepted historiography of the program in the Arkansas Delta, Pierce takes issue with the notion that the arrival of Mexican workers helped break down Jim Crow. Pierce shows that mechanization and federally mandated crop reductions led to the demise of the sharecropping system and caused a surplus of Black labor in cotton-growing areas. Fearful of a pool of poor, landless, and underemployed Black agricultural laborers, planters turned to braceros for their labor needs and then plotted to push the Black workers, who they had long denigrated and on whom they no longer depended, out of the region. As always, Blacks resisted, in this case with Ethel Dawson, an employee of the National Council of Churches, leading the way in Lincoln County. Although unsuccessful, Dawson's campaign shows how planters employed different racial groups as part of their scheme to maintain near absolute control in the region.

John Kirk's essay uses Lance Watson's "walk against fear," a protest march across eastern Arkansas that began almost exactly fifty years after the Elaine Massacre, to highlight both the continuity of Black resistance that stretched back to the Elaine Massacre (and before) and the discontinuities in white reaction. By the time Watson—also known as Sweet Willie Wine—walked from West Memphis to Little Rock to protest the lack of opportunity afforded Blacks in the Delta, overt white supremacist violence directed at demonstrators had dramatically declined. Kirk contends that the turning point in how whites responded to Black activism happened sometime after World War II. Violence directed at those who resisted white supremacy slowly decreased, giving way to the policing of Blacks' bodies and actions in the name of law and order. Kirk conveys both how overt violence receded in the Delta and how authorities devised new methods to regulate Black lives.

Greta de Jong's essay examines efforts to improve the living and working conditions of Blacks in Mississippi and Louisiana in the aftermath of the legislative triumphs of the 1960s that restored their voting rights and legal protections. She argues that violence against Black workers and their families took new forms in this era, emphasizing three. The violence of the market dehumanized African Americans and left them unable to find jobs with living wages as the fields became almost fully mechanized. There was also violence directed against those running and participating in the antipoverty programs that grew out of the Great Society. This violence weakened these programs, leaving most Black families in grinding poverty and the region poor. The white political reaction to these antipoverty programs formed the core of a third type of violence: an ideology that preached austerity at home and lavish military spending abroad. Ronald Reagan and his successors cut investments in people, claiming that the spending was wasteful and the recipients unworthy, while plunging the nation into debt to pay for weapon programs and overseas follies. This debt in turn became an excuse to cut domestic spending and make lives more precarious. Thus, de Jong roots the rise of the nation's current prevailing political ideology in the response of the Delta elite to the triumph of the Civil Rights Movement and the federal programs designed to improve the lot of the region's Black workers and their families.

Michael Honey's essay serves as the epilogue of the volume. Twofold in purpose, Honey places the Elaine Massacre in national context while highlighting the life of John Handcox, who, Honey asserts, represented the very personification of Black resistance to white supremacy in Arkansas. The violence Honey chronicles, although horrific and brutal, reveals that what occurred in Arkansas was part of a much larger wave of racial unrest overtaking America in 1919. Known as the Red Summer, violence against Blacks occurred in Washington, DC; Chicago, Illinois; Rosewood, Florida; and later, Tulsa, Oklahoma. Honey also offers a lens through which to view the violence, explaining that as African American soldiers returned from World War I, they had increased expectations of their country, while whites longed for a return to normalcy, placing the two at odds, which resulted in violence. Labor activities often served as the catalyst of such violence, as revealed in Elaine. Honey also shows that long after Elaine, Blacks continued to organize unions to combat white supremacy, and John Handcox's life personifies that effort. Born in 1904 in eastern Arkansas, Handcox learned at an early age the importance of the Black church and its usefulness in the fight against white supremacy. Consequently, songs and lessons Handcox learned from the institution later influenced his labor activities in Arkansas and beyond. As the Great Depression gripped the American economy, Handcox and his family found themselves facing many of the same conditions that prompted the events leading to Elaine. Honey reveals that in many ways John Handcox and his labor activities continued the tradition of resistance in Arkansas until the start of the national Civil Rights Movement. In fact, lessons and songs that had long been part of the labor movement were incorporated into and became synonymous with the Civil Rights Movement in Arkansas and beyond.

CHAPTER 1

Black Agricultural Labor Activism and White Oppression in the Arkansas Delta

The Cotton Pickers' Strike of 1891

MATTHEW HILD

ON SEPTEMBER 29, 1891, a posse of armed white men led by the sheriff of Lee County, Arkansas, stormed Cat Island in the Mississippi River and killed two African American men. The posse captured nine more Black men, all of whom would soon be lynched. This bloodshed marked the culmination of a strike by cotton pickers that had begun earlier in the month. The strike lasted less than two weeks, and the ensuing violence left approximately sixteen men—all of them African American except for one white plantation manager—dead.

Historians have typically associated this strike with the Colored Farmers' Alliance.[1] To do so is not incorrect; the Colored Alliance was active across the South when the strike occurred, and its leader, a white Baptist minister named Richard M. Humphrey, had, as historian William F. Holmes has noted, "worked to organize cotton pickers for [such] a strike" during the summer that preceded it.[2] But the emphasis on the Colored Farmers' Alliance overlooks the broader and longer history of activism among African American farmers and farm laborers in Arkansas and across the South. In Arkansas, such activism began before the Civil War ended, and it was particularly prevalent in (although not confined to) the state's Delta region. Like their brethren across the South, Black workers in the Delta joined a plethora of biracial organizations, including the Union League, the Agricultural Wheel, and the Knights of Labor, that served as vehicles for demanding economic and political rights. Black Arkansans also lined up behind white-led political parties—not only the Republican Party but also some short-lived producerist parties—to secure full citizenship and challenge the Democratic Party's ideology of white supremacy and elite control. Only after white racism narrowed the organizational opportunities for Black agricultural laborers starting in the late 1880s and Jim Crow was imposed in the early 1890s did they join segregated organizations like the Colored Farmers' Alliance. When viewed from this perspective, the Lee County cotton pickers' strike of 1891 assumes a greater significance than just being the deadly flashpoint of the Colored Alliance's brief career. Although white landowners had long resorted to violence to prevent Black laborers from organizing, the cotton pickers' strike signaled a new phase of Black worker suppression in the Delta—one in which it was easier for planters and their allies to employ mass violence to keep Black workers from demanding greater rights. Thus, the 1891 cotton pickers' strike foreshadowed the still bloodier Elaine Massacre in nearby Phillips County twenty-eight years later.

Tensions between Black agricultural laborers and white landowners began before the Civil War even ended. In dealing with landowners, the workers took advantage of new regulations issued by the U.S. Army that required a monthly minimum wage, and, even more importantly, they exploited a labor shortage on the plantations. Even when Black labor activists secured white support, the result could be violence and death. For instance, a group of newly freed Black farm laborers in Phillips County refused to work until their northern lessee agreed to their demands regarding wages and work rules. Shortly after the war, the formerly enslaved Bryant Singfield began organizing the newly free people in Phillips County who had stayed on the plantations of their former masters as contract laborers. Federal military commanders stationed in Helena "encouraged and assisted" Singfield in these efforts, according to the recollection of a former slave. Some of Singfield's followers then took the bold step of leaving their employers' plantations and moving onto abandoned land that they began farming as their own. A group of white planters, led by Singfield's former master (and future county sheriff) Bart Turner, retaliated, rounding up Singfield and several others who were involved in this budding labor protest and apparently killing them. Local legend later held that Singfield's ghost haunted a swamp where he was killed.[3]

Black agricultural workers also looked to the political arena to secure their civil and labor rights. While labor protests were isolated events, many more Black men in Arkansas asserted their rights by registering to vote in the wake of Congress's passage of the Third Reconstruction Act in 1867 and the granting of universal manhood suffrage in the state constitution of 1868. Assisted by the Union League, which was started by northerners during the Civil War, some twenty-two thousand Black men registered to vote in Arkansas between May and November 1868. This required a great deal of resolve and courage, as the Ku Klux Klan, which emerged in Arkansas in late 1867, began a campaign of violence and terror against Republicans of both races. As the presidential and congressional elections approached in 1868, the Klan and other groups associated with the Democratic Party killed more than two hundred Arkansans, mostly African Americans but also some white Republicans. Most but not all of this violence occurred in the Delta or other cotton-growing regions. For instance, along the Red River in southwestern Arkansas that summer, Klansmen killed about twenty men, most of them African Americans.[4]

African American support for the Republican Party paid dividends, though. African Americans served in the state's General Assembly as well as county and local offices. Perhaps more importantly, Republican governors and legislatures enacted some meaningful measures to benefit African Americans despite such violent opposition. For example, the Arkansas Civil Rights Act of 1873 preceded the federal Civil Rights Act of 1875 in barring segregation in most public venues. But after Democrats "redeemed" Arkansas in 1874 under the banner "A White Man's Party for a White Man's Land," the state's Republican Party soon became moribund. Fourteen years would pass before another competitive governor's race occurred.[5]

Nevertheless, a new political party—the Greenback Party—soon offered Arkansas farmers and workers, both white and Black, a new outlet for challenging the dominance of the state's Democratic Party and its planter-driven agenda. Agrarian reformers and, to a lesser extent, labor activists, primarily from Midwestern and mid-Atlantic states, held a series of conferences during the mid-1870s that culminated in the formation of the Greenback (later Greenback-Labor) Party. The Greenback movement began as a protest against the national banking and monetary systems, which had created an inflexible currency that exacerbated the problems of the working classes by making credit scarce and expensive. More broadly, however, the Greenback Party developed an anti-monopoly platform with planks that appealed to farmers and workers regardless of race. For example, the party called for the prohibition of contract prison labor and the reservation of public lands for actual settlers rather than their sale to railroads or other corporations. In 1876, the party held a national convention in Indianapolis and nominated a presidential candidate, Peter Cooper of New York. Arkansas sent nine delegates to the convention; the only other former Confederate state to send delegates was Tennessee. In September 1876, a small contingent of Arkansas Greenbackers held what they ambitiously deemed a "state convention" in Little Rock, and Arkansas was the only former Confederate state that counted any votes for Cooper in November, albeit a meager 289. But the Greenback Party's protest against the national system of money and banking and its anti-monopolist ideology nevertheless gained enough adherents to allow it to persist for the next several years.

While the Greenback Party never seriously challenged the Democrats' dominance in Arkansas—it never elected a congressman or state officer, and at its peak in 1878 it won only 7 of the state legislature's 124 seats— it nevertheless drew support from farmers and the state's nascent labor movement and appealed to voters across the color line.[6] In Little Rock, the party swept the municipal elections in 1878, and Isaac T. Gillam, a former slave and Union veteran who was serving as a Republican alderman in the capital city at the time, won election to the state legislature as a Greenbacker.[7] In 1882, the Greenback Party ran its last statewide campaign in Arkansas, as Rufus K. Garland of Nevada County received only 6.9 percent of the vote in a three-man race for the governor's office.[8]

Even as the Greenback Party collapsed in the early 1880s, Arkansas farmers and laborers began to form or join nonpartisan organizations that demanded similar reforms on behalf of producers. The National Grange of the Order of the Patrons of Husbandry had entered Arkansas in 1872 and organized only among the state's white farmers, but by the late 1870s it had already lost most of those members. In 1882, two homegrown farmers' groups emerged in the state to fill the void. A small group of farmers in Prairie County, located on the western edge of the Arkansas Delta, formed the Agricultural Wheel, while the Brothers of Freedom emerged in western Arkansas's Johnson County, an area of rockier soil where coal mining communities were emerging. The Wheel and the Brothers, which would merge under the name of the former in 1885, both expressed a producerist ideology that echoed the antimonopolism of the Greenback Party. They complained that nonproducers—bankers, gamblers, middlemen, monopolists, and stock speculators—were becoming rich while the farmers and workers that actually produced the nation's wealth were struggling. W. Scott Morgan, an early leader of the Wheel, succinctly expressed the outlook of many of his followers when he condemned "the infamous trusts that have become an incubus upon our body politic."[9]

Such a view of the political economy made these farmers' organizations sympathetic to the budding national labor organization of the day, the Pennsylvania-based Knights of Labor, which entered Arkansas at the end of 1882. The Knights declared in the preamble of its 1878 platform that "[t]he alarming development and aggressiveness of great capitalists and corporations, unless checked, will inevitably lead to the pauperization and hopeless degradation of the toiling masses."[10] The Knights of Labor entered the state by chartering a local assembly (or lodge) in Hot Springs of white men, mostly carpenters and clerks.[11]

Despite similarities in their producer-oriented ideologies, the Knights of Labor and the Arkansas farmers' organizations did not initially see eye to eye on issues of race. The Agricultural Wheel did not admit African Americans or women until 1886, by which time the organization had reached enough other southern states to call itself the National Agricultural Wheel. The Knights of Labor, however, had no such restrictions, welcoming Blacks and whites as well as men and women, skilled and unskilled alike. The second Knights local assembly in the state, also chartered in Hot Springs in January 1883, consisted of African American men, and soon women, both white and Black, joined the Knights' ranks in Arkansas as well. The Knights organized farmers as readily as industrial laborers and led the way in the organization of African American farmers and farm laborers in Arkansas, along with an all-Black farmers' group in the Arkansas Delta called the Sons of the Agricultural Star. (In Prairie County, the founder of the National [Northern] Farmers' Alliance, Milton George, established an all-Black lodge of that organization in 1882, but it apparently failed to last long.)[12] Thus, the Knights became the primary vehicle for African American farm labor activism across the South in the mid-to-late 1880s, most notably in leading a strike of predominantly Black sugar cane cutters in southeastern Louisiana that ended with the murder of as many as sixty Black men, women, and children at Thibodaux.[13]

In Arkansas, too, Black farm laborers struck for higher wages under the aegis of the Knights of Labor, and it is possible that its biracial structure prevented the outbreak of mass killing that characterized Thibodaux and later the Arkansas cotton pickers' strike. In June 1886, Dan Fraser Tomson, one of the founders of the first Knights local assembly in Arkansas, began to organize African American farmworkers on plantations south of Little Rock in Pulaski County. In the face of stiff resistance from planters,

Tomson procured the assistance of a Black Knight, G. W. Merriman, who had served two terms as the master workman of a local assembly in Argenta (later North Little Rock).[14] On Thursday, July 1, 1886, at the Tate Plantation, about thirty farmhands, men and women, went on strike demanding a raise from seventy-five cents to one dollar per day "until the [cotton crop] was out of the grass" and payment in cash rather than scrip that could only be spent at the plantation store. Knights of Labor from Little Rock assisted the striking farmhands, bringing meat, flour, and meal to feed families as they remained on the plantation over the weekend. On Monday, July 5, at 5:00 in the morning, Sheriff Robert Worthen arrived at the plantation with several deputies. The officers approached the house of one of the strike leaders, Hugh Gill, "called him out of bed and to the door," and then shot him with a double-barreled shotgun, wounding him in both arms. When this news spread throughout Pulaski County, about 250 Black men, many of them armed, rushed to the scene. Worthen and the deputies remained inside Gill's house and called for reinforcements to be sent from Little Rock. When the posse of twenty-seven men arrived that evening, some of its members fired shots. A few newspaper accounts reported that the strikers fired shots as well, but Arkansas Knights of Labor state master workman E. H. Ritchie claimed that the strikers, under the guidance of Tomson and Merriman, "refused to return fire, . . . preferring death rather than to violate the law or resort to violence." No one was seriously hurt that evening, but the posse dispersed many of the Black men on the scene. On July 7, the strike ended, as most of the strikers returned to work without their demands being met.[15] Given the propensity of white planters and officials to violently suppress Black farm labor activism in Arkansas, especially in the decades after the brief existence of the Knights of Labor, this episode stands out for its relatively peaceful resolution. Unlike most of the other episodes, though, a well-known white local labor leader (Tomson) was on the scene.

The Knights of Labor's efforts in Arkansas pushed it into closer contact with the Agricultural Wheel. The Tate Plantation strike came on the heels of the Great Southwest railroad strike, a much larger Knights of Labor conflict that occurred across several states from the Midwest to the Southwest, including Arkansas. The railroad strike witnessed not only widespread worker militancy but also gained popular support across the state. This would not be enough, though. The strike ultimately failed under the weight of heavy-handed oppression, from police forces, judges, and, in Arkansas, the state militia sent by Gov. Simon Hughes.[16]

In the aftermath of the Tate Plantation and Great Southwest strikes, the Knights of Labor informally joined the Agricultural Wheel's effort to challenge Democrats like Governor Hughes who had mobilized against the strikers. The challenge initially amounted to little. The Wheel's 1886 candidate for governor, former Granger and Greenbacker Charles E. Cunningham, received only 11.7 percent of the vote in a three-man race that saw Hughes's reelection.[17] But this modest Wheel–Knights coalition of 1886 grew considerably after several hundred agrarian and labor reformers created a new party, the Union Labor Party, at a conference in Cincinnati, Ohio. Even though that party never amounted to much nationally, it waged (with the support of Arkansas's Republican Party) spirited campaigns that attracted widespread support, only failing to take control of the state government in 1888 and 1890 because Democrats used fraud and violence, including murders, to remain in power. Most infamously, Democrats assassinated the Union Labor–supported Republican John M. Clayton in Plumerville (Conway County) in January 1889 while he was gathering evidence to support his contested election case before the U.S. House of Representatives. (The House later ruled that Clayton had indeed won the election and declared the seat vacant pending a special election, which the unseated Democrat, Clifton R. Breckinridge, won.)[18]

Arkansas's 1890 elections witnessed similar violence and fraud, prompting the state's Democratic lawmakers to take preemptive measures to crush the interracial, working-class challenge to their hegemony.[19] In 1891, the Democrat-controlled state legislature hardened the color line by mandating Jim Crow in Arkansas railroad cars (as well as waiting rooms in train stations) with the "separate coach" law and also began passing "election reform" laws that would disfranchise most Black men as well as many poor white ones. These efforts led to what historian Kenneth C. Barnes calls "a harsher, more inflexible form of white racism" that was accompanied by violent policing of the color line and increasing episodes of lynching.[20]

As Arkansas Democrats embraced Jim Crow and disfranchisement in the early 1890s, the Agricultural Wheel, which had been biracial since 1886 when it began chartering "colored Wheels," expelled its Black members. While the new political climate probably encouraged the expulsion, the process actually had begun in December 1888, when the Texas-based Southern Farmers' Alliance and the National Agricultural Wheel agreed to a merger in which the latter would be absorbed by the former. Ratification of the agreement occurred at the state level, and, not surprisingly, opposition to the merger proved strongest in Arkansas, where it was not ratified until early 1891. Unlike the Wheel, the Southern Farmers' Alliance restricted membership to whites only, which meant that white Wheel lodges were absorbed into the Alliance but "colored Wheel" lodges were not.

African American farmers in Arkansas thus had little choice but to turn to an all-Black organization that had begun in Texas, the Colored Farmers' Alliance. This process began before the merger of the Wheel into the Southern Alliance became complete, the white general superintendent (president) of the Colored Alliance, Richard M. Humphrey, claiming that his organization had twenty thousand members in Arkansas by December 1890.[21] The relationship between the Southern Alliance and the Colored Alliance, however, proved fraught, in part since many members of the latter organization worked for members of the former. As historian Charles Postel has noted, the Colored Alliance was both "segregated and subordinated."[22] On the other hand, the Knights of Labor, which still had about 3,500 members in the state in 1890, remained active among Black workers as well as white ones, albeit usually in segregated local assemblies.[23]

More so than any of the earlier producerist organizations, the Colored Farmers' Alliance was the target of violent attacks. In many respects, the Colored Alliance had less in common with the white Southern Alliance than it did with the Knights of Labor insofar as the South's Black agricultural laborers were concerned. The Knights and Colored Alliance both made attempts at cooperative enterprises among Black farmers and farm workers, they both mobilized their Black members politically, and they both led strikes among Black farm workers. But white landowners rarely targeted the biracial Knights as they did the Colored Alliance. In the Delta county of Leflore, Mississippi, Black farm workers began joining the Colored Alliance in the summer of 1889. At the urging of an African American leader named Oliver Cromwell, Colored Alliance members began taking their business away from local merchants in favor of a Southern Farmers' Alliance cooperative store in the railroad town of Durant, about thirty miles south of Leflore County.[24] In nearby Grenada County, newspaper reports suggested that Black cotton pickers, who were being paid fifty cents per hundred pounds, "have organized and will demand an increase in their wages or guard the fields with shotguns and prevent others from gathering crops."[25] The *Washington Bee* reported that the Alliance cooperative store at Durant had sold more than two hundred guns to African Americans on credit, and in early September 1889 newspapers warned that African Americans were plotting a race war in Leflore County. Gov. Robert Lowry sent National Guardsmen into Leflore, and what became known as the Leflore County Massacre ended with the murder of about twenty-five African Americans. Cromwell, a traveling Colored Alliance organizer, was not among the victims, having fled Leflore County before the bloodshed began and apparently succeeding in leaving Mississippi. After the massacre, a group of planters met in the Leflore County town of Sunnyside and passed a resolution in which they condemned the Colored Alliance for "being diverted from its original or supposed purpose and . . . being used by designing and corrupt Negroes to further their intentions and selfish motive[s]."[26] William F. Holmes, who examined the massacre in 1973, concluded that the reports of an impending Black uprising were a mere "pretext" for using violence to crush the Colored Alliance, and that white planters and officials took those measures because "the Blacks pursued policies aimed at bettering their economic conditions and lessening their dependence upon whites."[27]

While the Leflore County Massacre destroyed the Colored Farmers' Alliance in that part of Mississippi, the organization continued to grow elsewhere in the South. In Arkansas, by the summer of 1890, the Colored Alliance, the Knights of Labor, and Colored State Wheel lodges all coexisted, with some overlapping membership, and were all close to the Union Labor Party. Pending ratification of the Southern Farmers' Alliance–Agricultural Wheel merger, the Colored State Wheel held its annual meeting in July 1890, at which time it reelected its president, G. W. Lowe, who also represented Monroe County in the General Assembly as a member of the Union Labor Party. Likewise, the Knights of Labor, which had formed local assemblies in most Arkansas Delta counties in the latter half of the 1880s, continued to attract Black farm workers. For example, in St. Francis County, the Knights organized at least six local assemblies, at least two of which consisted of or included farmhands. Knights of Labor records often fail to indicate the racial composition of local assemblies, but since "colored Wheels" existed in St. Francis County, most likely at least one of the Knights locals of farmhands consisted of African Americans. In Phillips County, one of the two known Knights assemblies organized Black cotton oil mill, sawmill, and cotton compress workers. The Knights chartered at least three locals in Lee County, at least one of which, in LaGrange, existed at least as late as 1890.[28] In contrast to the national membership of the Knights of Labor, which was rapidly declining by 1890, membership in Arkansas fell much more slowly, from a reported peak of about 5,400 members in 1887 to about 3,500 three years later.[29]

Amid these organizational changes, Colored Farmers' Alliance superintendent (president) Humphrey issued a circular on September 6, 1891, calling for cotton pickers across the South to strike on Saturday, September 12, for a wage of one dollar per hundred pounds. Newspapers across the nation carried the story, along with Humphrey's claim that over a million African American cotton pickers would participate and his insistence that they were to "avoid all gatherings in public places and all insolent displays." Humphrey signed the circular with the title "General Superintendent Colored Farmers' Alliance and Cotton-Pickers' League."[30] According to William F. Holmes, Humphrey formed the Cotton-Pickers' League as sort of an adjunct organization "after he encountered opposition to the strike within the Colored Alliance." Holmes asserts that while African American tenants "had always formed a large part of the Colored Alliance, the organization had catered chiefly to the interests of landowners."[31] A more recent study by Charles Postel suggests otherwise, stating that most members of the Colored Alliance "suffered acute land hunger, mainly toiling on the land of white owners as sharecroppers and day laborers."[32] In the Arkansas Delta, judging from more readily available evidence about the composition of Knights of Labor and Agricultural Wheel lodges, Postel's assessment rings truer. In Woodruff County, where African Americans outnumbered whites, the Knights and Wheel jointly "petitioned the landholders for a reduction of land rent of 25 percent per acre."[33]

Not surprisingly, the major newspapers of the South treated Humphrey's strike proposal with a mixture of scorn and malice. For example, the *Atlanta Constitution* denounced the Colored Alliance leader's plan as "rash" and his demands as "absurdly extravagant." The newspaper also opined that "the negroes very generally understand the situation, and it will take something more than Humphrey's order to plunge them into a strike which promises so little and threatens so much of evil to themselves."[34] The *Houston Daily Post* reported that east Texas planters were "not a bit alarmed" by the proposed strike, adding, "Such a movement if successfully carried out would cause the planters to lose some cotton, but there would be great distress and poverty among the strikers this winter if they lost the wages for cotton picking."[35] In Little Rock, the *Arkansas Democrat* struck a more balanced note: "The demand for $1 per hundred pounds is excessive and unreasonable, although we are free to say that the price fixed by the Cotton Planters' Association at its recent session (50 cents per hundred) is too low."[36]

African American cotton pickers mostly ignored Humphrey's strike call. William F. Holmes suggests the possibility that "the majority of cotton pickers—most of whom were illiterate—never knew of the proposed strike." Colored Alliancemen in East Texas, where that organization had begun, debated whether to strike, most refusing. Cotton pickers struck on a farm near Palestine, Texas, but their employer simply fired them, thus scuttling the strike. Newspapers across the South, in Holmes's words, "ridiculed" Humphrey in the days following September 12, 1891.[37]

Without attracting much public notice, however, a thirty-year old African American labor organizer from Memphis named Ben Patterson —"most likely," according to historian Steven Hahn, "a member of the Colored Alliance"—arrived in Lee County, Arkansas, in early September 1891 and began organizing cotton pickers in preparation for a strike. Local pickers quickly took an active role in organizing activities. On September 20, eight days after Humphrey's proposed regionwide walkout had fizzled, a cotton pickers' strike began in Lee County. J. F. Frank, a Memphis resident who owned cotton fields in Lee County, told one of his Arkansas plantation managers, Tom Miller, that he would pay one dollar per hundred pounds if necessary to hasten the pace at which the pickers worked. Frank made this statement, which Holmes deems "probably . . . an idle boast," on the front porch of a general store. Some nearby cotton pickers overheard Frank's statement and reported it to Patterson, who decided that the opportune moment for the strike had arrived. Cotton pickers left the fields of the plantation managed by Miller as well as the nearby plantation of Col. H. P. Rodgers.[38]

Manager Miller settled the strike by giving the pickers a raise from fifty to sixty cents per hundred pounds, although Frank later received a letter from fellow planters warning that such a course of action was not permissible. Rodgers reacted the same way that the planter in Palestine, Texas, had earlier that month: he fired the strikers and made them leave his plantation. But the strikers soon came back, tried to convince other pickers to join their cause, and began recruiting pickers on nearby plantations. Meanwhile, Patterson went to Marianna, the county seat, and made a public speech attempting to garner support for the strike.

Violence erupted on September 25 as strikers entered one plantation and met resistance from the pickers at work. The melee resulted in the killing of two pickers. White men in Lee County then formed a posse, led by the county sheriff, in response not only to the violence but also to the increasing effectiveness of the strike, which had led to a noticeable decrease in the picking of cotton. On September 28, someone murdered Miller while he was riding on horseback to join the posse. Frank suggested that angry whites may have done this in retaliation for Miller giving pickers a raise, but most accounts blamed either Ben Patterson or two strikers, the brothers Mit and Early Jones, who had worked for Miller. The killing of Miller, of course, escalated white anger and panic and also drew "the condemnation of many Blacks in Lee County, some of whom joined the white posse to search for the strikers." Whites from neighboring Crittenden County swelled the posse's ranks as did deputy sheriffs from Phillips County.[39]

On September 29, the posse caught up with most of the strikers at a gin house on Cat Island in the Mississippi River just downstream from Memphis. The posse quickly killed two strikers and captured nine others. Two escaped, including a wounded Ben Patterson. As two deputies were ostensibly taking the captives to the Marianna jail, a mob of masked white men seized the nine men and hanged them. When Patterson boarded a boat docked at Cat Island later that night, crew members discovered his identity, and, when the boat stopped at Hackney's Landing, armed white men boarded and killed him. The cotton pickers' strike came to an end. Fifteen Black men, along with one white man, were dead, and six other Black men were imprisoned.[40]

The swift and severe repression of the Lee County cotton pickers' strike marked the end of the type of the African American farm labor activism that had found an outlet in organizations such as the Knights of Labor, the Agricultural Wheel, and the Colored Farmers' Alliance. In the aftermath of the strike, notes Holmes, "the Colored Alliance began to decline rapidly, and by 1892 only a remnant of the organization remained."[41] Neither the Southern Farmers' Alliance nor, more surprisingly, the Knights of Labor so much as issued a resolution of protest against the brutal manner in which the strikers were treated. Charles Postel suggests that the dismal failure of the cotton pickers' strike and its aftermath "put in stark relief the evolution of the Knights' leadership, which by this time had placed their fate in a coalition with white planters and farmers and had turned their backs on the Black poor."[42] By this point, the decline of the Knights in Arkansas was catching up to the organization's national deterioration. While a state labor convention in Little

Rock in June 1892 drew about seventy-five delegates, most of them craft unionists, the annual meeting of the Arkansas Knights of Labor State Assembly in the same city three months later drew only sixteen delegates. The Knights of Labor managed to maintain a presence in Arkansas for more than another decade, holding State Assembly meetings as late as 1906, but by the mid-1890s, its era of significance had passed.[43]

The year 1891, then, proved to be a bleak one for African Americans in Arkansas on several significant counts: the passage of the Jim Crow railroad coach law, the beginning of disfranchisement measures, the end of the Colored State Wheel, and the brutal suppression of the Lee County cotton pickers' strike and destruction of the Colored Farmers' Alliance. Not surprisingly, many African Americans in the state became interested in the "Liberia Fever" and the back-to-Africa movement; some actually followed through while more left for Oklahoma but, of course, most remained in Arkansas.[44] The events of 1891 marked more of a turning point than a nadir for Black civil and political rights in Arkansas, however; in 1892, voters approved a poll tax that made it still harder for the state's poor Blacks and whites to vote, and, as Kenneth C. Barnes has argued, violence directed against African Americans intensified.[45] Not surprisingly, the People's (or Populist) Party, which in Arkansas absorbed the Union Labor Party, did not draw the same level of support in the state's elections as its predecessor had, and by the end of the 1890s it too was finished. Its decline accompanied that of not only the Knights of Labor but also the Southern Farmers' Alliance.[46]

Nevertheless, the farmer and labor movements in Arkansas persisted even as these organizations withered. Coal miners, who had been, in the western part of the state, an important component of the Knights of Labor, formed Arkansas chapters of the United Mine Workers of America (UMWA) before the decade ended.[47] But while the UMWA did organize African American miners (into segregated locals), in Arkansas the union failed to match even the limited racial egalitarianism of the Knights. In fact, historian Guy Lancaster has found it "likely that the union had a hand" in the Bonanza Race War of 1904, in which riotous whites expelled African Americans (some of whom were apparently UMWA members) from that Sebastian County town.[48] During that same year, UMWA leaders took the initiative in organizing the Arkansas State Federation of Labor, which affiliated with the American Federation of Labor and was less inclusive of African Americans and women than the Knights had been.[49]

Arkansas farmers, too, found a new organization. Like the Farmers' Alliances (Southern and Colored) before it, the National Farmers' Union began in Texas in 1902 before entering Arkansas the following year. Also like the Southern Farmers' Alliance, the Farmers' Union did not admit African Americans, and a Texas-based counterpart, the Colored Farmers' Union, soon entered Arkansas as well. But the white Farmers' Union proved no more willing to support its African American counterpart than the white Alliance had; in 1906, the Arkansas State Farmers' Union revoked the commissions of some organizers who had been working across the color line and forming Colored Farmers' Union locals.[50]

The relatively greater racial egalitarianism of the Knights of Labor and the Agricultural Wheel lived on only in smaller segments of the Arkansas farmer and labor movements. In 1905, Arkansas Socialists helped to organize the Industrial Workers of the World (IWW), which combined the "one big union" approach of the Knights of Labor with a more radical critique of capitalism. The IWW recruited timber workers in southern Arkansas, who had been some of the state's last Knights, and, during the mid-1910s, the union endeavored to organize Black tenant farmers and agricultural laborers in the Arkansas Delta.[51] Around the same time, Socialists, former Knights, and former Populists formed the Working Class Union (WCU), the membership of which consisted largely of Black and white tenant farmers, sharecroppers, and farmhands. The WCU led a strike of farmhands in the vicinity of Moffatt, Oklahoma, just across the state line from Fort Smith, Arkansas, in 1916, to raise their daily wages from $1.00 to $1.25. The strike failed, but it did not meet with the violent reprisal that the Lee County cotton pickers' strike of 1891 did.[52] Nevertheless, during World War I, the Socialist Party, IWW, and WCU would all meet their demise in Arkansas (and elsewhere) over their opposition to the nation's involvement in World War I, in particular the Selective Service Act of 1917.[53]

In more than just the most obvious manner (namely, the murder of Black farmworkers for engaging in strikes or union activity in the Arkansas Delta), the cotton pickers' strike of 1891 foreshadowed the Elaine Massacre. When the strike occurred, the biracialism (albeit limited) that had characterized the Arkansas farmer and labor movements under the influence of the Knights of Labor and (beginning in 1886) the Agricultural Wheel already had faded. Thus, the cotton pickers were unprotected by white allies, as the striking African American plantation workers in Pulaski County in 1886 had been in the form of white

Knights of Labor leader Dan Fraser Tomson, who came to the scene to prevent bloodshed. Similarly, the WCU farmhand strike just across the state line from Fort Smith in 1916 included both white and Black workers. Neither of these strikes had taken place in the Delta, but there too, interracial farmer and labor movements had existed in the 1880s and again in the early twentieth century until World War I. But by 1919, when African American tenant farmers and sharecroppers organized themselves into the Progressive Farmers and Household Union of America in Phillips County, they did so, like their Lee County predecessors in 1891, without the presence of white allies. The cotton pickers' strike of 1891 had suggested what could happen when Black farmworkers in all-Black organizations struck with no support or solidarity—or, in fact, with hostility—from white farmers' and farmers' groups. Occurring just after a brief period of even limited interracial inclusion and cooperation in the Arkansas farmer and labor movements, the outcome of the Lee County cotton pickers' strike demonstrated the enormous danger and risk for African American activists in the state during the era of Jim Crow.

CHAPTER 2

"Night Riding Must Not Be Tolerated in Arkansas"

One State's Uneven War against Economic Vigilantism

GUY LANCASTER

IN OCTOBER 1887, a "party of masked men" attacked Black tenant houses in Clover Bend in Lawrence County, Arkansas, and ordered the residents to leave the country. These tenants were employed by F. W. Tucker & Co., which had reportedly been using Black farmers since Reconstruction. The company contacted both the sheriff and Gov. Simon P. Hughes, the latter of whom responded, "Citizens everywhere must be protected against lawlessness and violence."[1] Nothing more about this incident seems to have been reported in state papers, but this is not unusual when it comes to those events typically labeled "nightriding" or "whitecapping"—the first term named after the tendency of such vigilantes to carry out their deeds at night and the second from occasional reports that said vigilantes wore masks or sometimes even hoods to conceal their identities.

Part of the difficulty underlying any study of nightriding/whitecapping is the diverse array of behaviors that fall under this category, especially when compared to lynching. For Christopher Waldrep, "There is no single behavior that can be called 'lynching.' Any attempt to impose a definition on such a diverse, subtle, and complex reality will inevitably miss the point."[2] Likewise, nightriding/whitecapping encompassed an array of activities that could be related to matters of race and/or labor but that sometimes seem typical of the era's generalized rural violence. Although a formal case inventory of nightriding violence has not yet been assembled to permit more rigorous analysis, such violence appears to have tapered off in the 1870s only to return after the Democratic Party consolidated power in the early 1890s, defeating the interracial Republican–Union Labor Party challenge that attempted to unite African Americans and nonelite whites under the banner of class.

In general, though, nightriding/whitecapping consisted of acts designed to intimidate others (from violent assaults carried out by vigilante groups to the simple posting of notices or transmission of threats through the mail), employed for a variety of motivations (from economic retaliation to moral regulation, or at least claims of such), and perpetrated by a range of people (from the landless and jobless to small farmers and much more prosperous members of the local community). Because such acts were typically rural, they often evaded the same level of analysis afforded to lynching, a form of violence that did occur in rural areas but, especially in the late nineteenth and early twentieth centuries, as often occurred in towns and cities, where it attracted more in-depth media coverage.[3]

This is not to say that nightriding violence was entirely separable from that of lynching. Historian W. Fitzhugh Brundage includes whitecappers and nightriders in his category of "terrorist mobs," denoting one of the more common groupings of lynching perpetrators.[4] Especially when its target was an African American individual, family, or community, nightriding could manifest itself as punishment for some perceived infraction. As historian Kidada E. Williams writes, "When African Americans were called on by nightriders, some testifiers reported that they pretended they were not at home. If Blacks could not hide, then they were forced to deal with the white men. Whites responded by attempting to draw their targets out of their homes, presumably to have Black people perform antebellum rituals of subjugation by presenting themselves to the supposed white victims of their transgression and then accepting whatever punishment those men or women delivered."[5] However, the "transgression" in question need not always be an actual crime—it could be as simple as owning land or having a job desired by a white man. According to historian William F. Holmes, in Mississippi "whitecapping specifically meant the attempt to force a person to abandon his home and property; it meant driving Negroes off land they owned or rented."[6] In a similar manner, one scholar situated his analysis of nightriding in the context of racial cleansing, or the expulsion of African Americans from certain geographical areas and certain industries, acts that were sometimes predicated upon allegations of criminality. These wholesale expulsions often occurred in the upland areas of northern and western Arkansas, though they did also happen in those northern parts of the

Delta that did not develop until the late nineteenth or early twentieth centuries, such as the railroad and timber towns of Paragould and Trumann.[7]

Like lynching, nightriding was terroristic violence. According to philosopher Claudia Card, "Terrorism does not always succeed in rousing terror. But it creates an atmosphere of grave uncertainty and insecurity in the face of what could be imminent danger. Uncertainty and insecurity can make fears reasonable."[8] For example, the posting of notices warning local Black residents to leave the area could easily be followed up with the impunity of violence, thus leaving everyone targeted in a state of insecurity and wondering whether they should heed such notices. However, it is important to point out that nightriding, unlike lynching, never became a predominantly racialized phenomenon and was never sanctioned by the economic and political elite.

In 1909, the Arkansas General Assembly passed Act 112, a law that defined nightriding and attached specific punishments to the act (as I will discuss). However, that same year, the legislature also passed Act 258. Often cast in media reports as an "anti-lynching" bill, Act 258 sought to expedite trials for those who stood a chance of being lynched. In other words, if a man was accused of a crime "calculated to arouse the passions of the people," the state would quickly try and convict him in order to prevent a lynching. The law, though, did not require that any participants in a lynch mob, or those officers who allowed mobs to abscond with their prisoners, actually face consequences for their deeds.[9] The reason for the disparity between the legislature's actions on lynching, a lethal practice, and the typically nonlethal nightriding is clear. Lynching functioned to keep the Black population terrorized and thus submissive, in accordance with elite desires, in addition to serving as a ritualized form of violence that created a sense of white solidarity across class, while nightriding often constituted a significant threat to elites. According to historian Jeannie M. Whayne, "the wrath of white nightriders was often directed at [white] planters. Not only did whites in the Arkansas Delta attempt to drive Blacks from plantations so they could secure tenancies themselves, they sometimes destroyed planter property to make their point."[10] Nightriders kicked up as often as they kicked down, committing acts of violence targeting their economic betters, such as cotton merchants and the owners of cotton gins.

Although a highly diverse phenomenon, nightriding deserves scholarly attention not simply to reveal both the ubiquity of violence to which African Americans were subject during the same time lynching remained a popular American custom and the class stratifications of the rural South, but also because, unlike lynching, nightriding in Arkansas produced a significant legal legacy, manifest in both state law and (as the next chapter will explore) a decision from the United States Supreme Court, *Hodges v. United States* (1906), that fundamentally changed the federal government's relationship with American citizens.

Nightriding before Act 112 of 1909

Arkansas newspapers of the late nineteenth and early twentieth centuries are rife with accounts of nightriding and whitecapping. While some of these events expanded into weeks-long conflicts that resulted in sensational trials, most appear as little more than a few lines of text in the newspapers, with no follow-up. This makes it challenging to reconstruct the aftermath of threats or assaults. Although this work does not offer a full accounting of nightriding in the Arkansas Delta, it is worth highlighting an array of cases to illustrate the diversity of the violence. That nightriding could threaten both the elite landowner as well as the landless sharecropper fueled the push to curb such violence through legislation and the courts.

Although they constituted a minority of such cases, there are accounts of nightriding for purposes of alleged moral regulation (though its practitioners may have had other motives). For example, on April 1, 1893, Les J. Ware, Charles Henson, B. Ray, Al Counts, George Counts, Jim Ballentine, John Burrows, and K. Payne, who had reportedly organized a whitecapping band "primarily for the purpose of ridding the community of objectionable characters," murdered George Black, described as "an inoffensive man," near Jonesboro in northeastern Arkansas and were subsequently arrested and jailed without bail.[11] Ware was convicted of voluntary manslaughter and given two years in prison, but the judge in April 1894 granted his appeal. As the *Arkansas Gazette* reported, "On account of the circumstances connected with the case, and the social and professional standing of Ware, who was a member of the Jonesboro bar, this case has attracted quite a share of public attention."[12]

Sometimes, those whom newspapers identify as whitecappers or nightriders could differ very little—in either methods or motivations—from a lynch mob seeking to maintain the color line. Louis White, a Black resident of Brandywine Island on the Arkansas side of the Mississippi River, was visited in late April 1894 by whitecappers Hess Colbert, Will and

Babe Jett, and John and Joe Rast, who suspected the Black man of entertaining visits from "a white widow." Colbert and the Jett brothers entered White's house, and "White fired on the intruders with a Winchester, killing Colbert." The woman in question was not found in his company, "and this fact saved White from being lynched." He was, however, arrested and charged with murder.[13]

Moral regulation often had racial dimensions. On November 12, 1899, Sam Gray, the bell ringer at Second Baptist Church in Helena, received a notice "ornamented with a rough drawing of a coffin, with an attempted drawing of a skull and crossed bones," to wit: "Six Whites Caps will see thet you stop the bell. You may think this a goke. For the safty of yur sef and Church members and your House we tell you two stop it."[14] This could roughly fall into the category of moral regulation if the whitecappers in question objected to the ringing of the bell too loudly or too early in the morning, though it may also be indicative of racial animosity, with the ringing reminding local whites that this Black church did actually have a bell, a fairly expensive accoutrement.

Moral regulation also manifested itself in activities designed to imitate those of law enforcement. In the White County town of West Point in May 1900, whitecappers murdered a Black schoolteacher named S. A. Jenkins. Reportedly, two town businesses had experienced recent break-ins, and a group of men who suspected Jenkins "went to his home and called him and another negro named Durham out, telling them they were under arrest. When they asked to be shown warrants the negroes were told to wait until they reached town." On the way, "seven more men" armed with shotguns accosted the pair and demanded a confession. Jenkins ran in fright and was shot in the back. The whitecappers "tried to make Durham confess, but did not succeed and let him go."[15]

Of greater concern to legal authorities were those manifestations of nightriding that occurred when rural whites tried to prevent local merchants from foreclosing on their farms. On March 24, 1894, authorities arrested six men—Henry Young, Henry Watson, J. P. Chisenhall, Rice Gerow, Bob Hudspeth, and John Kavanaugh—"on warrants charging them with complicity in the whitecap outrages which have disgraced the western portions of this, St. Francis County, for several months past." The six men were allegedly ringleaders of an organized band that carried out murder and arson in the area.[16] By the following month, fifteen such alleged whitecaps in total had been arrested. According to the *Osceola Times*, "The trouble arose from the failure of some of the farmers to discharge their obligations to the merchants, and the consequent fore-closure of mortgages held by the merchants. This, it is said, led to the burning of a number of farmhouses owned by the merchants, and it is for this offense that the parties under arrest were indicted."[17] As the case developed, authorities also accused the men of "intimidating and whip-ping the tenants on the farms of planters who had fallen under their displeasure, and with other forms of deviltry." By the time of the October trial, which was moved to the Phillips County Circuit Court, eleven sus-pected whitecappers remained under indictment, and some 150 witnesses were scheduled to testify. The *Arkansas Gazette* reported, "The popular impression is that an attempt will be made to prove an alibi on the part of all the accused," given that the farmers called to testify viewed the case "as a species of persecution."[18] On November 6, 1894, jurors acquitted Jim Bell, who was charged with burning the homes of H. A. Martin and Henry Banks, despite his previous confession to those crimes, his testimony before a St. Francis County grand jury, and "the corroborating testimony of the three negroes who witnessed the burning." As a consequence, the prosecutors abandoned the remaining cases.[19]

Although the St. Francis County episodes suggest that nightrid-ing was not an explicitly racialized phenomenon, perhaps the greatest number of incidents, especially in the late nineteenth and early twenti-eth centuries, entailed violence against rural African Americans for pur-poses of driving them off land or out of sectors of the local economy. In September 1897, *Helena Weekly World* published one such account from Phillips County:

> It appears that there are a couple of negroes on Mr. C. F. Fisher's place, about eight miles above Marvell, whom the whitecaps are anxious to run off, as it is thought they know something which the whitecaps would rather they wouldn't know. Several times lately there has been a great deal of shooting heard of nights near the Fisher place, and some claim to have run across the whitecaps in the public roads.

The paper's editorial in the same issue concluded: "The WORLD believes in upholding the law, but if there is one offence which calls for the prompt use of the shot-gun, it is this night-riding, white-cap warfare against igno-rant and defenseless negroes."[20] The following week, Sheriff R. C. Burke offered rewards for information leading to the conviction of the vigilantes in question—"$25 for each conviction."[21]

In its February 23, 1898, issue, the *Helena World* reported on a "gang of irresponsible men" in the Connells Point neighborhood of Turner in Phillips County who had "been terrorizing the defenseless negroes of that vicinity until they have actually succeeded in driving them out of the neighborhood." The motivation behind this action was the refusal to rent land "at reasonable prices" to local landless whites rather than to African Americans. These vigilantes had fired into Black houses, burned a cotton pen, and destroyed cotton seed owned by local planter Joe Brown, yet, though several people had been arrested, there was not enough evidence to charge them. The *Helena World* editorialized that such vigilantes "should be shot down like dogs."[22]

Later that spring, whitecappers attempted to drive African Americans out of the community of Hunter in Woodruff County. Among the targets was H. L. Baker, who employed a Black man on his place. Baker ignored the notice to fire his employee, and "on the following night, his house was surrounded by a mob and a fusillade of Winchester bullets fired into the building." A few nights passed before the mob showed up again, shot into his house, and set fire to his corn crib.[23]

In January 1902, whitecappers attracted attention in Monroe County for trying to drive away African American workers. At the community of Glenwood, eight miles east of Brinkley, fifteen whitecappers, who "had white sheets thrown over their horses and wore white masks," fired shots into a Black-occupied home on "A. Garraughty's place" and attacked the place of Tom Bateman. The whitecappers posted notices "in several places warning all the negroes to leave the community within ten days or suffer the consequences of remaining."[24] Four men were later arrested for their role in the affair, which included severely whipping several people.[25]

Some whitecappers employed violence, but others seemed to bet that threats, most commonly posted notices, would suffice to change behavior, especially given the history of violence in many areas. The *Arkansas Gazette* reported on January 29, 1898, that "warning notices have been posted on the front gates of negro citizens" in the town of Lonoke, "threatening them with dire vengeance unless they emigrate within thirty days." Other notices were posted at the local Black school warning teachers to cease their work, while a letter received by the *Gazette* claimed that "certain parties" had "been shooting and whipping negroes in that county for the past three years."[26] In either late 1904 or early 1905, "whitecaps, who style themselves the 'Lonoke County Club,' " posted notices on the cabins of African Americans living along the border of Lonoke and Jefferson

Counties, warning them to leave the county by January 10, after which point "this is to be a white man's country." Worried planters contacted law enforcement, and Deputy Sheriff C. Mason Philpot ventured to Dudley Lake Township, while Sheriff James Gould conferred with people in Pine Bluff before issuing a statement "that any interference with anyone in this county while in the peaceful pursuit of their labor will be prosecuted to the limit of the law."[27]

The *Arkansas Democrat* published a letter in February 1898 from J. C. Fiddyment, apparently of the Brinkley Stave and Heading Company, to Gov. Daniel Webster Jones asking the state to offer a reward for the conviction of whitecappers who had recently threatened both his Black tenants and those of landowners John L. Smith and J. S. Cox: "Our tenants have been notified by written notices to leave the neighborhood within ten days, or be killed." In response, Governor Jones proclaimed:

> Whereas, it has been made known to me that certain persons in Monroe and Lee counties have entered into a conspiracy to frighten and drive away the tenants (both white and colored) upon certain plantations near the town of Brinkley . . . I, Daniel W. Jones . . . do hereby offer a reward of $50 for the arrest and conviction of each of the said, conspirators, or persons who may be convicted in any breach of the law in and about the attempt to frighten said inhabitants from said neighborhood.[28]

Act 112 of 1909 and Its Legacy

Nightriding continued to disrupt Arkansas into the twentieth century, occurring in many of the same places, for many of the same reasons, and mostly targeting Black tenants and sharecroppers. However, it was not anti-Black attacks that motivated the state legislature to pass a law against the practice of nightriding. Instead, the legislators were more likely motivated by the sort of white-on-white violence that began in September 1908 near Lake City in Craighead County, for these attacks threatened the larger economic structure of the cotton economy.

On September 10, 1908, "a band of night-riders" appeared in the Lake City area and "warned several farmers to hold their cotton for the minimum sale price established at the meeting of the National Organization of the Farmers' Union recently at Fort Worth, Tex." The nightriders also complained about land rental rates, telling one farmer, A. L. Counce, that five dollars, presumably per acre, was too much, and demanded that another farmer, William Winnifred, cut his cotton acreage, which totaled 100 acres, in half. Still another farmer, unnamed by the *Arkansas Gazette*, was taking a bale of cotton to Lake City when nightriders stopped him and told him to "hold it for the minimum price."[29] The Arkansas Farmers' Union sought to distance itself from the episode, quickly declaring that any member found to engage in nightriding would be "fired bodily."[30]

The violence continued into late September, when nightriders struck nearby in Greene County, just north of Craighead, setting fire to four bales of cotton near the community of Mainswood and visiting farmers at Finch and Herrinville regarding "the selling, raising and ginning of cotton." According to the *Arkansas Democrat*, men near Walcott, along the Greene–Craighead county line, were known for "the strongest sentiment of any section of the country in favor of the policies said to be those of the night riders" and had "been committing all the depredations in Craighead and Greene counties."[31]

These acts prompted area cotton buyers to suspend their activities. The Marmaduke Farmers' Union had encouraged the suspension of cotton buying as a means of discouraging nightriders in the area. Merchants agreed to suspend until October 2, 1908, the day that a mass meeting of farmers and businessmen was scheduled in Paragould, but expressed the belief that the whole matter was "a scare," especially since many Greene County farmers were taking their crop to sell in Jonesboro.[32] This belief manifested itself soon, with local merchants rejecting a Farmers' Union plan to store cotton in union warehouses and market it through union agents; such an agreement would have allowed union influence over the marketing of cotton produced by nonmembers. Too, an investigation (though who conducted it remained unsaid in contemporary reports) concluded that "there are no organized bands of night riders in any part of the county" but merely a few agitated individuals, who had posted the notices and warnings to create a general feeling of unrest.[33]

The Arkansas Farmers' Union had to walk a fine line. It could scarcely risk being associated with violence, but neither could it alienate its members by distancing itself from efforts to implement its agenda. The National Farmers' Union had been founded in Point, Texas, in 1902, and the Arkansas state chapter was established the following year. The union carried forward some of the populist spirit of the Agricultural Wheel and the National Farmers' Alliance and Industrial Union of America, both of which had petered out in the late nineteenth century as the Democratic

Party adopted the rhetoric, if not the policies, of populism.[34] The union was already frequently at odds with cotton merchants and bankers, and so outbreaks of nightriding provided opportunities for criticizing the union. As eager as the Farmers' Union was to distance itself from the vigilantes, some of its leaders acknowledged that nightriders might well be among their dues-paying members. R. B. Snell, the union's state lecturer, insisted that "the Farmers' Union is not in any instance officially responsible for night riding; but probably some members of the union, who do not come up to as high an order of intelligence as the main body of members and officers, are in part responsible for this lawlessness."[35]

The *Arkansas Gazette* demanded that all nightriding, even "anonymous threatening letter writing by alleged jokers," must be stopped, explaining that Arkansas could ill afford to "become a by word for lawlessness, riot, violence, arson and murder," much like Kentucky, which was dealing with a significant outbreak of vigilantism known as the Black Patch War. The paper insisted that Kentucky could survive the bad publicity as it had much more developed resources, a diversity of industry and agriculture, and an increasing population to buffer it, but Arkansas could not. In particular, the *Gazette* worried that reports of violence in Arkansas, circulated both nationally and internationally, might dissuade immigrants: "[Arkansas] wants desirable immigrants from other states and from Europe; it needs outside capital for the development of its resources, and it needs labor to gather its harvests. It can get none of these blessings if night riding and anonymous threatening letters and arson and violence prevail."[36]

The fervent wish of the *Gazette* was not to be, as nightriding in northeastern Arkansas may have inspired similar acts around the state in early October 1908. A notice threatening to burn all gins operated by the Arkansas Valley Cotton Oil Company resulted in the closure of twelve cotton gins in Yell County.[37] Similar threats were posted on gins in various Saline County locations, just southwest of Little Rock.[38] Likewise, R. D. Tucker, a Black planter who had recently been elected justice of the peace in Pulaski County, received a warning to "refrain from running his gin for a period of 30 days or suffer dire penalties."[39] Meanwhile, Judge Frank Smith informed the grand jury of Craighead County that any person convicted in his court for the crime of nightriding would receive the stiffest sentence in his power to bestow.[40] And a mass meeting of Jackson County "business men, bankers, farmers, merchants, lawyers and doctors" called by the county Farmers' Union met in Newport and declared their faith in the union while "urging the necessity of crop diversification to control the price of cotton and better the condition of the farmer."[41] Acting Gov. Xenophon Overton Pindall released a statement at the end of the month to the effect "that he was not at all alarmed over the alleged night riding in Arkansas" but was willing to meet the governors of other affected states "to devise means of putting an end to the lawlessness."[42] The following month, the Randolph County Farmers' Union, in northeastern Arkansas, offered twenty-five dollars for information leading to the arrest and conviction of nightriders following a threatening letter sent to County Judge S. M. White.[43]

The wave of nightriding prompted lawmakers to take a stand against vigilantism when the Arkansas General Assembly went into session the following year. Rep. A. G. Little of Mississippi County started off his term of service by announcing plans to introduce in January 1909 what the *Fort Smith Times* called "a red-hot bill against night riding."[44] The *Arkansas Democrat* featured the newly minted state representative, complete with picture, in its "Among the Law Makers" section on January 21, 1909, due to his measure to suppress nightriding and whitecapping, noting that "his bill proposes such stringent punishment as will prevent the occurrence of such acts of violence as have visited Kentucky and Tennessee."[45]

Debates over Little's proposal were informed not only by developments in Arkansas but also by an ongoing conflict in Kentucky and Tennessee known as the Black Patch War. As Christopher Waldrep writes, "Black Patch farmers grew their tobacco chiefly for export," and so were buffeted by the global market and economic turndowns.[46] Much like the Arkansas cotton growers who engaged in nightriding, some tobacco growers turned to cooperative efforts to assert some control over the market and targeted the buyers and "hillbilly" farmers who remained independent and refused to participate. Nightriding violence went on for several years in Kentucky and Tennessee, taking the form of attacks upon people and property such as barns, fields, and livestock. Not only did cooperative growers attack independent ones, but sharecroppers attacked landlords. As historian Suzanne Marshall explains, "Violent behavior in these cases might be directed toward people other than the landlord, such as relatives or neighbors." Violence only increased as people felt impotent in the face of an immense global economy.[47]

Nightriding and whitecapping alarmed the business class across the South. William F. Holmes noted that such vigilantism in 1890s Mississippi "taught many responsible businessmen, newspaper editors, and public officials the dangers inherent in such lawlessness. Not only was white-capping unfair and unjustified, it also hurt Mississippi economically. It forced some businessmen to leave the state, it discouraged others from coming, and it even caused some insurance companies to consider cancelling policies on cotton gins owned by merchants. Finally, it threatened to create a serious labor shortage by driving away Negro labor."[48] Granted, lynching was also unfair and unjustified, but it rarely ever threatened the upper crust during this period, and so it remained a permissible—if not encouraged—form of social control.[49]

Arkansas's anti-nightriding law began life amidst widespread elite concern that such violence threatened property and challenged to the economic order. Upon its introduction, Representative Little's bill made its way through the Arkansas General Assembly with remarkable ease, encountering no obstacles in committee and being approved unanimously in both the House and Senate. Gov. George Washington Donaghey signed the bill into law on April 6, 1909.[50] Dubbed "an act to suppress and punish nightriding and other riotous conspiracies," Act 112 sought to address not only those actions that were already illegal, such as burning down somebody's barn, but also acts of intimidation. For example, Section 1 of the law criminalized "going forth armed and disguised for the purpose of intimidating or alarming any person" as well as meeting or acting "clandestinely with any such band or order, be such organization known as nightriders, Black hand, white caps, or by any other name." Sections 2 and 3 specifically tackled the delivery of any "letter, notice or other written or printed communication intended to, or which by its nature, contents or superscription would, naturally alarm or intimidate any person," as well as the use of "any writing, drawing or printed matter, or . . . the delivery of matches or bundles of switches or other things" for purposes of intimidation.[51]

After the passage of Act 112, the *Arkansas Gazette*, in an editorial praising the punishment of nightriders in Tennessee, asserted: "The people of Arkansas have cause to congratulate themselves that the night rider spirit has not asserted itself in this state. Last fall there were faint outcroppings of it, showing that it existed in a dormant state, but there were no overt acts of a serious character." The editorial went on to praise the recently passed Act 112 as "an effective deterrent to any future manifestations of the night rider spirit in Arkansas."[52] Other newspapers endorsed the measure by reprinting the bill in whole or in part.[53]

Less than one month following the passage of the anti-nightriding law, the deputy prosecuting attorney of Lonoke County made use of it, indicting George Granberry Jr., Verbon Leggett, and Frank Rexer.[54] The three were alleged to have traveled "to the home of Henry Beavers, a negro, and called for him late in the night," telling him "that he was under arrest." When Beavers came out, "they surrounded him, cursed him and told him to pray," and, when he fled, they fired at him but could not determine "whether any of the shots took effect."[55] The *Democrat* reported, "There are four charges against Granberry, two for night riding and one each for carrying a pistol and resisting an officer, while only two charges of night riding are preferred against the two others."[56] Although the trial was set to begin on August 13, it was continued until the February term on account of the lawyer for the accused, U.S. senator Jeff Davis, being unavailable. The Granberry family was prominent in the county, and having a former governor and current U.S. senator serve as the family lawyer signified their status. By February, however, the senator was still in Washington, DC, and the case was continued yet again, until the August 1910 term, the judge announcing that the trial would absolutely take place then.[57] In the end, Granberry was fined fifty dollars for carrying a pistol and twenty dollars for impersonating an officer.[58]

The honor of being "the first white man to be given a penitentiary sentence in this state under the new law against night riding" went to one J. R. Bush of Jefferson County. Bush was "engaged to work at a sawmill" but allegedly became troubled over "differences between white and negro labor," likely the lower salaries of Black laborers, which made them more attractive for employers and probably earned them longer hours. Bush, in response, fired shots into "a negro settlement of millworkers, it appears, for the purpose of intimidating them." For that, he received thirty days in the state penitentiary.[59]

Northeastern Arkansas continued to be an epicenter of nightriding, but convictions were still hard to come by. In October 1911, a Black cotton picker working on the farm of John Rice near Bono in Craighead County received a "threatening letter telling him he must leave the country." Although Sam S. Ratton was arrested and charged with nightriding in connection to this affair, jurors acquitted him.[60] The following May, forty-eight "well known farmers" in western Craighead County were arrested and charged with nightriding after allegedly giving notice "to all the negro help of John W. Whipple and J. Reidman to 'skiddo' quick from those parts and not come back." However, the grand jury did not find sufficient evidence to warrant a trial.[61]

A major incident of nightriding occurred in April 1912 near the northeastern Arkansas town of Walnut Ridge in Lawrence County. There, a vigilante group styling itself "Kit Karson and Band" posted notices ordering Black residents to leave the community. Despite a committee of leading white citizens asserting that "white people will arm their servants with instructions to shoot the first intruders who disturb them," unidentified white men terrorized the Black part of town for several hours on the night of April 19, dynamiting one Black-owned home and firing shots into another." Governor Donaghey called out the local militia to restore order, but, by the time it arrived, about half of the Black population had fled. Later in the month, authorities arrested thirteen men on charges of nightriding, including Robert McCall, the alleged leader of the gang. On May 1, 1912, however, the first trial—that of George Nance—ended in acquittal, and all the other men were soon released on the condition that they "keep the peace."[62]

In August 1913, Craighead County sheriff Mark Phillips arrested four white men—George Broadaway, George Woodruff, B. F. Woodruff, and V. S. Kingston—who allegedly "posted a notice at the mill of Barney & Hines at Anderson's Spur," in a remote part of western Craighead County, "ordering all negroes to leave the mill and threatening them with death if they did not obey." Reportedly, the fact that management at the mill employed Black labor had created "ill-feeling" among the people of Anderson's Spur for some time.[63]

Lonoke County also continued to be a hotspot for nightriding activity, even after passage of Act 112. In early 1914, authorities arraigned John Beavers, Hard Lyons, and Matt Thomas on charges of nightriding. The three men were alleged to have shot into a local plantation with the aim of driving Black laborers away.[64] On September 9, 1914, one Jess Cook reportedly made "a demonstration" at "a negro settlement six miles north of England," for which he was arrested on a charge of nightriding.[65]

On November 7, 1914, a group of vigilantes went to a timber camp of the Weona Land Company, located in the St. Francis River bottoms in eastern Poinsett County, "where negro laborers had been imported a few days previously." Prosecutors alleged that the men "exploded dynamite bombs around the camp," in addition to posting notices "giving warning that negroes would not be tolerated in that community." Twenty men were charged, but thirteen of those were freed after examination.[66] Six men were later acquitted and sued the prosecutors, for which they were each awarded $100 in damages.[67]

Nightriding and whitecapping often occurred at the nexus of labor and racial concerns, but sometimes people were charged with the crime of nightriding for carrying out acts of moral regulation. For instance, in May 1913, Fenlon Wood, in the Greene County community of Finch, allegedly "wrote a note, to which was attached a bundle of switches, warning Mrs. Nannie McClure . . . that if she again received attention from certain persons she would be punished."[68]

While many juries refused to convict those accused of nightriding, sometimes prosecutions were successful. In early March 1915, nightriders posted notices around the O'Donnell Bend area northeast of Osceola in Mississippi County warning that houses would be burned if Black workers were not turned out. Authorities moved quickly against the vigilantes, arresting five and later bringing in two more suspects; three of these seven (Mark Rogers, Jesse Swafford, and Giles Simpson) were later indicted. Swafford turned state's evidence against the others, and all three men were thus convicted and received sentences ranging from one year for Swafford to seven and a half years for Rogers. While delivering his instructions to the grand jury, Judge W. J. Driver announced that "if anyone ever loses his life while engaged in night riding, the man who kills him in defense of his home shall never go to jail for the act so long as the court has the power to set aside the verdict of guilty."[69]

The difference between how the state—and the South in general—regarded nightriding versus how it regarded lynching continued to expand as the years passed and more and more men were arrested, charged, and even sometimes convicted. Starting in March 1915, a wave of nightriding charges hit Arkansas County. It began when authorities arrested a white man by the name of Smith for having allegedly posted notices in the town of Gillett, warning African Americans to leave.[70] Over the next few months, Sheriff E. B. LaFargue charged more than a dozen men with nightriding. An editorial in *The Monticellonian* observed: "Usually night riders first direct their energies toward negroes. And if they are allowed to go unwhipped of punishment for this they grow bolder and attack any other person who may have aroused their displeasure."[71] Attorneys from neighboring counties traveled to Arkansas County to assist in prosecuting the alleged nightriders, six white men—brothers Ben, George, Garland, and Harvey Bulley, Bryant Harrison, and Glen Morris—who were each indicted on murder, arson, and nightriding charges growing out of the murder of an African American and the burning of his home.[72]

Ongoing violence led Gov. Charles Hillman Brough in October 1920 to denounce "lawlessness in some of our counties growing out of the prevailing low price of cotton" and to issue a proclamation "calling upon the adjutant general of the state and the sheriffs of all counties in which there have been disturbances to use every effort in upholding the law."[73] He later told the *New York Herald*, however, that farmers were justified in holding back their cotton in an effort to reestablish the cotton market.[74] The state commissioner of mines, manufactures, and agriculture, Jim Ferguson, had a similar message following an October meeting of state agricultural commissioners in Washington, DC, insisting that "prejudice is being created in the North . . . against the Southern farmer" as a result of nightriding and that "farmers would never solve the problem of obtaining higher prices for their product by such methods." He urged farmers, instead, to organize and build bonded warehouses where cotton could be stored the year around, rather than dumping it on the market all at the same time.[75] In Jackson County, the county farm demonstrator, A. W. Milling, circulated a petition that, as of late October 1920, had been signed by twelve of the largest cotton growers, committing them to reducing "the yield at not less than 50 per cent of their holdings" as a means of trying to raise the price of cotton." The report in the *Democrat* connected this sort of collective action with keeping violence at bay, writing, "So far Jackson County has had no trouble with the night riding gang."[76] Pressure to take "prompt and vigorous action" against nightriders was also coming from insurance companies, who were threatening "a withdrawal of insurance policies from cotton, cotton gins and warehouses" unless local authorities guaranteed "a proper measure of protection."[77]

During the same month that Milling was circulating his petition and the insurance companies were threatening to cancel policies, White County authorities charged eight local farmers with nightriding, and seven allegedly confessed. Those who confessed said that the campaign of intimidation had been planned at a Farmers' Union meeting, which had to be a blow to union officials who had worked for years to distance themselves from vigilantism. The nightriders sent letters containing matches to gin operators in and around Bald Knob, writing, "These gins must cease to run until cotton is 40 cents a pound. If these gins do not stop them [*sic*], these matches will." Among those arrested was one J. W. Fuller, who, according to the *Arkansas Democrat*, had been charged with burning down a barn at the town of Denmark two years earlier and received a suspended sentence for the deed. Reportedly, the confessions included information on additional persons who had favored stronger measures against gin operators.[78] The eight men were eventually fined twenty-five dollars for violating an anti-anarchist statute passed in 1919.[79] Meanwhile, in Crittenden County, three men—T. H. Smithson, J. R. Shepherd, and R. B. Shepherd—were arrested two days after visiting three Black families "picking cotton in a field near Earle," telling them "to quit picking cotton and to leave the community at once, under penalty of being killed." The three families were said to have fled that night. Charges of nightriding were later reduced to disturbing the peace, and each man was sentenced to a $500 fine and twelve months in jail.[80]

On April 11, 1921, authorities in Craighead County issued arrest warrants for thirty-nine men near the town of Bay in the eastern part of the county who had allegedly threatened cotton growers and burned gins, barns, and some dwellings during the slump in cotton prices the previous year. According to the *Democrat*, "There was also much bitterness over alleged unfair treatment of sharecroppers by landlords in the division of the crops. Nearly all the farmers in the section involved are tenant farmers." Gov. Thomas McRae sent a deputy fire marshal to the area to investigate the arson. By April 12, nine people had been arrested, including E. Bowman, whose trip to Jonesboro on April 9 had aroused suspicions that he was giving information against the nightriders. His fellow vigilantes held him captive upon his return and threatened his life before releasing him, and, when Bowman mentioned this to some of his neighbors, these neighbors traveled to Jonesboro to inform the prosecuting attorney of what they had learned.[81] By the morning of April 13, ten more people had been arrested on charges of nightriding, arson, or both, all of them living in the vicinity of Bay, Lake City, or Lunsford.[82] By week's end, twenty-six of the thirty-nine charged had been arrested by Sheriff Walter Johnson, and bond was placed at $2,000 each.[83] The circuit court term began on Monday, April 18, by which time thirty had been charged. Judge R. E. L. Johnson instructed the grand jury that "lawlessness had been going on for three years in and around Lake City and that it had been impossible to get a jury that would indict the guilty persons. He urged the jury to do its full duty in all cases."[84]

By the start of the trial, thirty-one men had been indicted. The first man on the docket was DeWitt Garrett, charged with both arson and nightriding. The star witness for the prosecution was Chester Freeman, who was stopped by the nightriders near the house of Dr. H. H. McAdams and was compelled to take part in burning the house. Fellow vigilantes William Moon and Heeke Bowman turned state's evidence against

Garrett and testified to being at the burning of the house, as did Bob Story, who, like Freeman, insisted that he was forced to take part with the threat of violence.[85] Among the other witnesses was General Greeson, a farmer near Lake City, who testified that he had received a notice in handwriting he recognized as Garrett's, warning that he would "suffer the consequences" if he planted more than one-third of his cultivated area with cotton. On the stand, Garrett denied any involvement and insisted that "he had offered to assist financially in running down the night riders." His mother testified that he had never left the house on the night the McAdams place burned. However, before the case went to the jury, Garrett pleaded guilty and threw himself upon the mercy of the court.[86] This created a cascade as twenty of the accused followed suit, while ten were exonerated due to lack of evidence. The sentences ranged from two months to one year in the state penitentiary; ten men had their sentences deferred so they might make a crop on their farms.[87] Following this trial, authorities issued warrants for the arrest of twenty more Craighead County farmers on charges of nightriding.[88] Governor McRae pardoned DeWitt Garrett and another man, Everett Kincade, each of whom had been sentenced to one year. Garrett, by this time, was "said to be suffering ill health in addition to having incurred a paralyzed arm" resulting from being shot by notorious outlaw Tom Slaughter during Slaughter's September 18, 1921, attempt to escape Tucker Prison Farm.[89]

The highly publicized trials of Garrett and his co-conspirators in April 1921 did not have the desired effect of bringing an end to nightriding in the Arkansas Delta. That same month, a Craighead County grand jury indicted John Coward on a separate charge of nightriding, having been arrested for posting notices on a gin at Bono in the fall of 1920.[90] In September 1921, J. W. Barnett of Hickory Ridge in Cross County was put on trial for nightriding after having allegedly "placed several sticks of dynamite under the residence of W. R. Malone . . . with whom he had quarreled."[91] Seven men who resided in the Butlerville area of Lonoke County were arrested on November 24, 1922, on various charges following their alleged attempt to assassinate the local sheriff; two other suspects were still at large. The sheriff had been called to the door of his home and shot in the face. As the *Pine Bluff Daily Graphic* reported, "The attack supposedly resulted from his aid to prohibition officers."[92]

Aftermath

If the purpose of a law is to dissuade individuals from perpetrating criminal activities, then Act 112, in the estimation of Jeannie M. Whayne, "had been ineffective." Part of this lay in its implementation, for "although passed at the behest of planters who felt powerless to conserve their labor force, the law was used as often to quell vigilante violence perpetrated by whites against other whites. In at least one case it was used to suppress striking workers."[93] However, the law also has a darker legacy that makes visible the same superstructure of white supremacy and elite rule underlying the *Hodges* case covered in the next chapter. Act 112 of 1909 was rife with the potential for abuse, given that it specifically condemned "intimidating or alarming any person," and white elites may well have found any number of activities intimidating or alarming when conducted by African Americans. Thus, charges of nightriding were at times leveled against the very victims of terrorism and oppression.

Nearly a month after the Elaine Massacre of 1919, a Phillips County grand jury charged 122 African Americans "with crimes ranging from murder to night riding," the latter, in the eyes of historian Grif Stockley, having "its own ironic implications, since in Phillips County it had been brought on behalf of planters against whites who tried to run off their Black labor."[94] Historian Brian K. Mitchell rediscovered the indictment book in the Phillips County Clerk of Court's office and found that a hundred men were charged with "unlawfully and feloniously confederating for the purpose of going forth at night armed to commit a felonious act," or nightriding—the highest number of charges to come out of the massacre's aftermath.[95] In a similar manner were eleven African American men charged with nightriding following the Catcher Race Riot of 1923, during which whites rioted in a rural Crawford County community near the state's western border and ended up driving off the entire Black community. The men in question had, for purposes of self-defense, holed themselves up in a log cabin armed with two shotguns and little ammunition and surrendered at once upon the appearance of the Arkansas National Guard. Nonetheless, they were charged and convicted of nightriding, although the Arkansas Supreme Court in 1924 overturned their convictions, asserting that "the State has wholly failed to sustain the charge of nightriding."[96] During a September 1938 strike in Mississippi County, authorities arrested and charged members of the Southern Tenant Farmers' Union, an interracial sharecroppers' union, with nightriding for distributing strike notices.[97] Certainly, such action was threatening to the local planter elite, but the purpose of Act 112 of 1909 was always to protect the elite from unrest coming from below.

As political scientist Michael G. Hanchard has written, "political inequality is not simply an epiphenomenal feature of social and economic inequality. Instead, political inequality is often the result of deliberate actions to exclude specific groups from participation in a polity and to deny their access to the same social and economic opportunities afforded to members of dominant groups."[98] The structure of Arkansas's economy already prevented most people, Black and white, from enjoying the social and economic opportunities afforded cotton merchants, landowners, and bankers—and the politicians who served them. When poor whites responded to their situation with violence or threats against their social betters, the law could be used to prosecute them. And when these same poor whites took out their wrath against African Americans—either seeing them as objects worthy of hatred on their own or attacking them as a means of harming their white employers—the law could step in there, as well, if somewhat inconsistently. However, when African Americans attempted to unite for self-protection against exploitation and violence, the law functioned to keep them in their prescribed place. In Arkansas, the law afforded the lowest of the low no recourse from violence. In fact, the law was violence itself.

Black Workers, White Nightriders, and the Supreme Court's Changing View of the Thirteenth Amendment

WILLIAM H. PRUDEN III

IN 1903, AN AMBITIOUS U.S. attorney determined to bring the practice of nightriding under control in Arkansas. He was reacting to a series of incidents starting the year before on the plantations of R. R. Fallis and a few of his neighbors in White Chapel in Cross County. The first incident began when a group of disgruntled workers burned the Christian Church where Fallis worshipped. Things soon escalated and, when Black workers received the contract to harvest Fallis's crops, a decision that left numerous white workers jobless, Fallis and his fellow planters became targets of nightriding attacks aimed at forcing them to fire the African American workers. To protect their property and families, Fallis and his neighbors hired a private detective, J. H. Brown of Memphis. In March 1903, Brown and several associates set up at the Fallis plantation, hoping to catch the nightriders in the act. Confusion among Brown's forces, though, eliminated the element of the surprise, and Brown was killed. The death prompted local law enforcement officials to double their efforts to bring the nightriders to justice. The local sheriff quickly expanded his force and within just a few days brought in twelve suspects. But reflective of the cultural and economic divide that was at the heart of nightriding, popular protests arose in response to those arrests.[1]

At the same time, another wave of nightriding struck in Whitehall in nearby Poinsett County as whites mobilized to prevent the employment of Black workers at a lumber mill. The local justice of the peace rebuffed the mill's owner, Jim Davis, when he sought protection for his Black workers, and Davis fired the Black workers rather than see them or his mill be continued targets. Perhaps because of the brazenness of the mob, which included the justice of the peace who had turned down Davis's request, this incident caught the attention of local federal officials and would soon become a turning point in the campaign to bring nightriding in Arkansas under control.[2]

William G. Whipple, the U.S. attorney for the Eastern District of Arkansas, got wind of the incident at the mill in Whitehall and seized upon it and the Cross County episode to send a message. So determined was Whipple to restore order and rein in the growing practice that, in a move that ran directly counter to the South's deep-seated reluctance to invoke federal authority, he contacted the U.S. Justice Department and the attorney general's office seeking support for an effort to combat nightriding, specifically funds to employ a special prosecutor for such cases. Attorney General Philander C. Knox, a McKinley appointee retained by Theodore Roosevelt, responded quickly and affirmatively. Praising Whipple's responsiveness to the problem, he approved both the requested funding as well as the appointment of Whipple's choice as prosecutor.[3]

Thus began a legal saga that, although based in local concerns, would upon reaching the U.S. Supreme Court result in *Hodges v. United States*, a decision that not only gutted what was left of the federal Civil Rights Act of 1866 but also shackled the Thirteenth Amendment, eliminating it as a vehicle for protecting the rights of the nation's African American population. While *Hodges* was certainly part of the Supreme Court's long retreat from protecting the civil rights of African Americans, it should also be read as part of the Court's embrace of laissez-faire constitutionalism— the insistence that governmental entities remain neutral as unfettered market forces work themselves out, especially in the realm of labor relations. Embodied most fully in the Court's *Lochner v. New York* decision (1905), laissez-faire constitutionalism gave the nation's most vulnerable workers little hope of securing government protection in their economic confrontations with either capital or competitors.[4] A Court faithful to laissez-faire ideals could hardly allow Congress and the Department of Justice to become involved in a dispute between lumber mill workers in a small Arkansas Delta town. Thus, as legal scholar Pamela Karlan has pointed out, the curtailment of Thirteenth Amendment protections has to be understood not only as part of the Court's long retreat from civil rights but also as bound up in the *Lochner*-era jurisprudence that stymied workers' efforts to use democratic processes to regulate labor relations in order to improve their situations.[5]

Whipple's efforts to curb nightriding began in the fall of 1903. Once he had secured the support of the Department of Justice, Whipple undertook a full-scale investigation, one that led to the presentation of two sets of indictments. The investigation indicated that the defendants—a group of working-class whites struggling to compete with Black workers for the limited work available in an economically impoverished part of Arkansas—were motivated by both economic and racial concerns, and that they had undertaken the nightriding in an effort to drive away new competitors.[6] Yet, however true it was that nightriding was never an explicitly race-based phenomenon, most incidents, especially in the late nineteenth and early twentieth centuries, targeted African Americans with the ultimate goal of driving them off the land and out of the area. To the white working-class defendants for whom Black labor represented competition, a good economy was a white economy; at the same time, that was not necessarily a universal feeling among the area's whites. For many landowners and mill operators, the employment of African Americans and the ability to stoke competition between white and Black workers offered the opportunity to drive down wages and realize greater profit. Unsurprisingly, local newspapers and most of the Delta elite sympathized with the employers and expressed concern and outrage at the extralegal violence.[7] All of this undoubtedly emboldened Whipple while also likely leading him to invoke the Civil Rights Act of 1866 to solve the problem.

In the first of the two cases, *United States v. Morris*, the government charged a group of eleven whites with the intimidation of Black sharecroppers. In the second case, *United States v. Maples*, the government asserted that on August 17, 1903, fifteen men had descended upon a sawmill in the Poinsett County community of Whitehall and threatened a group of Black workers in the hope of getting them to abandon their jobs. After being rebuffed in his efforts to convince a justice of the peace to protect the Black workers, the sawmill's owner advised the Black workers to leave their jobs. With the indictments set, the legal maneuvering began. The defense attorneys sought to have the charges dismissed on the grounds that the statutes under which the indictments had been brought—portions of the 1866 Civil Rights Act—were unconstitutional. Specifically, the defendants' lawyers asserted that the statutes represented an infringement upon the rights of both the states and the individual defendants.[8]

The motions were denied by federal district court judge Jacob Trieber, a German immigrant and the first Jewish person to be named to a federal judgeship.[9] In denying the motions, Trieber ruled that the Thirteenth Amendment in fact marked "a great extension of the powers of the national government." From the outset of the legal proceedings, the question centered on the scope of the Thirteenth Amendment, all parties acknowledging that the actions in question had been committed by private citizens rather than a government entity. Trieber asserted that the amendment allowed the federal government to protect the well-recognized freedom of individuals to contract for their labor, maintaining that such a protection was a central part of the freedom it granted. For Trieber, the amendment protected that freedom by allowing Congress to enact measures like the Civil Rights Act of 1866 and for the prosecution of those—private parties and governments alike—who violated those measures. Trieber also asserted that responsibility for protecting the right could not be left to the states, for it was under their authority that the now banned practice of slavery had operated and had only been abandoned under the military-enforced directive of the federal government.[10]

With Trieber's dismissal of the motion, the cases moved to trial. The prosecution asserted that the harassment of the victims was racially motivated, suggesting that the primary purpose of the government's action was to protect the right of African Americans to contract their labor. However, the case was more likely pursued at the behest of prominent whites who viewed nightriding as something that ran counter to their economic interests.[11] The defendant's lawyers included L. C. Going, who represented the nightriders in both of the trials and then argued on behalf of one of them, Reuben Hodges, in the U.S. Supreme Court. Going was a well-respected local attorney who in fact won election in 1904 to the post of prosecuting attorney for the district and then won reelection as the case went before the Supreme Court. In addition, U.S. senator James P. Clarke, a former Arkansas governor, joined the defense team right after the initial *Morris* decision and, alongside Going, represented the nightriders before the Supreme Court. Clarke's participation was not surprising. Like his political ally Jeff Davis, Clark styled himself as the protector of working-class whites against the aggressions of corporations, bankers, and planters from above and African Americans from below.[12] Thus, in many ways, the trials functioned as contests between two types of white supremacists—those who wanted to exploit inexpensive African American labor and those who wanted to protect white labor from Black competitors.[13] But in the end, the racial identity of the victims, coupled with the government's race-focused argument, made the case a test of just how far the government would and could go to protect the rights guaranteed by the Reconstruction Amendments.

Not surprisingly, given the vagaries of local justice and the competing visions of white supremacy, the initial trials yielded differing results. In the *Morris* case, the defendants presented a united front, a tactic that left the government unable to present any direct testimony about the alleged intimidation and thus prevented even a single conviction. However, in the *Maples* case, the prosecution was more successful, using the testimony of coconspirators to convict three of the defendants, Reuben Hodges, William Clampit, and Wash McKinney, on charges of conspiring to intimidate the Black lumber mill workers. Each of the three was sentenced to one year and a day in prison and fined $100. However, those verdicts were quickly appealed, and in March 1904 the U.S. Supreme Court agreed to hear the case.[14]

Central to the Court's willingness to review the case was the expansive interpretation of the Thirteenth Amendment that Trieber had made in his initial rulings.[15] In retrospect, given his fierce devotion to the protection of the nation's Black citizens, Trieber was the wrong judge, in the wrong place, at the wrong time. His lower court ruling in favor of the expansive interpretation of the Thirteenth Amendment and the federal government's powers to protect Black workers threatened both forms of white supremacy. Neither those who sought to take advantage of low-wage Black labor nor those who wanted to run off African American competitors could tolerate the federal government protecting the labor rights of Black Arkansans. Consequently, Arkansas's power brokers had little choice but to appeal the case all the way to the Supreme Court, a body that, had anyone really looked, offered little hope of a ruling that would protect the South's Black population. But with the Court's rulings on racial issues in the aftermath of the Civil War having been mixed, white leaders had ample reason to see the effort through. Another consideration was that, while there had been changes in its membership, the Court that heard *Hodges*—Chief Justice Melville Fuller and Associate Justices John Marshall Harlan, David Brewer, Henry Brown, Edward Douglass White, Rufus Peckham, Joseph McKenna, Oliver Wendell Holmes Jr., and William Day—included six members who had heard *Plessy* a decade before, although Brewer, who had sat on the *Plessy* Court, was not involved with the decision given his daughter's sudden death and his subsequent absence. But there was little reason to think that the substitutions of McKenna for Stephen Field, Holmes for Horace Gray, or Day for George Shiras would tilt the Court in a new direction. Indeed, despite the Department of Justice's determination to see the effort through, the ruling in *Plessy*, membership changes notwithstanding, left the nightriding forces with considerable hope. Yet few could have predicted such a complete victory.

Indeed, it was the totality of the defeat that was the most dispiriting part of the case for those seeking to protect the rights of Black citizens, for the Court's ruling did not represent a small setback or the next logical step back in a gradual erosion of protections. Rather, while the Court had been wavering in its commitment to the use of the Reconstruction Amendments as a means to protect the rights of freedmen and their descendants, *Hodges* represented a major turnaround. Indeed, *Hodges* reversed earlier decisions, especially *Civil Rights Cases* and *United States v. Cruikshank*, that had offered expansive readings of the Thirteenth Amendment. Admittedly, the expansive interpretation had seen some setbacks, most prominently the *Slaughter-House Cases*, but, from almost any perspective, *Hodges* was a giant leap backward.[16]

The first judicial consideration of the Thirteenth Amendment had come in 1866, albeit at the circuit court level, but it was Supreme Court associate justice Noah Swayne who upheld the amendment's power to protect a Black individual's right to testify in court. Swayne asserted that slavery's abolition must inevitably lead to "hostility of the dominant class," which by its very nature endangered the freedmen.[17] Consequently, under section two of the amendment, Congress was empowered to combat the efforts rooted in that hostility which might make the "gift of freedom . . . a curse instead of a blessing."[18] Swayne's broad view of the Thirteenth Amendment was cut back a bit in the *Slaughter-House Cases* in 1873 when the Court determined that the amendment did not reach servitudes that were imposed on property rather than people.[19] But in *United States v. Cruikshank*, decided three years later, the Court affirmed a lower court ruling in which Associate Justice Joseph Bradley had taken a broad view of the power of the Thirteenth Amendment, declaring that it gave Congress the power both to eliminate the "badge[s] of servitude" and "give full effect to this bestowment of liberty on these millions of people."[20] However, inklings that change might be in the offing came with the 1883 decision in the *Civil Rights Cases*. There, Justice Bradley backed off his earlier assertion that the Thirteenth Amendment gave Congress the power to eliminate the "disabilities" that had been incidental to slavery as well as "the effects flowing for them," adding that Congress had the authority to "instate the freedmen in the full enjoyment of that civil liberty and equality which the abolition of slavery meant."[21] Instead, in the *Civil Rights Cases*, he wrote, "it would be running the slavery argument into the ground" to expand the protections afforded by the Thirteenth Amendment to include every act of personal discrimination like those protected in the Civil Rights Act of 1875.[22] He also noted that the amendment's application was limited to "those fundamental rights which are the essence of civil freedom."[23] Then, in a rather chilling foreshadowing, Bradley noted that at some point in time the nation's Black population "ceases to be the special favorite of the laws" and must instead find its protection in state law.[24] But the Supreme Court's decision the following year in *United States v. Waddell*, a case coming out of the Circuit Court in the Eastern District in Arkansas, seemed to indicate that the federal government had the power to protect victims against nightriding, in this case by a group of whites who sought to drive off a Black man who was trying to settle and establish a homestead on federal land.[25] However, the fact that the conflict was based in federal law made the Court's determination that yes, the federal government had the power to protect the homesteader, a decision different and distinct from the developing conflict between state and federal authority that the Court would soon see.

The Court's next major pronouncement in this area came in 1896 in *Plessy v. Ferguson*. While its infamous "separate but equal" doctrine was based in the Fourteenth Amendment, the Court offered some telling thoughts that seemed to imply that the Thirteenth could be used to protect the labor rights of former slaves and their descendants. It declared, "Slavery implies . . . a state of bondage . . . and the absence of a legal right to the disposal of his own person, property, and services."[26] The Court noted that a state law that required separate but equal public accommodations "has no tendency to destroy the legal equality of the two races, or re-establish a state of involuntary servitude."[27] It was against this evolving legal background that the appeal of the Arkansas nightriding case was argued and decided.

As the case, now labeled *Hodges v. United States*, headed to the U.S. Supreme Court, the fundamental issue to be addressed was the right of African Americans to contract for their labor. But in conjunction with that issue was the equally if not more important question of whether the Thirteenth Amendment made the right one guaranteed by the

Constitution or federal laws and thus subject to protection by the federal government, rather than the states. And if it was, then the Court faced the question of just how long was the reach of the Thirteenth Amendment. It had to determine whether the amendment was intended only to secure the freedom of the enslaved African Americans or whether the prohibition against slavery and the protections central to that edict applied to all people. This was a question of no small relevance at a time when reports of abuses against Italian immigrants and Chinese laborers were commonplace. Ultimately, the Supreme Court had to confront the question of the Thirteenth Amendment's intent as well as the question of whether the federal government had the power to protect the newly granted rights.

The Supreme Court's *Hodges* decision threw out the convictions of the three men—Hodges, Clampit, and McKinney—but more importantly it imposed substantial limitations on both the reach of the Thirteenth Amendment and the federal government's power to protect the labor rights of Black citizens. Central to the Court's ruling was the distinction between the imposition of slavery—something clearly prohibited by the Thirteenth Amendment—and the denial of freedom, in this case the freedom to sell one's labor that was less clearly expressed in the amendment. Such an inquiry required the Court to define slavery. While relying more on the common usage of the word "enslavement," the Court acknowledged that a central component of slavery, as previously practiced, was the act of rendering individuals unable to sell their labor, and, while the government argued that the defendants had done just that, the Court majority found that not "every wrong done to an individual by another . . . operates . . . to abridge some of the freedom to which the individual is entitled."[28] The Court ruled that while an individual is entitled to the safety of his property and as well as being personally safe from assault, violation of these rights cannot be said to "reduce the individual to a condition of slavery."[29] In addition, the Court determined that the protection of these rights was the responsibility of the states rather than the federal government. Finally, in determining whether the Thirteenth Amendment served to protect only the rights of the African Americans, the Court declared that the Thirteenth Amendment was not intended to "denounce every action done to an individual which was wrong if done by a free man and yet justified in a case of slavery and to give to Congress the authority enforcing such denunciation."[30] Rather, in conjunction with the Fourteenth Amendment (which defined citizenship and contained clauses relating to privileges and immunities, due process, and equal protection) and the Fifteenth Amendment (which prohibited the denial of suffrage based on race or previous condition of servitude), the Thirteenth Amendment sought to give the African Americans full citizenship, so that their interests would be best served by "taking their chances with other citizens in the states where they should make their homes."[31]

Writing for the seven-member majority, Associate Justice Brewer argued that the conviction could not stand because the Fourteenth Amendment had given the federal government no authority to address action of private individuals and the Thirteenth Amendment could not be read so expansively as to allow it to prohibit the conduct the state was seeking to address. Noting that attorneys for the federal government had argued that the defendants' action had been based in racial animus and imposed the badge of servitude prohibited by the Thirteenth Amendment, Brewer departed from previous Courts that had required a race-based motive for any indictments coming under the Thirteenth Amendment. Instead, he argued that the amendment outlawed slavery in all forms and of all groups, an especially important recognition in an increasingly ethnically diverse nation. But as Brewer expanded the populations protected by the Thirteenth Amendment, he weakened those protections.[32] Indeed, he asserted that in looking past their color he was in fact recognizing Blacks' status as full American citizens. In contrast, he suggested the government sought to treat Black citizens as a special ward of the federal government and that an expansive reading of the Thirteenth Amendment would give to the federal government the authority to ensure the "protection of the individual rights which prior to the Thirteen Amendment was unquestionably within the jurisdiction of the States."[33] Brewer's concerns about this shift in power failed to address the fact that, while the states had had the authority to protect Black rights, they had of course not done so prior to the Thirteenth Amendment, a reality that Judge Trieber had clearly understood when he asserted that those states under whom slavery had operated could not be entrusted with the protection of Black liberty. Brewer concluded that allowing the federal government to pursue this result would make it the protector of individual rights, a role, he asserted, that was well beyond the intentions of the congressional framers of the amendment. Brewer insisted, as one scholar put it, "African-Americans should be left on their own to struggle for their rights in the state rather than federal courts."[34]

In the Court's view, *Hodges* boiled down to the question of whether it was "the intent of the [Thirteenth] Amendment to denounce every act done to an individual which was wrong if done to a free man and yet justified in a condition of slavery, and to give authority to Congress to enforce such denunciation."[35] The Court's answer in Brewer's opinion was an emphatic no.[36]

In addition, while the trial court had found the defendants guilty of conspiring to prevent the workers from exercising their right "to make and enforce contracts" on the same basis as whites, a protection provided by the Civil Rights Act of 1866, Brewer and the Court's majority determined that the act exceeded the authority granted to Congress under the Thirteenth Amendment. To come to this conclusion, Brewer relied on a very narrow definition of slavery, taking the basic definition from Webster's dictionary, which defined slavery as "the state of entire subjection of one person to the will of another" and "servitude" as "the state of voluntary or compulsory subjection to a master."[37] Given the Black laborers who had been attacked had no master, they could not be considered slaves. Thus, the attacking whites had not violated the amendment, and the Congress had no authority to reach their behavior. As scholar James Gray Pope notes, the decision echoed the opposition's arguments during the congressional debates over the Civil Rights Act of 1866, when Brewer argued that "if the Amendment reached racially motivated interferences in the right to make contracts," then it must reach even further.[38] As Pope continues, "Although Hodges involved violent and intentional interference with Black labor freedom, the Amendment's core concern, Brewer chose to worry instead about the possibility that the national government might seize on the Thirteenth Amendment as authority to displace the states' authority over all personal rights."[39] Indeed, Brewer warned, it meant that "every wrong done by an individual to another would become the responsibility of the federal government."[40] And that, he reminded his colleagues, would then include the "protection of individual rights which prior to the Thirteenth Amendment was unquestionably within the jurisdiction of the states, would, by virtue of that Amendment, be transferred to the nation, and subject to the legislation of Congress."[41]

But that was not where the Court was going. Rather, Brewer's opinion gutted the "badges and incidents doctrine" at the center of the more expansive interpretation. It ended efforts to use the Thirteenth Amendment as a vehicle for protecting Black civil rights and invalidated what was left of the Civil Rights Act of 1866. Decades before, in 1866, Frederick Douglass, in an essay titled "Reconstruction," warned a nation still recovering from the Civil War that while the radical Republicans in

Congress were engaged in an admirable effort to rid the nation of the vestiges of slavery, those efforts might prove meaningless so long as "there remains such an idea as the right of each state to control its own affairs." Unhappily, the *Hodges* decision did just that, refusing to "render the rights of the state compatible with the sacred rights of human nation."[42]

Not only was Douglass's warning ignored, but so too was Justice John Marshall Harlan in his *Hodges* dissent, which ran three times the length of Brewer's opinion. Echoing his dissent in *Plessy*, but without a memorable invocation along the lines of "our Constitution is colorblind, and neither knows nor tolerates classes among citizens," the former slave owner offered a very different vision of how the Reconstruction Amendments should be viewed, one that was rooted in precedent. Recalling the *Civil Rights Cases*, Harlan declared, "I stood with the Court in the declaration that the Thirteenth Amendment not only established and decreed universal, civil and political freedom throughout this land, but abolished the incidents or badges of slavery."[43] In order to secure this freedom, the Court had recognized Congress's authority to "reach and punish individuals whose acts are in hostility to rights and privileges derived from, or secured by, or dependent upon, that [Thirteenth] Amendment."[44] Echoing Judge Trieber, Harlan took the traditional expansive view of federal power, asserting that only the federal government could adequately protect the rights promised by the Thirteenth Amendment. But Harlan's argument fell on deaf ears.

All of this makes clear that the *Hodges* decision was a turning point or, perhaps more accurately, a dispiriting exclamation point in civil rights–based litigation. It effectively shut the door on the legal effort to put the power and authority of the federal government behind the effort to energize the Reconstruction Amendments, specifically the Thirteenth, so as to provide the protection Black citizens needed to make real the promises of those amendments as well as the other legislative initiatives of Reconstruction.

While its place in civil rights jurisprudence cannot be denied, the *Hodges* decision is also part of the Court's embrace of what legal scholars call "laissez-faire constitutionalism"—the idea that the Constitution requires governments to remain neutral, especially concerning labor relations, so as to allow the natural workings of the free market to reward the industrious and punish the sluggish. The author of the *Hodges* opinion, Associate Justice David Brewer, was one of the fiercest advocates of this laissez-faire view of the Constitution. In 1891, soon after he was appointed associate justice, he warned of the "spoliation and destruction of private property through the agency of that undefined and perhaps indefinable power, the police power of the State" and made it his mission to use the Court to curtail almost all state power in economic matters.[45] Trieber and Harlan's understanding of Congress's expansive powers under the Thirteenth Amendment could hardly stand alongside a series of rulings that rolled back the ability of the states and federal government to regulate the relationship between employee and employer. Only by understanding the Court's adherence to laissez-faire constitutionalism can we make sense of its dramatic curtailment of the scope of civil rights legislation permissible under the Thirteenth Amendment.

The Court signaled the primacy of laissez-faire constitutionalism in *Lochner v. New York* in 1905, just a year before *Hodges*. A five-man majority ruled that a New York statute regulating working conditions for bakers violated the Constitution's guarantee of the liberty of contract—that is, the right to make economic agreements free of government interference. The Court located the source of this right—which is not explicitly enumerated in the Constitution—in the Fourteenth Amendment. As Associate Justice Rufus Peckham wrote for the majority, "The general right to make a contract in relation to his business is part of the liberty of the individual protected by the Fourteenth Amendment of the Federal Constitution. Under that provision, no State can deprive any person of life, liberty or property without due process of law. The right to purchase or to sell labor is part of the liberty protected by this amendment." Peckham and the majority did acknowledge that liberty of contract was not absolute; it could be abridged by laws "necessary for the preservation of the health of employees" as long as courts found those laws to be reasonable, a standard known as substantive due process.[46]

At first glance, there appears to be a tension between *Lochner*'s defense of the "right to purchase or to sell labor" and *Hodges*'s refusal to use the Thirteenth Amendment to protect African American lumber mill workers from nightriders intent on preventing them from working. In fact, Harlan pointed this out in his *Hodges* dissent: "[T]he liberty protected by the Fourteenth Amendment against state action inconsistent with due process of law is neither more nor less than the freedom established by the Thirteenth Amendment."[47] But the key to reconciling the two decisions can be found in Associate Justice Oliver Wendell Holmes Jr.'s dissent in *Lochner*. Holmes criticized the Court's majority for substituting its economic values and vision for a careful reading of the Constitution. The decision was driven by laissez-faire thought, an "economic theory which a large part of the country does not entertain."[48] Holmes continued that the "constitution is not intended to embody a particular economic theory, whether paternalism and the organic relation of the citizen to the state or of laissez faire."[49]

The *Hodges* decision reinforces Holmes's insistence that the doctrine of liberty of contract was a product of the Court's desire to implement a particular economic theory, one that fettered governmental power, celebrated the unregulated marketplace, and privileged the powerful. The cases can certainly be distinguished on a number of fronts—one invalidated a federal law, the other a state statute; one dealt with the Fourteenth Amendment, the other the Thirteenth Amendment; one concerned state action, the other private action; one protected the right of employers and employees to enter into contracts free of interference, the other prevented the federal government from preventing such coercion. But taken together, the cases show that for the Court liberty of contract was a sword that only swung one way. It could be wielded by capital when employees sought protection from the state but not to protect vulnerable workers from violent competitors or exploitative employers. The Court considered neither New York bakers nor Black Arkansas lumber mill workers to be so impaired as to need protections from the state. To reach this understanding, the Court relied on abstract economic theory, ignoring both the piles of evidence submitted to the Court about the deleterious effects of long hours on bakers and the fact that disfranchisement, Jim Crow, and extralegal violence had drastically restricted the ability of Black Arkansans to compete in the marketplace or seek state-level relief. As one scholar examining *Hodges* asserts, "Because the Court was unwilling to align the law with the world in which it operated, the Court remade the world so as to align it with an abstract notion of what the law should do."[50]

In Arkansas, the impact of *Hodges* was immediate and disturbing. As the case was winding its way through the courts, Whipple's prosecution of nightriders had continued. In one instance, he secured the convictions of three nightriders on charges of threatening to shoot Black workers at a lumber company if they did not leave their jobs. But these men were released after the Court issued the *Hodges* decision. Soon after *Hodges*, the Supreme Court in *Boyett v. United States* overturned the convictions of another set of Arkansas nightriders without issuing a formal opinion.[51] Reports throughout the state (and Texas) suggested that federal prosecutors simply dropped investigations into nightriding in the aftermath of the ruling. With no federal prosecutions, nightriding returned with a vengeance, threatening not only Black laborers but also white property owners.[52]

With Justice Brewer's opinion restricting Congress's power under the Thirteenth Amendment, the Supreme Court insisted that the African Americans were best served by "taking their chances with other citizens in the states where they . . . make their homes."[53] In Arkansas, it took three years for the state legislature to address the problem. Worried about the rising tide of nightriding not only in Arkansas but also nearby Tennessee, Rep. A. G. Little of Mississippi County introduced a measure to make nightriding a felony, punishable by a prison sentence of no less than two years and no more than ten and a fine of up to $5,000. Labelled House Bill 80 upon its introduction, it was quickly embraced by members of both the House and Senate. After the Senate Judiciary Committee reviewed its constitutionality and deemed it "a necessary bill for public safety," the bill passed overwhelmingly, and Gov. George Donaghey signed it into law as Act 112 of 1909 on April 6.[54] The unanimous support that the bill received suggests that legislators were more concerned with protecting property owners who drove down wages by forcing Black and white labor to compete and were sometimes the targets of nightriders than with the disfranchised African Americans who were more often the victims.

That Act 112's purpose was to protect powerful whites rather than Black laborers became most apparent in the aftermath of the Elaine Massacre, an event sparked when a white posse disrupted a meeting of Black sharecroppers seeking ways to guarantee their ability to exercise their right to contract. The law against nightriding became a central part of the prosecution's arsenal as it convicted hundreds of Black victims, people who were, as one analyst observed, guilty of nothing more than being in the wrong place at the wrong time.[55] Brewer's faith that the victims of nightriding could find relief through state-level democratic processes was always naïve, but never more so than in the wake of the Elaine Massacre. The Supreme Court's abhorrence of governmental interference with the workings of the market, under the pretense that governments should remain neutral and treat all citizens the same, enabled the powerful to exploit the vulnerable.

Reuben Hodges and his gang of whites ran off the Black workers at the lumber mill in Poinsett County because they were both African American and economic rivals. The mere presence of Black people did not trigger this sort of violence on the part of whites, and it is doubtful that white economic rivals would have met the same fate. It was this toxic combination of racial animosity and economic jealousy that made nightriding so violent and so rampant in the Delta. In a similar fashion, *Hodges v. United States* must be understood as the product of the Supreme Court's jurisprudence on both racial and economic matters. The Court's traditional expansive (albeit waning) reading of the Thirteenth Amendment—one that allowed Congress to attack the "badges and incidents" of slavery—ran up against the Court's embrace of laissez-faire constitutionalism, and laissez-faire won. The Court would not begin to roll back the legal underpinnings of white supremacy until after the era of laissez-faire constitutionalism ended in 1937. The New Deal Court quickly signaled the start of its new orientation toward civil rights the following year in the famous *Carolene Products* footnote: if it was going to defer to Congress on economic matters and relinquish its role as protector of property rights, the Court had to ensure that "racial minorities" were treated equally before the law and had access to democratic processes.[56] At the Supreme Court, as on the ground in the Delta, civil rights were entwined with the economic rights of all workers. Progress on one could not be made without progress on the other.

CHAPTER 4

Henry Lowery Lynching

A Legacy of the Elaine Massacre?

JEANNIE WHAYNE

FIFTEEN MONTHS AFTER THE Elaine Massacre, a gruesome lynching occurred in Mississippi County, the northernmost Delta county in Arkansas. The lynching of Black sharecropper Henry Lowery, though, was not a legacy of the Elaine Massacre. Rather it was more likely merely "business as usual" on Delta plantations. Violence, including lynching, was one of several mechanisms planters used to try to force Black compliance with the plantation labor regime, but their power was insufficient to discourage activism on the part of African Americans. Indeed, the Elaine Massacre followed the founding of a union of sharecroppers, a direct challenge to the supremacy of whites and the economic system that disproportionately rewarded the planters. The precipitating event was an exchange of gunfire between white deputies and Black guards at a meeting of the Progressive Farmers and Household Union of America, but the planters knew of the union activism and intention to file suit for a fair settlement of the crop. Planters would not tolerate this sort of collective action, and government, army, and local authorities dispensed violence to serve the interests of planters. Over two hundred African Americans lost their lives in the worst rural massacre of Black people in American history.[1]

Before the Elaine massacre and afterward, however, individual African American sharecroppers addressed their grievances directly to their planters, and sometimes violence was the result. This individual, rather than collective, action will be explored in the case of Henry Lowery, who approached his planter on Christmas Day 1920 to demand a written "settlement of accounts" so that he could seek employment elsewhere. We have mostly biased white reports of what happened next, but, suffice it to say, once the smoke cleared, the planter and his adult daughter were dead, his two adult sons were wounded, and Lowery, though himself wounded, had escaped to the swamps with bloodhounds and mobs on his trail. With the help of his Odd Fellows lodge brothers, he miraculously eluded capture and made his way to El Paso, Texas. There, he was later arrested and returned to Mississippi County where he was burned to death at Nodena Landing on January 26, 1921.[2]

The Lowery lynching and the Elaine Massacre were similar in that they were challenges to planter power and the workings of the sharecropping system, but there were important differences. Lowery's temerity in demanding a written statement stipulating that he had "paid out" at the end of the 1920 crop year was an individual act against a specific planter. On the other hand, the Farmers and Household Union represented a bold and rare collective challenge: Black sharecroppers formed a union, hired a prominent white attorney to file suit for fair settlement of the crop, and, in doing so, struck at the heart of planter control over plantation labor. Regardless of these differences, both tragedies attracted the attention of the National Association for the Advancement of Colored People (NAACP). Just a decade after its founding in 1909, the NAACP became actively involved in the pursuit of justice for the Elaine Twelve, the Black men convicted and sentenced to death after Elaine Massacre. When Lowery was arrested in Texas, the NAACP attempted to prevent his return to Arkansas until some guarantee was made that he would receive a fair trial. After his lynching, as historian Karlos K. Hill has persuasively argued, the episode became a key feature in the organization's antilynching campaign with the NAACP producing a pamphlet, "An American Lynching," that detailed Lowery's brutal murder. While the Lowery lynching contributed to a renewed effort to secure passage of a federal antilynching bill—one that would fall short—the Elaine Massacre led to a U.S. Supreme Court decision that struck a blow against unfair trials and asserted a new interpretation of the Fourteenth Amendment.[3]

Behind the efforts of the NAACP in both situations was a keen understanding of the obstacles facing African Americans in the South, one based on careful observation of the situation in Arkansas. Walter White, an investigator for the organization since 1918, authored a particularly astute account of the Elaine Massacre.[4] William Pickens, who became a field secretary for the NAACP in 1920, wrote a cogent analysis of the circumstances surrounding the Lowery lynching in *The Nation* in March 1921, placing it in the context of the exploitation of African American sharecroppers on Arkansas plantations. It stands as an indictment of the plantation system in the South. Pickens, an African American who spent much of his childhood in Woodruff County, Arkansas, was quite familiar with the workings of the sharecropping system as his father had been lured to Arkansas by the promises of a labor agent. The landowner had paid the family's fare to Arkansas, so he began his sojourn there in debt and was unable to "pay out." The family struggled mightily until his father found a planter willing to assume his debt and rent him a farm near Little Rock. Young Pickens left the state to secure one degree at Talladega College (1902) in Alabama and another at Yale University (1904). He taught at various colleges and became an active member of the NAACP. In 1918, he became the NAACP's director of branches, traveling the South to establish chapters of the organization. He was appointed field secretary in 1920, and in that capacity traveled to Arkansas to investigate the Lowery lynching in 1921.[5]

Pickens's understanding of the pernicious sharecropping system hinged on his personal association with it, but his intellectual appreciation for its vagaries was greatly enhanced by his NAACP activities. Not only did Pickens have a keen understanding of how African Americans were exploited on plantations in the American South; he also was able to grasp the macro-level forces at work, calling the lower Mississippi Valley "the American Congo." In fact, both the sharecroppers of Elaine and Henry Lowery were confronting the larger edifice of the global cotton complex. Sven Beckert's *Empire of Cotton: A Global History* argues that cotton was essential to the development of capitalism both in the United States and globally. From the cotton growers in the American South and elsewhere to the textile mills of England and thence distributed as cloth to a global market, cotton was fundamental to a new global network of finance and commerce. The world had never seen anything like it. Between the plantation owner and the textile mills, however, was an important intermediary: the cotton broker. Cotton brokers served eastern Arkansas out of cities like Memphis, Tennessee, and Greenville, Mississippi, and played pivotal roles not only in selling the crop to the textile mills but also providing credit services to planters—at a price, of course. It was through this mechanism that planters found themselves locked into the global cotton economy, and they passed on their own dependency on broker financing to their sharecroppers by requiring them to grow a cotton crop and to mortgage any mules and implements they might own to the planter.

Neither sharecroppers nor planters had a lot of maneuvering room within the global cotton complex, an entity that had no conscience, no heart. The mechanisms of the market were not curbed by justice to any of the individual players. Each was left to struggle within the system and, particularly for the Black sharecropper, on unequal terms.[6]

While Beckert writes of the global cotton complex, historians of the "global plantation" offer an elaboration on the workings of plantation economies around the globe. They do not argue that the plantation economies are necessarily interconnected but rather function independent of one another with remarkable similarities. Wherever they exist, they dominate the region in which they operate, politically, economically, and socially. They have considerable influence over politicians and the police apparatus; they own the best land and control other resources like water, often driving out smaller farmers; and they exercise power over labor, whether ethnic or racial minorities, immigrants, or local indigenous labor. This is certainly true of plantations in the American South and particularly in the Mississippi Delta region.[7]

The key component of control over labor in the American Congo was the sharecropping system, which arose in the wake of the Civil War, replacing the contract labor system that had maintained the plantation system in the South even as war raged. Northerners who had come South to run cotton plantations or southerners who took an oath of allegiance to the United States employed Black workers who had taken advantage of the war to secure their own emancipation. The arrangement illustrates the importance of the cotton economy not only to the South but also to the financiers in centers like New York City. The contract labor system had severe shortcomings, however, as planters had little cash to offer in wages, and freedmen wanted land of their own to farm. But the former slaves had no resources to purchase land, only their bodies to offer in labor, and they resented the fact that they were forced to live in the old slave quarters and often worked under overseers, just as they had under the slave regime. Out of this dissatisfaction of both sides, the sharecropping system was born. In its initial configuration, African Americans moved away from the old slave quarters onto roughly twenty-five-acre parcels of land that they farmed and were paid their wages in cotton. The planter marketed the crop and paid the sharecropper what they said they were owed.

Given that wages came only at the harvest, sharecroppers became indebted to plantation commissaries until the crop came in. There was plenty of room for chicanery, of course, as few freedmen could read or write given that it had been against the law or custom to teach enslaved people to read. Using lessons they had learned as slaves in resisting slavery's dehumanizing conditions, freedmen maneuvered as best they could under these circumstances and frequently exercised their freedom by moving to other plantations, hoping for a better deal. Southern legislatures passed "Black codes" to impede the movement of freedmen. For instance, in the 1870s most legislatures passed laws that made it illegal for a sharecropper to leave the employment of the planter for whom he worked if he owed a debt. If a sharecropper was lucky enough to acquire some mules and implements of his own, he could move into the ranks of tenant farmers and demand a larger share of the crop. If a sharecropper or tenant failed to break even at the end of the year and attempted to leave, it was commonplace for a constable, sometimes in the pay of prominent planters, to pursue "absconded" tenants and sharecroppers and force their return. This led to the development of a system of debt peonage and was precisely what Henry Lowery was rejecting when he confronted seventy-year-old Oscar Craig on Christmas Day in 1920. He wanted a written statement to the effect he had fulfilled his contract and did not owe Craig anything. A simple enough request, it might seem, but to Craig it was an affront. Besides, cotton prices were already on the way down in late December 1920, and Craig was likely in no mood to be challenged. He threw a billet of wood at Lowery as his two sons charged out the front door, guns blazing.[8]

Craig's violent response to Lowery's audacity in demanding a written accounting was entirely in keeping with the norms of plantation operations. Vagrancy statues, laws making it illegal for a sharecropper to leave an employer to whom he owed money, and the practice of sending constables after absconding sharecroppers were all mechanisms planters used to keep labor in place. Violence was another. Admittedly, violence could get out of hand, such as in the situation in Elaine, where the murder of hundreds of Black workers could hardly have served planter interests. In its aftermath, African Americans in Phillips County departed in larger than usual numbers. The Black population in the county dropped by 17 percent between 1920 and 1930, though some of that was surely the result of other factors, and other southeastern Arkansas Delta counties were experiencing similar declines. Meanwhile, in the northeastern part of the state where Mississippi County and Lowery were located, the plantation system was expanding as drainage enterprises opened tens of thousands of acres for cotton production. An increasing labor supply was acutely necessary, and there the African Americans population increased by 31.3 percent. These were the forces prevailing when Henry Lowery confronted Craig. Labor was in great demand, and Oscar Craig was determined to keep Lowery in place.[9]

Henry Lowery's escape after the confrontation with the Craig family led to sensational stories that threatened to expose the injustices that existed on Arkansas plantations. The state was still dealing with the fallout over the Elaine Massacre and, once again, national and international outrage was aroused. Ironically, the lynching might have been avoided had the agreement reached between the governors of Texas and Arkansas been adhered to. Pat Morris Neff, the newly inaugurated governor of Texas, had been pressed by a prominent white attorney in Texas who was representing the NAACP to demand a guarantee from recently inaugurated Gov. Thomas McRae of Arkansas that Lowery would be returned to Little Rock, where he would receive a fair trial. McRae, for his part, was preoccupied by the legal ramifications of the death sentences facing the Elaine Twelve and most likely preferred to avoid another such controversy, so the prospects of a "fair trial" probably resonated with him. On the same page where a story appeared about Lowery's seizure by the mob in Sardis, Mississippi, the *Arkansas Democrat* ran a separate story concerning pressure being applied on McRae to stay the executions of the Elaine Twelve.[10] Having assured Neff of a fair trial, McRae was genuinely outraged when the train with Lowery aboard was intercepted at Sardis and Lowery was seized and rushed back to Mississippi County, where he faced a crowd of hundreds eager to see him die.[11]

As Karlos Hill suggests, a "climate of fear" in Mississippi County made many African Americans reluctant to talk about the lynching.[12] Nevertheless, Pickens traveled there—just as Walter White had traveled to Phillips County in 1919—and secured enough information to write the account that was published in *The Nation*. While local and regional white newspapers offered various versions of Lowery's motivations, they never probed the economic system in place. Instead, with one exception, they portrayed Lowery as deranged or drunk at the time of the shooting. In fact, Lowery was neither. As Pickens notes, "even the Memphis newspapers admitted finally that he [Lowery] was an honest, hard-working, inoffensive Negro. They admitted this to make it sound reasonable to assert that he ran a still and got drunk."[13]

Little is known about Lowery's background beyond the fact that he asked to be buried in Magnolia, Mississippi.[14] If that was his home and if he was farming there before 1918, the year he moved across the river to Arkansas, he was almost certainly experiencing what other farmers faced in southern Mississippi. Magnolia, the seat of Pike County, is along the border of Louisiana. Like much of south Mississippi, it was facing the boll weevil infestation, something planters, farmers, and agricultural scientists were struggling to conquer. Farmers in southeast Arkansas were also struck with the boll weevil blight, but it had yet to move into the northeastern portion of the state and that may have been what attracted Lowery to Oscar Craig's Stonewall plantation in the spring of 1918. Lowery quickly integrated into the Black community there, joining the local African American Odd Fellows and Knights of Pythias, and attending lodge meetings of the Masons. He gained his reputation as an "honest, hardworking farmer," and his first year on the Stonewall plantation passed without incident.

The trouble began the next year, which saw a precipitous drop in cotton prices—from 35.3 to 15.9 cents per pound—and, as was the custom, planters often passed their losses on to their sharecroppers and tenants. That apparently happened in the fall of 1920. Lowery discovered that Richard "Dick" Craig, Oscar's son who was then running the plantation, was a difficult man. Lowery probably turned his crop over to the younger Craig, as was required by the typical contract, and Craig had it ginned and marketed and reported to Lowery the price he had secured. If Lowery had owed money to the company store for the year's furnish, that would have been subtracted from the amount due him. Lowery may or may not have accepted the reckoning of the figures—meaning, agreed with what Craig said the crop had fetched at the market and what he had coming to him—but he made his first demand for a written statement from Dick Craig that he had "paid out." This would have verified that Lowery's share of the sale had been greater than the amount he owed to the plantation commissary. Dick Craig not only refused to give him that statement but also "struck Lowery and admonished him not to come again for settlement."[15] His treatment both angered Lowery and made it dangerous for him to leave Craig's employment. Had Lowery done so, local law enforcement officials, in keeping with practice, would have been dispatched to return him to the plantation to work off any debt Craig claimed he owed. In this case, the official likely would have been Jesse Greer, who served as a part-time constable and worked full time for Oscar Craig's brother-in-law, Lee Wilson. Wilson was the largest plantation owner in Arkansas and one of the largest in the South. Craig banked at the Bank of Wilson in the nearby town of Wilson, and may have marketed his cotton through Wilson & Ward Cotton brokerage of Memphis, Tennessee, a Lee Wilson entity that attempted to sidestep the important broker middleman in the cotton trade.[16]

Despite the obstacles in his way, Lowery was desperate to leave Craig's Stonewall plantation, and on Christmas 1920 he went to the Craig home to demand, once again, a written statement. He arrived as the family assembled for their Christmas dinner, including Oscar Craig, his wife, and their three adult children, Dick, Hugh, and Mrs. C. O. "Maybelle" Williamson. One of the Craig servants, a Black woman who, according to William Pickens, was known to be "on perfectly friendly terms" with Dick Craig, saw Lowery coming down the road and ran to the house to warn of his arrival.[17] Oscar Craig went out on the porch to speak to Lowery, exchanged some words, and then threw a billet of wood at him. Hearing a commotion, Dick, Hugh, and Maybelle rushed to the porch, the sons firing their guns. Lowery returned fire, killing Oscar and Maybelle and wounding Dick and Hugh. Although injured himself, he escaped into the swamps and over the next few days was tended to and fed by his Odd Fellows lodge brothers. A posse of hundreds combed the swamps, and Lowery later reported that "they nearly stepped on me once. It was cold and once or twice I had to crawl through puddles of water."[18]

At this point, the relationships Henry Lowery had forged with the Black community came into play. Despite the power of the planter class and the high stakes incurred by the deaths of two prominent whites, his Odd Fellows lodge brothers did not fail him. They enabled him to stay hidden in the swamps, supplied him with medical care and food, raised money for his escape, and transported him to the Earle, Arkansas, train station where they hid him in a load of cotton heading south. When he reached El Paso, he took a job as a janitor under an assumed name. He planned to cross the border into Mexico, but he wanted his wife and daughter to join him. However, he made a fatal mistake by writing a letter to one of his lodge brothers, Morris Jenkins: "I want to hear from my wife. I don't know how she is fairing. I left her with a plenty, but you know how it is with the white people in a case like this."[19] He sent the letter by way of an acquaintance who was instructed to deliver it directly to Jenkins. But Jenkins was in jail, along with his own wife and four lodge brothers, for having helped Lowery to escape. The acquaintance, unable to find Jenkins, mailed the letter to him instead, a tragic error. The letter, which included Lowery's assumed name (Sam Thompson), his address, and his place of work, was intercepted and read by the postmaster at Terrell, who notified authorities. When arrested, Lowery was "firing a furnace in a bank building" and reportedly said, "Please kill me, boss. If they take me back to Arkansas, they'll burn me sure."[20]

Lowery might have escaped the fate he so clearly foresaw but efforts made on his behalf were undermined by Arkansas parties determined to wreak an awful vengeance on him. At first there seemed to be some hope for Lowery after Lawrence A. Nixon, an African American physician in El Paso and leader of the local NAACP chapter, visited him in jail and then convinced a prominent white attorney, Fred C. Knollenberg, to make overtures on his behalf to the Texas governor, Pat Morris Neff. Knollenberg had represented Black clients in various capacities but his most famous case was one he and Nixon would later launch to end the white primary in Texas. That saga began when Nixon sought to vote in the 1924 Texas Democratic primary, a direct challenge to a law the legislature passed the year before, which restricted the primary to white voters. Election officials turned him away from the polls, and he brought suit with Knollenberg representing him. In *Nixon v. Herndon* (1927), the U.S. Supreme Court overturned the Texas law, but the state simply rewrote it and, again, Nixon sued. In 1932, in *Nixon v. Condon*, the Court again overturned the law. This case was instrumental in the 1944 ruling in *Smith v. Allwright*, a Texas case that overturned white primary laws across the South.[21] Clearly, these men made a powerful partnership, and Lowery had some reason to trust them. It was Knollenberg who convinced Governor Neff to intervene with Governor McRae of Arkansas to secure a promise of a fair trial.[22]

Despite McRae's assurances that Lowery would be returned to Little Rock where he would stand trial, the Arkansas governor found that he had little influence upon the officers who traveled to Texas to take charge of the prisoner and no influence over a group of men determined to interfere with his transfer. The Mississippi County officers dispatched to return Lowery to Arkansas—Jesse Greer and D. H. Dickson—were directed to bring the prisoner to Little Rock but ignored those instructions.[23] As mentioned, Greer was the part-time constable whose full-time job was working for planter Lee Wilson, Oscar Craig's brother-in-law. Instead of taking a train from El Paso through Texarkana, which would have been the direct route to reach Arkansas's capital city, Greer and Dickson took Lowery on a circuitous route to New Orleans and north up the Illinois Central Railroad. According to one account, Mississippi County sheriff

Dwight Blackwood, who would come under fire for failing to prevent the lynching, later defended himself and the circuitous route, saying, "I knew several days ago that they [the mob] had men at Texarkana, Hoxie and Jonesboro and that we wouldn't have a chance going that way, so we took the only route left open. We found later that they had men at New Orleans and were tipped off when my men left that place."[24] The governor remarked that he had "asked that Lowery be brought direct to Little Rock from El Paso for safe keeping and he could not understand why the negro should have been taken that round-about way through New Orleans, Mississippi and Tennessee instead of direct to Texarkana and thence to Little Rock and the state penitentiary."[25] Blackwood, though, was in frequent contact with the governor in the days leading up to Lowery's transfer, and it seems likely he would have shared any genuine misgivings about the route and the details of the transfer with McRae. In response to the governor's criticism, Blackwood blamed the "activity of certain negro lodges and the free publicity of the actions of Governor McRae in behalf of Lowery from the time he was placed in jail at El Paso until he was taken from my deputies at Sardis, Miss., were solely responsible for the mob's action."[26] It is unclear precisely what Blackwood meant by the reference to the "activity of certain negro lodges" but it is certainly true that the NAACP was exerting considerable pressure and that Governor McRae was in contact with that organization. In fact, there was some initial confusion about whether Greer and Dickson had received a telegram the governor sent to El Paso, but it was later confirmed that the communication had been delivered to them.[27]

Whether the sheriff and the deputies responsible for delivering Lowery safely to Little Rock for trial were culpable or not, their failure to protect him had tragic consequences. At 5:00 a.m. on January 26, just half an hour before the train was due to stop in Sardis, six mud-covered automobiles carrying between twenty-two and twenty-five armed men arrived at the station. The leader of the group told the night watchman that "he had been appraised by a telegram from New Orleans that the officers and the negro were on the train." He indicated that the group intended to take Lowery from the train rather than allow him to reach the safety of the penitentiary in Little Rock.[28] When the train arrived thirty minutes later, they boarded it and seized Lowery from Greer and Dickson. Although the two officers claimed that they were taken by surprise, their quick and easy surrender astonished Governor McRae, who complained of their "lamb-like docility."[29] According to some reports, the posse intended to parade him through the streets of Memphis, but, with feelings running high because of the inflammatory newspaper accounts of the murders, that city's authorities wanted no part of that spectacle or the disorder certain to accompany it and set up a roadblock. The posse, somehow alerted to the existence of the barricade, skirted the city and stopped at Fowler's Restaurant in Millington, Tennessee, just northeast of Memphis, for lunch. Lowery was taken into the restaurant "and kept under observation while the party ate." An observer remarked he "said nothing, but showed the intense strain he was under. He realized he was on his way to death."[30]

From Fowler's Restaurant, the men and their prisoner headed to the Mississippi River where they boarded boats and crossed at Nodena Landing, which was in sight of the Craig home. Somewhere between five hundred and six hundred men, together with Dick and Hugh Craig, who were still recovering from their wounds, were on hand in a large grassy area that formed a natural amphitheater. A few women were among the crowd, and, at Lowery's request, his wife and daughter (in some accounts "his children") were brought to the scene, presumably so he could say his goodbye. He was chained to a log and "questioned," but no transcript of that interrogation survives. As the *Osceola Times* later reported, no one was willing to identify those present. Lowery was placed "on top of a huge pile of dry leaves and cracker boxes. Gasoline was applied to his body and a torch lighted. As the flames ate away his abdomen, a member of the mob stepped forward and saturated Lowery's body with gasoline. When he burned too fast, water was splashed on him." Although some reporters indicated he screamed and begged them to end his life, others claimed that he remained remarkably silent and only uttered a distress call common to one of one of his fraternal lodges.[31] The brutal nature of the retribution was not simply to punish Lowery for the deaths of two white people but also to serve as a warning to the Black community of sharecroppers. The system of plantation agriculture would brook no defiance on the part of labor, no challenge to the power of the planter class.

In the end, similar to the situation in the Elaine Massacre, no white man was held to account for the Lowery lynching. Immediately following the lynching, Governor McRae declared his intention to "recommend to the legislature that any Sheriff or officer who permitted or did not prevent the lynching of persons within his jurisdiction should be removed from office."[32] A Little Rock newspaper, however, suggested prophetically that the effort to pass such legislation "would meet bitter opposition from the legislative delegations from the so-called 'Black-belt' counties or counties having large negro populations." So incensed was the governor, in fact, that he suggested that the incident might attract federal attention. "Inasmuch as the negro was taken from an interstate train and brought from Mississippi into Arkansas where he was killed, the matter may come within the purview of federal authorities, and it is possible that this occurrence may result in the enactment of federal statutes for the prevention of crimes which should be prevented by our county officers."[33] Whether intentionally or not, he was offering an argument for the passage for a federal antilynching law—or near enough to it—something the NAACP was attempting. As Karlos Hill has argued, the NAACP pamphlet "An American Lynching" included appalling details of the lynching precisely to appeal to the sensibilities of the public and officials, all in an effort to buttress their campaign for an antilynching law.[34]

Neither state nor federal action was taken, however, and, with one exception, the perpetrators remained unidentified. A *Chicago Defender* article named Oscar Craig's brother-in-law, Lee Wilson, as playing a role in the lynching. The article reported that an arrest warrant had been issued for Wilson, whom the paper described as a sawmill owner, in connection with the lynching, but there is reason for skepticism. No record of such an arrest warrant could be located, the *Defender* article was published without an author byline, and it is not known who provided the newspaper with this information.[35] Even without confirmation from the public record of an arrest warrant, the *Chicago Defender*'s account cannot be entirely dismissed. First, Wilson was the most powerful man in the region, and it was his brother-in-law and niece who had been killed in the confrontation with Lowery. He had the prominence and moral authority as a relative to demand a trial and prevent the lynching. He did not. Second, his son, Lee Wilson Jr., was the commander of the American Legion Post at the town of Wilson, to whom the governor addressed a telegram calling upon him to "to use every means at your command in assisting civil authorities to uphold the law and prevent lynching of the negro who will arrive at Nodena tonight."[36] Instead, the younger Lee Wilson indicated to a local reporter that "feeling against Henry Lowery was so acute that he doubted if the lynching could be averted."[37] Third, Jesse Greer, who worked for Lee Wilson & Company and had been charged with returning Lowery safely to Little Rock for trial, had taken a route that seems to have been calculated to coincide with the plans of a posse. If it is true that an arrest warrant had been issued for Wilson, it would have come from Sheriff Blackwood, who was himself under scrutiny for having allowed the lynching to take place.[38] If Blackwood secured a warrant for his arrest, it might explain the animus Lee Wilson developed toward Blackwood, a hatred that survived into 1932 when Blackwood was running for the Democratic nomination to the governor's office.[39] Wilson did everything in his power to secure the nomination for Blackwood's rival. Though not solely due to Wilson's efforts, Blackwood lost the nomination. If Blackwood did indeed attempt to arrest Lee Wilson, it challenges assumptions about the power planters exercised in plantation areas or, at the very least, suggests that the Lowery lynching was a step too far.

And what of Lowery's lodge brothers who had been implicated in Lowery's initial escape? They survived, unlike many members of the Farmers and Household Union and hundreds of other innocent Black men, women, and children in Phillips County. The Elaine violence led to a mass exodus of Black labor from the county and an ongoing crisis in its plantation economy, a crisis that was not lost on planters elsewhere. It is likely that the effort to contain the violence after the Lowery lynching was motivated as much—or maybe more—by a desire to protect the plantation system rather than some altruistic pursuit of justice. Nevertheless, the survival of Lowery's compatriots was not without drama. Mississippi County authorities arrested Morris Jenkins and his wife, Jenny, along with Mott Orr, Walter Johnson, and John Redditt and incarcerated them in the Crittenden County jail in nearby Marion. By the time the mob that burned Lowery turned their attention toward his friends, the lynchers were exhausted, and "the almost impassable dirt roads" probably saved the prisoners. Meanwhile, John Williams and Henry Corbin were being held in the north Mississippi County jail in Blytheville on charges of abetting Lowery's escape. Believing that the lynch mob at Nodena was on its way to Blytheville, the "courthouse and jail were barricaded," and Sheriff Blackwood and Circuit Judge R. H. Dudley stood with "forty armed men" prepared to fend off any effort to reach the prisoners.[40] A reporter from the *Memphis Press* was on the scene in Blytheville and described the frenzied effort to protect the prisoners. Sharpshooters were placed on roofs and "squads of men were stationed at points of vantage thruout [*sic*] the building." Other men were stationed inside the jail and "rushed thruout [*sic*] the building guarding doors and flashing lights in each other's eyes. The guards in the building were under instructions to shoot the minute that an attempt was made to rush the jail." The reporter claimed to be "more afraid that they would start shooting each other before the mob arrived. . . . The majority of them were a bit excited, and with the building in darkness, it was impossible to tell which were guards."[41] In the end, muddied roads stymied what remnants of the Nodena mob tried to reach the jail, probably preventing an attack.

The two men in Blytheville were soon transported to the Pemiscot County jail in Caruthersville, Tennessee, for safekeeping but eventually moved to Little Rock. The five prisoners in Marion were moved to Memphis a day or so after the Lowery lynching in order to place them on the train to Little Rock. They were briefly held in the city jail—the sheriff refused to take them at the Shelby County jail—before being transported to the Memphis Grand Central Station "in a closed car." Once at the station, "they were led down a long freight chute and taken to the track level in the freight elevator, just in time to board the fast Rock Island train . . . for Little Rock."[42] According to one report, they were to be tried in late February, but no record of their prosecutions has been located. Two of them, Morris and Jenny Jenkins, could be found in the 1930 census, working as sharecropper and wife on a Pulaski County plantation. It may well be that they served time in prison for having aided Lowery, but that was not the only possible price they paid. Prior to being discovered as a Lowery confederate, Jenkins had been a caretaker for a Memphis hunting club in Crittenden County, a position of some authority. His status as a sharecropper at age sixty-five was a step down.[43]

Given the association of his lodge brothers with Lowery's escape to El Paso, there was "considerable talk [throughout southern Mississippi County] . . . to start a campaign to break up the various negro fraternal lodges throughout the state."[44] One white observer, clinging to the unfounded conviction that southern African Americans were docile and content, alleged that the lodges were "said to have been organized by smart eastern negroes for the double purpose of inciting the southern negro and for getting what money they could out of him."[45] It was a common white delusion shared with the Phillips County whites who said virtually the same thing about the Farmers and Household Union. It remains unknown whether an effort to eliminate Black lodges occurred elsewhere in Arkansas, but records of the Universal Negro Improvement Association establish that there were no Garvey clubs—organizations formed in southern rural areas under the association's auspices—in southern Mississippi County. The Garvey clubs focused on self-improvement, promoted the segregation of the races (to maintain the purity of Black women), and supported a back-to-Africa movement. It was more than a fraternal club, as women were often heavily involved, and it was more public facing than traditional Black fraternal organizations. Wearing military regalia, Garveyites paraded on the streets, calling attention to themselves in a way that south Mississippi County African Americans may have found too dangerous in the aftermath of the Lowery lynching. Nevertheless, the formation of Garvey clubs in the northern portion of the county may be, as historian Kenneth Barnes suggests, connected to the Lowery lynching.[46]

Without the "testimony" that Lowery allegedly provided his inquisitors at Nodena Landing, there was no word from him as to the circumstances of his confrontation with Craig, no "possible" record of any indictment of the plantation system as it operated in the Arkansas Delta. Ironically, Lowery's lynching and the Elaine Massacre occurred just as the global cotton complex started to unravel and sharecropping along with it. Other industries were already in the process of displacing cotton as global operators, and other agricultural commodities were soon to overtake cotton as the dominant crop in the old cotton South and the Mississippi River Valley. Cotton and the sharecropping system had barely another two decades of life left in them. Government programs that arose out of the 1930s New Deal bailed out planters and land-owning farmers and—circumventing the workings of the free market—extended them an economic safety net through farm programs. Cotton planters would use the funds they received from the government to diversify, mechanize, and, after World War II, begin to use chemicals, all of which eliminated the need for the sharecropping system. Sharecroppers would become a burden to planters in the post–World War II South, who no longer needed year-round labor. Historian Don Holley calls the New Deal, in fact, the "second great emancipation"—an emancipation of planters from the burden of labor-intensive cotton farming.[47] But it was not an emancipation that beckoned a better future on the farm for Black sharecroppers.

CHAPTER 5

Black Women, Violence, and Criminality in Post–World War I Arkansas, 1919–1922

CHERISSE JONES-BRANCH

IN FEBRUARY 1921, Gov. Thomas McRae appointed reformer, educator, and farmer Laura Conner to serve on the Arkansas Penitentiary Commission. During her tenure, she often received clandestine notifications about the sexual and physical abuse incarcerated Black women endured. Conner remembered, "Letters were slipped to me and one girl told me personally of her abuse by free white men working on the farm."[1] The sexual and physical violence these Black women experienced was often tied to their exploitation as sources of labor in the plantation areas near the Tucker Prison Farm in Jefferson County and the Cummins Prison Farm in Lincoln County. Penitentiaries became sites of exploitation and abuse for Black female inmates who were often hired out as domestic servants, even though this practice was forbidden under state law.[2]

In one particularly egregious situation, a former inmate, Torressia Dancler McDowell, revealed to Conner in a 1921 interview the conditions under which she was forced to serve her sentence as a domestic servant for the Tucker Prison Farm's physician. Tucker, first opened in 1916, was actually for white prisoners. Most African American prisoners were housed at Cummins Prison Farm, but Black women prisoners were frequently sent to Tucker to cook and perform other domestic duties.[3] McDowell labored daily in the physician's private home from 4:00 in the morning until 11:00 p.m. or midnight. She was also beaten by the Tucker Prison Farm superintendent, Dee Horton, after she protested being accused of theft. Horton often referred to McDowell and other Black women inmates as "bulls," a racist term meant to defeminize and

81

dehumanize them and to justify their subsequent sexual assault and rape. McDowell resisted by declaring that they were women and not bulls, and for this she and the other women were forced to get up and run when, as she said, "I couldn't hardly pick myself up . . . was sick nearly all the time with female troubles." She sought temporary refuge by running away. Unfortunately, she was caught in nearby Wabbaseka and returned to Tucker, where she was taken into a room full of men, forced to undress, and beaten.[4] McDowell recalled that her clothing was "torn into shreds" and that she was struck "until the blood came."[5]

Black women prisoners were subject to the authority of white prison officials, who inherently possessed what scholar Sarah Haley called "a sovereignty that was enforced by the unfettered power to injure."[6] And injure they did. After Horton raped and impregnated McDowell, he and the prison physician repeatedly attempted to abort her unborn child by opening her womb with forceps and inserting gauze into her cervix. At one point, Horton insisted that he did not "want the curse of a Damn nigger brat on him" before attempting to "mash the child out." Horton threatened that if she ever told anyone he was the child's father he would kill her.[7] The child was born in December 1920 just after McDowell's release from Tucker.[8]

The sexual abuse of Black women inmates was an open secret in Arkansas prisons. In 1921, an investigation at the Tucker Prison Farm, which prompted Laura Conner to call for Horton's removal, revealed not only the horrendous conditions in which prisoners lived but also "charges of alleged misconduct by wardens and guards with negro women."[9] In a 1922 letter to the *Arkansas Democrat*, Conner recalled what had happened to McDowell and requested that her charges against Horton be investigated in "the pure name of our citizenship." She additionally said that this was just "one instance of the abuse of the chastity of these helpless creatures" and recommended to the "good people of Arkansas" that "some of the gold being coined from the backs of the convicts be spent in providing a Negro female camp just as is provided for white women at Jacksonville, Ark." Arkansas authorities, as historian Ryan Anthony Smith has found, not only ignored Conner's charges but also silenced her by forcing her to resign from the prison board.[10]

Sexual and physical violence was pervasive among Black female inmates, and Arkansas prisons were notorious for their deplorable conditions and high inmate mortality rates. Using the story of the African American women prisoners who empowered themselves by offering their testimony to Conner as an important starting point, this essay is a foray into a little-explored topic about Black women, violence, and their presumed criminality in post–World War I Arkansas. It is informed by a deep reading of Talitha LeFlouria's *Chained in Silence: Black Women and Convict Labor in the New South*. This excellent book written by a stellar scholar focuses on African American women's presence in Georgia's prison system. Such a study has never been done on Arkansas, a state notorious for having one of the most brutal prison systems in the nation.[11] For the most part, authorities (and most white Arkansans) tolerated and even encouraged the abuse of women like McDowell because they saw Black females, especially those convicted of crimes, as deserving of it. White-owned Arkansas newspapers sensationalized Black women's crimes and portrayed them (and the entire race) as prone to violence, immorality, and in need of policing. But Black women's lives did not reflect inherent criminality. Rather, they were products of the difficult times in which many African Americans lived after World War I, as opportunities for jobs and land ownership vanished and whites violently reinforced Jim Crow laws to uphold the racial hierarchy and stem the tide of Black assertiveness. Thus, Black women's attempts at social and economic mobility often got them sent to the penitentiary and placed under the violent authority of people like Superintendent Horton.

Many of these Black women—whose parents may have been enslaved or lived through Reconstruction—were born into lives of struggle and resistance. As LeFlouria has argued, "Freedwomen and their daughters' lives were broadly circumscribed by racial hostility, violence, terror, poverty, and exclusion. The confluence of these menacing social and economic forces, combined with a predatory legal establishment, fostered a fertile environment for notions of Black female crime to emerge."[12] These Black women lived during an era of heightened concerns about "Black criminality" and along with it an increased dedication to reducing what many whites generally considered a moral defect among African Americans. Although much research remains to be done on this topic, a cursory glance and a gendered analysis reveals much about Black women's social and economic lives and the reality of their exposure to crime and violence in Arkansas in the aftermath of a major international war. Black women's criminality and incarceration almost always resulted from the clash between their determination to maintain their independence and move up the economic ladder and white efforts to keep them dependent, poorly paid, and under control.

In May 1919, the *Daily Arkansas Gazette* recorded the number of convicts in the state penitentiary system as 855: 272 white men, 550 Negro men, and 33 Negro women. No white women were included; in fact, when white women were incarcerated, newspapers noted it as an exception, portrayed them as victims of misfortune, and focused on efforts to pardon or rescue them.[13] Mary Dewees, who from 1920 to 1924 was the superintendent of the all-white Arkansas State Farm for Women in Jacksonville, wrote that "the work of the reformatory is one of changing old patterns into new, of reforming new habits of work, of play, of thought, and of developing principles of character which may enable a woman to feel her responsibility as a potential being in the community."[14] Dewees imagined transforming white women prisoners into wholesome citizens—that is, they were considered to be redeemable. Such possibilities, however, were typically not extended to Black women. It remains unclear what crimes the thirty-three Black women were charged with, but they—unlike white women—were incarcerated in a space where the vast majority of inmates were male.[15] It is also likely that their numbers were higher than what the newspapers reported. Black women prisoners routinely were inadequately documented and sent to county work farms or jails to serve their sentences.[16]

Most studies of African Americans in post–World War I Arkansas have emphasized Black men's experiences. While there exists an ever-growing body of scholarship on African American women's history, woefully little of it explores Black female criminality and violence.[17] Court and prison records bring much to bear in fleshing out the contours and complexities of the lives of those whose voices have been rendered silent. This piece is an important and necessary exploration into how Arkansas newspapers chronicled Black women's lives within a shifting economic and political milieu. LeFlouria has correctly assessed that most scholarship "elude[s] any in-depth discussion of women's experiences . . . within the carceral regimes of the post emancipation South," likely because the sources that could be used to examine their unique positioning during these years were either unavailable or inaccessible. The ever-increasing digitization of newspapers, however, provides a useful tool to help understand the ways that race and gender shaped and complicated Black women's lives in post–World War I Arkansas.[18] They allow us to rescue stories that might otherwise be lost to obscurity. They make Black women visible.

Much of Black women's "criminality" was rooted in their fight for wages and economic justice for their families. This was clearly the case for the women arrested during the 1919 Elaine Massacre. One Black woman was driven from her home and jailed in Helena, where Black women were routinely "whipped as well as the men." When she returned to Elaine to collect what was left of her families' belongings and receive payment for the crops she and her family had harvested, the farm manager told her that if she did not "get out and stay out he would kill her, burn her up and no one would know where she was." She was later rearrested, incarcerated for eight days, and forced, along with other Black women, to work from three in the morning until nine or ten at night. In another example, a female Progressive Farmers and Household Union of America member was dragged from her home, beaten, and then jailed. Gender clearly did not protect Black women from physical and possibly sexual violence.[19] They were rarely perceived as worthy of protection. A racially defined moral weakness was mapped upon them that permitted some whites to assume their actions were always criminal, their bodies deviant and accessible, and their femininity assailable.[20]

As World War I came to an end, so too did many Black women's opportunities for lucrative employment beyond spirit-depleting and sexually exploitative labor. As a result, some Black women were forced by the deeply oppressive social environment in which they lived to resort to theft as a way to sustain themselves.[21] Pearline Moss, a former employee of Mrs. E. N. Sparks, who resided on State Street in Little Rock, confessed to stealing several sheets and towels from Sparks's home because she did not have any of her own. She was also accused of taking a watch, a charge she denied, but for this crime she was fined ten dollars and sentenced to fifteen days on the county farm.[22] Soldiers with money as a result of their military service were often desperate Black Arkansas women's best victims. In November 1919, Little Rock police chief Burl C. Rotenberry ordered his officers to arrest two Black women who allegedly had violently robbed Sgt. Garra A. Laster, a soldier at nearby Camp Pike. Rotenberry accused the two women of striking Laster in the head in an alley on Second and Chester Streets and robbing him of $220 in cash and a Liberty Bond worth $100. While the emphasis was on the women's criminal act, it is less clear what Sergeant Laster was doing in the alley.[23]

For many people, including some African Americans, women like Pearline Moss and those accused of robbing Sergeant Laster were unworthy of protection because they did not operate within the confines of respectability. That is, their behavior repudiated middle-class notions of racial self-determination and in fact hindered the Black elite's resolve to prove to white Americans that members of their race were entitled to full citizenship and equal opportunity. But if read against the grain, Black women's criminal actions actually reflected their own sense of self-help and determination in a social and political context that provided them with few honest opportunities to better their circumstances. This was particularly the case among working-class Black women who, because they were either unemployed or poorly paid when they were employed, resorted to criminal activities.[24]

Black women's criminality often resulted from disputes with employers. In the absence of economic opportunity and political power, Black women sometimes exacted revenge to settle their grievances. In October 1921, police arrested Minnie Williams and Alice Jenkins for setting fire to Mrs. J. T. Gillespie's home at 1217 Louisiana Street in Little Rock. Both had been fired as cooks in the Gillespie home, which was also a boarding house. Henry Clark, a Black employee who lived in the rear of the boarding house, informed police that he saw the women, who were dressed in long black cloaks, pour kerosene on the house and then set it aflame. Clark extinguished the fire before it caused any damage, and fire department employees set bloodhounds on Williams and Jenkins, who were discovered and apprehended. Clark was then arrested as well, although the account does not explain why.[25] While what these women had done was a crime, it can also be read as an act of resistance. At a time when the only lawful vocation available to most Black women was domestic service, it was entirely likely that they were underpaid or that their employer had stiffed them on wages. Existing in a system that did not value the back-breaking and soul-crushing labor required to cook and clean while carrying the risk of sexual violation, these Black women upended the system. Unlike white women who could avail themselves of the police or civil court, Williams and Jenkins registered their discontent and animosity with their former employer and settled their score in the only way they could.[26]

When they were arrested, Black women often attempted to liberate themselves from the horrid conditions of their incarceration in an attempt to preserve their dignity. According to one study of Black prisoners in Alabama, women often courageously professed their own vision of freedom by challenging and defying prison officials. They did so in groups or pairs, which suggests that women prisoners encouraged and supported each other.[27] In March 1919, Salina Collins and Laura Sessions escaped from the Pulaski County jail in the chaos following the shooting of another inmate named Guy Craig. The women, who had been convicted of highway robbery, were being held in the jail until they could be transferred to the state penitentiary. They took advantage of the opportunity to escape during the melee surrounding Craig, who had attempted to escape as well.[28] Escape was also a necessary act of resistance because, as Daina Ramey Berry and Kali Nicole Gross have noted, Black women spent more time in prison than white women. In fact, they persuasively argue that Black women were overrepresented in the prison system. When they were released, it was often to work under exploitative conditions in white homes. While Berry and Gross speak specifically about Black women in northern urban areas, this appears to have been the case in Arkansas as well.[29]

The limited economic opportunities afforded Black women in Jim Crow Arkansas often forced them to engage in illegal activities or underground economies, which subjected them to criminal prosecution. In the era of Prohibition, no activity offered Black women a greater chance to make enough money to survive as bootlegging. In one 1920 example, the police chief and the military police detachment from Camp Pike arrested Anna Rodgers and Cora Harrison for bootlegging or transporting whiskey. Each woman allegedly had a pint of moonshine, a small amount usually associated with personal use rather than sale. Nonetheless, they were convicted and fined $200 each, a sum that was prohibitive for the two women, who for that reason were remanded to jail.[30] Similarly, Millie Pendleton and Fannie Price were arrested in Pine Bluff in 1921 for transporting five gallons of liquor, which the deputy sheriff found in their homes.[31] The arrests of Rodgers, Harrison, Pendleton, and Price clearly reveal how Black women, facing limited economic opportunities, undermined African American respectability politics, middle-class norms, and white patriarchal culture when they resorted to criminal activities in order to survive.[32]

And indeed, many of these women were not adults at all, but in fact teenagers. Their youth, however, did not protect them from arrest. In 1922, Alberta Forrest, a fifteen-year-old runaway from Georgia, was found guilty and fined $100 for "procuring whiskey." Forrest, though, had a turn of seemingly good fortune. The jury recommended suspending her sentence if she elected to return home, an option that proved impossible for her and many unhoused young women during these years.[33] Forrest had clearly identified a lucrative trade in whiskey because she had been arrested the previous month and charged with "selling liquor," which landed her in jail with a $1,000 bond.[34]

Following the Civil War and emancipation, authorities began arresting newly freed African Americans, including women, for vagrancy. Such charges criminalized Black people generally and delimited their agency and autonomy as free people. This was especially true for Black women who were convicted. Saidiya Hartman has described vagrancy as "status criminality" that was "tethered ineradicably to Blackness." Race defined criminality. The police widely utilized vagrancy as a means to target and control young Black women and others. It did not matter if they had committed a crime; their presence in urban spaces and their free movement was enough to threaten the racial status quo.[35]

The enforcement of vagrancy laws to police the lives of Black women continued in Arkansas after the Great War. In February 1921, "18 negroes and four negro women" were arrested on vagrancy charges as part of several raids ordered by the police chief to round up all of Little Rock's unemployed. Some of those caught, including one Black woman, were also arrested for gambling.[36] In Pine Bluff, Estelle Smith and Georgia Streeter were arrested in a raid and fined fifty dollars for "running and disorderly rouse."[37] Intentionally vague, these charges were an excuse to justify monitoring Black women's actions.

Limited economic prospects and the impoverished living conditions resulting from them often led to African American women's arrests for "disturbing the peace," another vague charge that often gave authorities the power to keep them marginalized. In most instances, newspaper accounts list the names and races of those arrested but do not describe the disturbance. When articles did provide details, they marked Black women as unfeminine. For example, in Little Rock in May 1920, local police arrested Artie Black and Hattie Griffin, each identified as a "negro woman," for disturbing the peace after breaking up a fight. The *Arkansas Gazette* used it as an opportunity to call the women "embattled amazons" and to perpetuate the myth that Black people were impervious to pain by detailing the severe blows inflicted on each woman "with neither showing the effects of the punishment."[38]

Black women also got into trouble with the police when they resorted to violence to protect and defend themselves during the domestic disputes that frequently occurred in the unsanitary and unsafe residential spaces where poor Black people with few resources and many frustrations were forced to live. Seventeen-year-old Mable McGraw was arrested and held in the city jail for killing Willie Haynes, twenty-five, who had threatened and beaten her on numerous occasions. McGraw had been living with Haynes as his wife since she was fourteen years old. When he refused to work, McGraw was forced to provide for both of them. Haynes usually spent the pathetically little money she earned shooting craps. Whenever McGraw refused him, Haynes beat her; in fact, when she was arrested, her right eye was badly discolored and her neck bore a mark. McGraw, however, had defended herself as Haynes choked her by grabbing a small pocketknife and stabbing him.[39]

Arkansas newspapers were rife with articles about Black women's incarceration for violent crimes in the late 1910s and the 1920s. The stress resulting from extreme poverty and deprivation in the postwar years created a flourishing environment for women to become involved in non-domestic conflicts with each other as they struggled to survive. Talitha LeFlouria has argued that these entanglements were the byproducts of "unintelligible causes" that "escalated from minor skirmishes into lethal altercations."[40] This was especially true when women were fueled by alcohol consumption and verbal sparring that too often devolved into violence. In November 1920, during a drunken confrontation, Beatrice Douglas assaulted Pearl Richardson by hitting her in the head with a bottle because she had unceasingly "nagged her." Richardson consequently spent several days in the hospital. Douglas, whom Little Rock police arrested in her home, was charged with assault with intent to kill. She remained in jail until Richardson was well enough to testify against her.[41]

Black women were sometimes arrested for defending other members of their race against white violence. For example, in August 1921, Little Rock authorities arrested a Black man and a Black woman who intervened on behalf of a Black woman, Mary Carter, who was being assaulted by a white man, W. F. Smith. Smith accused Carter of robbing him of twenty-five dollars and chased her down in Little Rock, at which point things became violent. While Carter may have committed a crime, she also defended herself. During the ensuing scuffle, an African American man and woman who lived in nearby servants' quarters rushed to Carter's aid. Unfortunately, they were rewarded for their assistance by being arrested for "disturbing the peace."[42]

Because they could expect little protection from the police, Black women engaged in criminal acts and violence to regulate behavior in their own communities. In Newport, Arkansas, Black women punished an African American man who deserted his sick wife. He returned a few days later but displayed no remorse for abandoning his partner. A young woman "possessing the powers to beguile" lured him to a secluded spot near the levee where "a half score or more of Negro women" beat him with sticks and whips. After he had been soundly thrashed, he was allowed to "crawl to his feet and stagger away." It is not clear if these women were prosecuted for their actions, but their readiness to assume such a risk suggests that Black women were willing to engage in criminal activity to protect themselves and each other.[43]

Sexual violence also defined the lives of many Black women, but authorities only stepped in to protect the extremely young. Authorities in the Clark County town of Gurdon charged Jim Estes, a fifty-year-old white timber company employee, with statutory rape after a mixed-race infant whom he had fathered with a young Black girl was found buried in the woods. The unnamed girl, who claimed Estes was the father and whom the *Arkansas Democrat* article described as a "half-wit," was only fourteen years old.[44] A Pulaski County grand jury charged African American shoe repair shop owner James Kindle with assaulting fifteen-year-old Bertha Byrd, an orphan living in a boarding house on Broadway Street, after the police found the back door open, the interior in disarray, and blood spots "at various points." In December 1922, Frank Miller was found guilty of "carnal abuse" for attacking a twelve-year-old Black girl in North Little Rock. The jury, unfortunately, was unable to agree on a sentence and left the decision up to the court.[45]

Unlike the orphaned, most Black women were presumed to be immoral and, for this reason, their reports of rape or assault were typically not taken seriously. Thus, they were often prosecuted for sex crimes even when they were the victims.[46] Willie Lee Johnson, for instance, was charged with immorality and fined ten dollars on Christmas Eve in 1922, then released after serving only three days of her sentence. Although the "Christmas spirit," as per the title of the article from which this story is taken, may have entered the First Division Municipal Court, it is possible that Johnson either had been sexually assaulted or compelled to engage in prostitution to support herself in the face of extreme deprivation and poverty. It is unlikely that Johnson had the money to pay her fine and probably had no place to go once she left jail.[47]

Many of the African American women languishing in Arkansas's carceral system had been arrested for soliciting or prostitution. The prostitution charges were often false and, according to Saidiya Hartman, frequently utilized to "establish the boundaries of what a Black woman could and could not do."[48] In February 1921, two Black women testified that they had been robbed by two white men—a soldier, Pvt. J. M. Collier, and his companion—who had held up a bus at Camp Pike. Collier maintained his innocence, although he was charged with "highway robbery" and held on $1,000 bond. The women were fined ten dollars for soliciting.[49] Whether they were actually guilty of this crime is irrelevant. What was clear is that because of their close proximity to white men and soldiers in particular, whom they may have assumed were flush with cash, they were presumed by default to be involved in illicit activity.

The prostitution charges meted out to Black women were often false, but widespread beliefs about Black women's hypersexuality and criminality made it difficult for those charged to defend themselves.[50] In 1920, the aforementioned Beatrice Douglas was arrested and fined ten dollars for soliciting after she and another young woman were seen getting into a car with two white men.[51] Noted as "a young negro girl with a long police record," Douglas was arrested again in 1921, this time for vagrancy. She was sent to the women's reformatory in Jacksonville, only to be refused because the facility was for white women. The judge before whom Douglas appeared had grown weary of repeatedly seeing her in his courtroom. He fined her again and then said, clearly registering little concern for the young woman's wellbeing, "I suppose we have to put up with her until an automobile runs over her or someone shoots her."[52] With this declaration the judge had effectively determined Douglas' life and worth as a human being were inconsequential.

Furthermore, concerns about sexually transmitted disease (STD) resulting from prostitution were racialized, and Black women's alleged promiscuity was specifically blamed as the culprit. In Little Rock, for instance, white leaders discussed plans to convert state penitentiaries into hospitals and detention homes for women suffering from STDs. Police chief Burl C. Rotenberry deemed this necessary because "99 per cent of all negro women arrested in the city were victims of venereal disease and that some place should be provided where they may receive adequate treatment and at the same time be self-supporting."[53]

While Rotenberry could not possibly have known how many Black women suffered from STDs, what is patently demonstrable is that these reports reveal much about how they engaged in sex work to support themselves and their families in the face of limited economic opportunities. But seemingly uncontrolled and unbridled women troubled middle-class sensibilities, even more so if the women were Black because some read their very existence and that of African Americans generally as the source of contagion. During and after World War I, white southerners were particularly concerned about reducing STDs, an anxiety that was exacerbated by boll weevil infestations, a steep fall in cotton prices, and the migration of African Americans seeking improved circumstances.[54] What Black migrants found in Delta towns and the nearby cities was chronic unemployment, desperation, food insecurity, and disease. In places like Little Rock, this was especially true for Black women migrants, who regularly disregarded Victorian standards of middle-class respectability as impractical. They did so, however, in the midst of an intensifying nationwide movement to reform indigent and unhoused young women.

Although reformers attempted to assist white women migrants by establishing reformatories throughout the South, they were not as concerned about young Black women. Many white people in general believed that criminal behavior and sexual delinquency were endemic among Black women and hence could not be reformed. In fact, one historian has argued that it was not even considered delinquent behavior.[55] Thus when fifteen-year-old Dorothy Anderson, also known as Josephine Harris, was charged with forgery, the court likely would have sentenced her to prison had the victims, the Dubisson brothers, not intervened. The brothers, African American undertakers in Little Rock, likely understood that Anderson/Harris's youth, race, and gender offered her little protection from the harshness of the carceral system. They took pity on her and asked the judge to send her to the Black industrial school in Memphis instead, because there was "no such institution for negro women in Arkansas." The brothers even offered to pay her transportation costs.[56]

The responsibility for creating reformatories or industrial homes for Black women fell to African American organizations like the Arkansas Association of Colored Women (AACW). Founded in 1905 and affiliated with the National Association of Colored Women, the AACW lobbied before and after World War I on behalf of young Black women who, when arrested for crimes, were usually incarcerated with hardened male criminals.[57] When Jennie Thomas was arrested in Little Rock in 1922 for leading a group of young African American men in criminal activity and stealing eleven dollars from a store, she was fined ten dollars and sentenced to eleven months on the Pulaski County farm.[58] Thomas had previously done time at the farm after being arrested for stealing a revolver from Little Rock police chief Rotenberry while cleaning his office when she was a trusty at city hall. The weapon was recovered but Thomas was charged ten dollars and sentenced to six months at the county farm.[59] Unfortunately, young Black women continued to be jailed, instead of being placed in reformatories, for many years to come, despite the AACW's best efforts. Although a reformatory was established for young Black men by 1922, one was not available for Black women until 1949.[60]

What does all of this reveal about Black women, violence, and criminality in post–World War I Arkansas? For starters it demands that scholars contest the archives and the ways in which we read such sources as mainstream newspapers to instead view them through a lens that contextualizes the circumstances under which Black women were criminalized and subjected to violence. As Kali Gross asserts, we must combine "archival research with an expansive interpretive analysis," one that "enables historians to delve more deeply into text and histories that otherwise might be discarded"—or, in the case of Arkansas newspapers, completely overlooked.[61] White-owned newspapers routinely vilified Black women arrested for petty crimes by describing them in unflattering and racist language, their crimes considered a product of inherent Black criminality. Absent in these descriptions was any sense of the context—not only Jim Crow laws and disfranchisement but also the lack of access to well-paying jobs and economic mobility—that pushed Black women to engage in "criminal" acts. Moreover, Black women could not expect protection from sexual violence. Public indifference to the rapes of Black female prisoners like Torressia Dancler McDowell, for instance, was another way to maintain white supremacy.

Most crimes ascribed to this era's Black women—bootlegging being the best example—are evidence of their desire for economic independence and opportunity in post–World War I Arkansas. They deployed these acts as strategies to ensure their survival in the face of extreme racism. When Black women's criminal activity is understood in this way, incarceration takes on a different meaning. While their seemingly antisocial behavior was an affront to white and often Black people, economically marginalized Black women rejected the burden of middle-class sensibilities in favor of their need to survive the difficult circumstances they endured because of their race and gender. By doing so, they created and accessed the best opportunities available to them in post–World War I Arkansas.

CHAPTER 6

Steadily Holding Our Heads above Water

The Flood of 1927, White Violence, and Black Resistance to Labor Exploitation in the Mississippi Delta

MICHAEL VINSON WILLIAMS

ON APRIL 15, 1927, the Memphis *Commercial Appeal*, a white southern newspaper, warned its readership, "The roaring Mississippi River, bank and levee full from St. Louis to New Orleans, is believed to be on its mightiest rampage. . . . All along the Mississippi considerable fear is felt over the prospects for the greatest flood in history." Six days later, army district engineer Maj. John Lee wired the head of the Corps of Engineers, "Levee broke at ferry landing Mounds Mississippi eight A.M. Crevasse will overflow entire Mississippi Delta." This would prove to be one of the most devastating levee breaks of the nation's most horrific flood, and in its wake racialized violence and exploitation increased exponentially.[1]

To deal with the flood and aftermath, whites intensified the labor exploitation, abject violence, and daily brutalities they practiced against African Americans. In response, Black men and women demanded systemic and immediate change and used the flood as a platform for engaging in more national resistance movements for labor equality and an end to white oppression. On June 14, 1927, Walter White, assistant secretary for the National Association for the Advancement of Colored People (NAACP), wrote to Secretary of Commerce Herbert Hoover, who headed up relief operations. White pointed out the atrocities practiced against Black men and women in the flood zones and the need for Hoover and the federal government to provide assistance: "In brief, we are requesting that Negro refugees be permitted full freedom of movement as American citizens, and a checking of the efforts by selfish persons to use the Red

Cross towards retention of Negroes as though they were chattel."[2] Black resistance to labor exploitation and white brutality proved immediate and sustained. The Mississippi Flood of 1927 became the focal point in the NAACP's fight against labor exploitation and push for federal legislative change, a process that would focus organizational leaders' attention on the national Democratic Party leadership as well.

This essay briefly focuses on whites' violent subjugation of the labor of African Americans—tied to the land through economic and, in many instances, environmental circumstances—and their various means of resistance. As a way of highlighting the extreme levels of labor exploitation and the brutality used to enforce it, the Mississippi Flood of 1927 and the consequent federally funded program to rebuild the river's levees provide an important point of analysis. Labor exploitation and white violence were constants for African Americans, as was their resistance to them. Roy Wilkins, NAACP assistant secretary in 1931, noted the important role the Mississippi Flood had on the NAACP's determination to bring about change: "Images of what I had seen in Mississippi [as an undercover investigator]—the grim little river towns, rain-soaked levees, suspicious white faces, poverty-beaten Negroes—stayed fresh in my mind for a long time. I returned from the delta determined to do something about them. The first problem, as it would be all through the [Great] Depression, was to broaden the range of the N.A.A.C.P., to get the association down to where the people were, where race cut the deepest, where the suffering was the worst."[3]

The NAACP dedicated resources to protecting the rights of levee workers and in 1933—during the New Deal —successfully won them higher wages and shorter work hours. "For me," Wilkins noted, "the reward was even more substantial: we had proved that if you pushed the government long enough, hard enough, and in enough of the right places, change could be accomplished. I felt hope and renewed energy. If we could bring a few dimes to Mississippi, perhaps we could one day bring freedom."[4] African Americans, however, would not only bring pressure to bear upon the NAACP to act, but also upon organized labor, including the Brotherhood of Sleeping Car Porters, the National Agricultural Workers Union, and later the Southern Tenant Farmers' Union, and civil rights organizations such as the Urban League. They also engaged prominent Black newspapers and magazines such as the *Chicago Defender*, *The Crisis*, and the *Pittsburgh Courier* in the overall fight for full citizenship rights. By 1933, the federal government felt the crushing pressure exerted by African Americans and the many strategies they employed to expose labor inequality and to bring about real change. Although New Deal programs often failed to meet the needs of African Americans, the NAACP continued to use the issues associated with the Mississippi Flood to challenge inequality.

The resistance measures African Americans deployed against labor exploitation and violence after the flood had their roots in much earlier struggles against white oppression. In the words of historian Vincent Harding, there truly was a river of resistance chronicling the Black Freedom Struggle and that struggle, like its metaphorical river, remains long, wide, and deep.[5] On November 27, 1858, the *Natchez Dailey Courier* ran the following advertisement: It promised "a choice selection of slaves, consisting o[f] MECHANICS, FIELD HANDS, COOKS, WASHERS AND IRONERS, and GENERAL HOUSE SERVANTS." The same advertisement also listed for sale "Mules! Mules! Mules!" which were "raised in Missouri, and recommended for their size and condition."[6] For whites, what this and advertisements like it represented were the realities of Black exploitable labor. They also publicly reinforced whites' belief that they could indeed buy, sell, exploit the labor of, and oppress Black people without repercussions or consequences. Yet African Americans did resist, as the many advertisements for the capture of runaways attest. They also engaged in revolution, broke tools, killed livestock, burned down houses, barns, and fields, and, in some instances, killed their tormentors. The Civil War, however, provided African Americans with additional opportunities for seizing their freedom and for controlling both their labor and their lives. The Reconstruction era also provided the newly freed population with the hope of sociopolitical inclusion; however, they would be disappointed.

For African Americans, the Reconstruction period provided a glimpse of what participatory democracy, freedom, and economic independence could mean; yet it proved short lived. Sociologist and historian William Edward Burghardt Du Bois argued that for a moment the "slave went free; stood a brief moment in the sun; then moved back again toward slavery." For white southerners, particularly white Mississippians, the loss at Appomattox signaled a need to transform battle tactics from an emphasis on guns and cannons into economic and political war with Black labor and Black bodies as the prize. The planter class, in many instances, precipitated the move to control Black labor post-1865. These "planter-capitalists," Du Bois noted, "proposed to protect themselves from further loss by dominating the labor of their former slaves." As a result, in Mississippi there would be "no labor dictatorship or dream of one. White labor took up arms to subdue black labor and to make it helpless economically and politically through the power of property." In the South, it would be "the policy of the state to keep the Negro laborer poor, to confine him as far as possible to menial occupations, to make him a surplus labor reservoir and to force him into peonage and unpaid toil."[7]

Mississippi's 1890 constitutional convention disfranchised African Americans and established means for the continued exploitation of Black labor. T. P. Gore, quoted in *The Daily Clarion-Ledger*, argued that since "the object of the present Convention is to continue white supremacy and discontinue the fear and possibility of black domination, it is well for them to make our 'calling and election sure.'" As a way of avoiding the "indignity of being controlled by black officials," Gore noted that perhaps it would be wise "to incorporate in the new Constitution, a clause forbidding all black citizens or citizens of African descent the right to hold office in the State."[8] The tactics put into place in 1890 to repress Black political power in Mississippi were tied to labor. Unrestrained by Black political strength or economic independence, the planter class believed it could take Black labor outright and without any political or social repercussions. Thus, the plantation system continued to be the bedrock of labor oppression. It was, as historian Neil McMillen wrote regarding Black and white Mississippians' thoughts on labor and race, "a remarkably resilient institution scarcely touched by either civil war or reconstruction."[9]

The Mississippi River's catastrophic flood in 1927 highlighted the power of the plantation system, and whites' unfettered attempts to control and exploit Black labor. It also exposed the pervasive economic and labor exploitation that, unlike the flood waters, did not readily recede. Heavy rains, beginning in August 1926 and continuing into 1927, caused the Mississippi River to crest in April, overwhelming the levees and inundating 170 counties in seven states; this disaster had a particularly profound impact upon Black communities in the Mississippi Delta region.[10] Yet the racial divide that marked the Jim Crow South followed the "refugees" into the hastily erected camps. The racialized way in which African Americans were treated within the camps upheld the tenets of the segregationists' system. The *Pittsburgh Courier*, a Black northern newspaper, reported that in Vicksburg, Mississippi, alone, "6,000 Negroes are living in tents and 4,000 whites are being cared for in the hotels."[11] African Americans bore the brunt of flood-related discrimination and violence; furthermore, they represented a large portion of camp refugees. For example, in Greenville, Mississippi, "90 percent of refugees were Black."[12] Many of those confined to the camps vocalized their desperation. One victim noted, "In many instances our homes are gone. In practically every case, whatever we possessed has been washed away. Already we were in debt up to our necks under the plantation system. We are being fed now by the Red Cross. What can the future hold for us?"[13] There were two converging viewpoints regarding the flood: African Americans who saw it as an opportunity to escape white repression and whites who saw it as a hindrance for controlling their Black labor force; both would eventually collide.

In many ways, the flood serves as a microcosm for understanding how whites generally saw Black labor and their entitlement to it by whatever means they devised. Planters needed Black men and women to fortify the cities and to build and protect their property and, in that, saw no need for further discussion. The Associated Negro Press, the *Pittsburgh Courier* reported, informed its readers that "White planters who see in the devastation wrought by the flood another blow at their labor supply are planning ways and means to make it difficult for the Negroes to leave." To stem the flow of Black labor out of the state, whites issued orders to ensure "that railroad tickets be not sold to black men." Whites' strategic placement of Black men and women in hastily established camps and temporary living facilities also served a calculated purpose. The Associated Negro Press surmised that Negro "refugees on the levees have been placed there for two reasons, first because the levees are high enough to keep them out of the water and second because it makes it easy to guard the Negroes and keep them from getting away."[14] Walter White, NAACP assistant secretary in 1927, was also "informed that the Boy Scouts at Greenville were armed by the Scout Master to stand guard over the Negroes working on the levees until troops came."[15] Not only were African Americans dealing with the catastrophe of the flood itself, but they also were trying to avoid further repression, violence, and death.

Individuals in charge of refugee camps, such as those in Greenville, used conscription to tighten their control over Black labor and tied work to commodities distribution.[16] Whites forced Black men to unload Red Cross supplies, protect white homes, and work on the levees irrespective of their own needs or their families'. When asked about the reliability of Black and white levee workers, one white foreman explained that "you can get more out of the Nigger than you can out of the whites, because you can force the Nigger and get the maximum of work done, while the damn white boy is not inclined to do any more than he has to; and as a rule he is not able to do levee work, anyhow."[17] Once in charge, William A. Percy, "chairman of the Flood Relief Committee and the local Red Cross," worked to secure and control "Negro" labor. He remained committed to ensuring that whites maintained control of Black labor at all cost and be able to conscript it in whatever manner they chose: "All Negroes in Greenville outside of the levee camp who are able to work should work. If work is offered them and they refuse to work they should be arrested as vagrants. Names and addresses of those refusing to work should be telephoned to police headquarters."[18]

In further support of his directives, Percy announced that no rations would "be issued to Greenville Negro women and children unless there is a man in the family, which fact must be certified to by a white person." He also gave white planters the power to deny assistance to their Black workers, threatening "if the 'boss' says you can eat you can and if he says 'no,' then you starve." Also, no Negro men in Greenville or their families would "be rationed unless the men join the labor gang or are employed." Those "Negro men" not working on the levees were to "be given labor tickets which will be punched each day they labor." Percy, in effect, was an admitted "dictator" who used the Red Cross's control of food supplies and transportation services to "enforce" his orders.[19] There were additional constraints that were just as repressive, placing pressure upon African American families. Mandates such as these also created resentment and, in some instances, open resistance. Nannie Clark Peters objected to her husband being conscripted and forced to labor on the levee. In response to "her disapproval," a police "officer threatened to knock her down." Reacting to this verbal threat, several "refugees" came to her aid, but she was still arrested and held overnight. None of this impacted her husband's situation as he remained at work on the levee. The Peters' home had not been impacted by the flood, but his labor was taken all the same.[20] Such actions happened throughout the camps, and when Black men resisted, both they and their families faced dire and sometimes violent consequences.

Case in point, James Gooden was well respected in Greenville's Black community. He was sitting on the steps of his home when police officer James Mosley approached him and demanded that he "come along and work as a garbage cleaner." Although offered a dollar a day, Gooden refused, having already worked all night. He then rose up and walked into the house where Mosley followed him with gun drawn. "*Nigger! Get your black ass in that truck,"* Mosley shouted. Gooden responded in kind with, *"White man. Don't pull no gun on me!"* The two men argued, and, before long, Mosley shot Gooden in the stomach; he "died three hours later at the King's Daughters Hospital." In protest, Black workers stopped all work and demanded that the officer "pay for the slaying." Although arrested, Mosley was later released on bail and many believed that he would "be freed . . . when he . . . [pled] self defense."[21] Even with the death of a Black man who had exercised his right to control how much of his labor he gave and to whom, whites could not fathom the legitimacy of his right to do so.

Although Black men and women fled the camps whenever possible, those who escaped sought help for those still trapped in the system of repression, and activists like Ida B. Wells-Barnett played an integral role in rallying help for camp sufferers. The individuals Wells-Barnett spoke to by phone, the letters she read requesting help, and the personal testimonies she recorded bolstered her sense of urgency. As a journalist, she in turn transformed the pain and anguish she saw and heard into words on paper for the nation to see. The tales of woe and violence she encountered were sickening. Wells-Barnett recalled a particular meeting with one "John Jones." He was twenty-three years old and had escaped from one of the camps in Louisiana. The men, he remembered, were rounded up and taken to work on the levee where they were promised one dollar per day and board. He worked this way for fifteen days without pay. In response to asking for his money and expressing a desire to leave, the foreman shot him in the leg to prevent his escape. His wife rushed to his aid and stopped the bleeding while another man helped him into the tent. Jones later escaped, leaving his wife and children behind until he could later spirit them away.[22] His story was one of many Wells-Barnett heard that inspired her to render aid in any way possible.

Yet there was a larger responsibility at play for Wells-Barnett that typified the work of other organizations and the hope of those directly subjected to labor and racial exploitation. Wells-Barnett challenged her readers to take responsibility for aiding those in need: "Have you readers here in the North no duty to perform for these, our suffering people?" The key lay in publicizing the extent of the suffering itself. "The only way to bring public opinion to action is for those whose race is suffering to cry aloud, and keep on crying aloud until something is done." Crying aloud required, in Wells-Barnett's words, "the combined influence of all our people in the North, East and West, where our votes count, to put a stop to the slavery that is going on right now in the government camps in

Arkansas, Mississippi and Louisiana."[23] In response, African Americans wrote, called, and visited representatives of the Black press and contacted political leaders.

The stories Black men and women shared and the pressure that followed helped publicize their plight and brought the NAACP to full attention. This was, in fact, Black resistance. In June 1927, Walter White wrote Herbert Hoover, who oversaw relief operations in the Mississippi Valley, regarding the forced labor of "some of the Negro flood sufferers." With blue eyes and fair skin, White easily passed for a white man, which allowed him unfettered access to white spaces; he used this to his advantage when investigating camp conditions. His interactions with Gen. Curtis Green, the Mississippi National Guard officer who oversaw the Vicksburg camps, revealed some disturbing facts regarding Black labor and white control. Green informed White that Negroes were "to be held in the camps until the landlords for whom they were working at the time of the flood, came to the camps and 'identified their Negroes.'" Once identified, he continued, "their landlord or his authorized agent would take these Negroes back to the plantation from which they had come, and that no man would be allowed to talk to any other than 'his own Negroes.'"[24]

As multiple news outlets reported that African Americans were in fact being held against their will and forced to labor, white officials attempted to justify such detainments. The *Chicago Defender*, a Black northern newspaper, reported that Dr. Felix J. Underwood, who oversaw the Mississippi Board of Health, tried to explain the need to guard "Negroes" to prevent their leaving the camps. It was necessary to guard them, he noted, "because after the flood they would be needed to get the plantations in shape. Every refugee must return to his respective town and do reconstruction work."[25] The planter class, as historian Robyn Spencer points out, "relied on the presence of an exploitable labor force not only for profit, but as the foundation of their very existence."[26]

African Americans were under constant surveillance, and many planters took extreme measures to ensure they maintained their labor force. The *Chicago Defender* reported that Del Weber, a white man from Greenwood, witnessed between the Mississippi towns of Moorehead and Inverness "more than two thousand [Black] refugees . . . in boxcars. That white planters refuse to allow them to leave, fearing they will never return. Guards are stationed around the cars and the planters have issued warnings that anyone attempting to escape would be slain."[27] Influential Delta resident Oscar Johnston, head of the Delta and Pine Land Company, proved powerful enough to have his 450 tenants sent by train from the Vicksburg camp. They were transported to Deeson, Mississippi, some 260 miles, at no charge, to his personally established "refugee camp, supplied by the Red Cross, patrolled by the National Guard, and managed by his foremen."[28] Through such methods, Walter White acknowledged that Negroes are "bound to the land and to the landlords for whom they were working at the time of the flood as though the Civil War had never been fought or the Emancipation Proclamation never signed."[29]

African Americans' attempts at escaping from the camps, or gaining some type of economic foothold, were also hampered by the Red Cross. Investigative reporter John Louis Spivak noted that the Red Cross often distributed supplies directly to the planters who "were authorized . . . to distribute them among their tenants. The planters thereupon either distributed the food, using it as a weapon to force obedience, or charged the share cropper [sic] for it on his private books, deducting these charges from the money the Negro cropper was supposed to get at the end of the season."[30] In this manner, African Americans often found themselves in greater financial distress after receiving supposed assistance from the Red Cross.

Planters' concern with controlling Black labor proved paramount. General Green's statement to Walter White illustrates how important Black labor was to the Mississippi Delta and thus why whites were so willing to do anything to keep it. Green noted that "the delta region is one of the richest farm sections of the entire country and 'we do not propose to have it stripped of labor.'"[31] Such a statement illuminated the thinking of white business interests in the region regarding control over Black labor. This revelation proved even more significant given the fact that in the Delta lowlands, African Americans comprised 75 percent of the population yet provided 95 percent of the plantation and farm labor power. The Colored Advisory Commission "estimated that out of the 637,000 people forced to flee" due to the floods, "94% lived in three states, Arkansas, Mississippi and Louisiana; and that 69% of the 325,146" housed in the "concentration camps," who depended on the Red Cross for food and shelter, "were colored."[32] Green also provided Walter White with report sheets listing the name of Negroes who had been removed from the camp for use at local industries where "they were put at the heaviest kind of work" and brutally treated and beaten when they refused to labor. " 'It aint [sic] the work,' said one of these refugees, 'we's willing to work. It's the kickin' and cursin' makes it so hard.' "[33] African Americans resisted such treatment and informed the NAACP of the many atrocities they suffered.

Yet many Black men and women took matters into their own hands rather than wait on the NAACP to act. In Memphis, Tennessee, Negroes were tired of the treatment they received and left refugee camps despite attempts by whites to prevent them. They, Walter White reported, eluded "guards at the refugee camp at the Fair Grounds [sic] and escaping, preferring to forego food, shelter, clothing and medical attention rather than go back to the plantation from which they had been driven by the flood."[34] For White, the "greatest and most significant injustice [in this forced labor system] is in the denial to Negroes of the right of free movement and of the privilege of selling their services to the highest bidder. That, if persisted in, would recreate and crystallize a new slavery almost as miserable as the old."[35]

Whites oppressed Black men and women with one economic hand, while reaching out for governmental assistance for themselves with the other. The sheer devastation of the flood caused powerful politicos such as William Hale Thompson, mayor of Chicago, to seek federal assistance for the Mississippi River Valley.[36] However, President Calvin Coolidge proved extremely protective of the federal budget and cared little for committing to any project that might endanger it. In his message to Congress on December 6, 1927, Coolidge argued that local governments were tasked with providing relief in their areas and the federal government's role was to provide "generous relief" when "the sources directly chargeable cannot meet the demand."[37] In response, Mississippi senator Byron Harrison argued that Coolidge's "message does not give to the people of the flood-stricken Mississippi Valley the hope and assurance that the situation warrants and which they have been led by universal public opinion to expect." Political pressure eventually led Coolidge to sign the Jones–Reid bill on May 15, 1928. Also known as the 1928 Flood Control Act, the measure earmarked $325 million for key construction projects and strengthening of levees.[38] This type of federal response demonstrated the government's commitment to rebuilding the levees and addressing flood-related needs of the white property-owning class. However, this act of political goodwill meant little to African Americans as local officials continued forcing them to labor under slave conditions to rebuild levees and conduct other flood-related work.

Coolidge's hands-off demeanor regarding "Negro" suffering played a key role in the political stance some African American leaders took during the 1928 presidential election. Walter White believed that the Republican Party had taken African Americans for granted over the years and, with Coolidge deciding not to run for reelection, the Republican nominee would be Herbert Hoover, who had overseen the Red Cross's flood relief effort. White argued that the "Republicans believe that they own us, body and soul, and will keep on believing that until we ourselves do something about it. Hoover's record during the flood . . . give[s], it seems to me, little or no ground for even slight hope. . . . I do believe that we would fare at least as well under [New York governor and Democratic nominee Al] Smith as president as under Hoover or any other Republican, perhaps a great deal better. I have no illusions as to either party—politics is a matter of expediency and not of principle."[39] For White and the NAACP, the Mississippi Flood continued to be a focal point for expressing discontent with Hoover and the Republican Party:

> Then there is the matter of the repeatedly broken promises of the Republicans, their lies and treachery. There is Hoover's surrender during the flood to the peonage barons of the Delta. There is the rapid decrease of consideration of the Negro by recent Republican administrations. Mind you, I do not for a minute wholly blame the Republicans. Much more do I blame Negroes themselves. No man works for a thing which is already his. So long as Negroes blindly vote any ticket regardless of the treatment of the party whose ticket he votes, so long will [they] be . . . despised and ignored.[40]

Democratic nominee Al Smith seemed a plausible alternative.

The growing issues White and the NAACP had with Herbert Hoover and the Republican Party pushed him and NAACP executive secretary James Weldon Johnson toward supporting Al Smith. White sincerely believed that it was time for Negroes to focus less on party and more on what individual candidates could do for the good of the race. In that sense, Smith proved more promising than Hoover, and White explained his support:

> The nomination of Smith seems to me to offer a fair chance for Negro independence. In the first place I have been promised that Smith will make as strong a pro-Negro statement as he can, considering the bitter fight certain elements in the South are making upon him. . . . Smith's election would, it seems to me, be a long step towards wresting dominance of the Democratic Party from

the southern bourbon and vesting it in the hands of the North and East. Eventually it appears to me that we are going to have an entirely new political alignment—the Republicans will absorb the anti-Negro South and become, through the compromises necessary to gain that end, the relatively anti-Negro party, while the Negro will find refuge in the Democratic Party controlled by the north where in ten states the Negro today holds the balance of power. . . . Finally and more immediately, if ever the Negro demonstrates that he can no longer be regarded as the chattel of any one party, he will never again be so completely disregarded and so impudently insulted as has been the case within recent years.[41]

Although Hoover won the election by a landslide, White's notion of Black support for the Democratic Party would happen after the election of Franklin D. Roosevelt. The 1930s, however, would produce increased scrutiny on the part of the NAACP and labor organizations regarding the atrocities inflicted on Black men and women who were rebuilding the levees destroyed by the flood and housed in the refugee camps.

Full investigations of the camps and their work abuses, as it pertained to Black men and women rebuilding the levies funded by the 1928 Flood Control Act, increased in both quantity and veracity during the early 1930s. In 1931, the American Federation of Labor (AFL) investigated work conditions in Mississippi and Louisiana. The probe revealed extreme abuse and exploitation throughout the camps and workers laboring for wages well below subsistence levels. The amount for some "was as low as $1.25 for a 12 hour work day" and less in some camps. Investigators also received information that "at least ten men were unmercifully beaten in Roach's camp near Greenville, Miss. and run off their jobs without any part of the pay past due them."[42] Daily beatings were common throughout the camps.

Such exploitation ruled these makeshift living and working spaces, and during the summer of 1932 the NAACP sent Helen Boardman to further investigate camp conditions.[43] Boardman, a white woman and former Red Cross worker, visited twenty-two camps on levees between New Orleans and Memphis to gauge the types of treatment workers received. She discovered that African Americans considered the R. T. Clark Company in the Mississippi town of "Myersville" (the report's misspelling of Mayersville) to be one of the most brutal. " 'Clark will pick up a stick and beat a man just for looking at him,' one man said. The men are paid $1.50 to $2.00 a 12-hour day. There is a $3.00 commissary check, $.50 a week tent-rent, $.75 for [a] cook, $.05 a day for ice water. Pay-day is irregular. . . . One man . . . received $12.35 for two months work of 12 hours a day, seven days a week. He had not missed an hour." Boardman found that another camp in Mayersville, under the control of J. W. Noble Contractor, oppressed its workforce as well. Here the men complained "that they work overtime without extra pay, the usual working day being 14 hours. Only twenty minutes are allowed for dinner. The week before this visit (July 6 or 7), two men were whipped for refusing night work after working all day." Boardman found common threads linking the workers, particularly Negro laborers, in the camps she visited: long hours, low wages, overcharging, physical violence, and unsanitary living conditions.[44] In August 1932, the NAACP sent copies of Boardman's report to U.S. senators and key politicians including President Herbert Hoover, Gov. Franklin D. Roosevelt, Secretary of War Patrick J. Hurley, and Attorney General William DeWitt Mitchell to garner support for ending the exploitation on government-contracted jobs.[45]

The NAACP's efforts on behalf of levee workers had already won support from Sen. Robert Wagner of New York. In a letter to White, Wagner noted that if the alleged conditions were true, such "conditions cannot be tolerated. They would call for immediate correction even if they occurred in a purely private enterprise. Surely, the American people will refuse to have it on their conscience that such conditions were permitted to flourish on government work." As such, Wagner proposed that the best course of action would be "an impartial public inquiry by the United States Senate" and he planned "to secure such an investigation."[46] However, his call for an investigation into the abuses the NAACP reported stalled in the Senate, and the NAACP's new assistant secretary, Roy Wilkins, and his colleagues believed additional witness testimonies would help to move along Wagner's "corrective legislation." Wilkins chose Black journalist George Schuyler as his undercover camp investigative partner. In December 1932, both men traveled to the Mississippi Delta with Wilkins going to Greenville and Schuyler to Vicksburg. Walter White had warned Wilkins that this was a dangerous undertaking and "that a black man who meddled around the river camps in 1932 might easily wind up dangling from a tree."[47]

Wilkins published his findings the following year in *The Crisis* magazine under the title "Mississippi Slavery in 1933," concluding that "the conditions under which Negroes work in the federally-financed Mississippi levee construction camps approximate virtual slavery." Much like the investigators before him, he also found that twelve-hour workdays were the standard and it was quite common for men to work over twelve hours in a day. One laborer had worked for one contractor, as a caterpillar tractor driver, for a few weeks on an eighteen-hour long shift. Contractors controlled the time clock and workers suffered because of it. Wilkins recalled that "one lad told me: 'Sometimes they comes and rousts you out at 3:30 in the morning, telling you it's too cold to work the night crew any longer. You got to get up and hit it.' "[48]

Wilkins discovered that in many places in the Delta a seven-day work week proved the rule. Yet in some Mississippi counties, religious practices prevented working on Sunday. This paradox, for Wilkins, was odd to say the least: "It is that good old-fashioned religion which sees nothing wrong in working the hearts out of God's children and robbing them for six days a week, but insists the seventh day must be for rest and worship—to say nothing of counting profits and figuring out the exploitation of the next six days." Of all the issues that the men complained about—beatings, cursing, long hours, little pay, and commissary fleecing, to name a few—they reserved their most venomous scorn "for the contractor who 'won't pay you even that little you got coming.'" Investigations revealed that some men had not been paid in months.[49]

The irregularity in pay schedules was a calculated strategy whites used to weaken Black economic power. The longer the period between paydays, the more workers had to rely on the commissary for food and clothing at robber-baron prices. This limited the amount of actual cash they had coming to them when payday finally arrived and thus left little option for leaving or demanding work-related changes. Pay delays, Wilkins observed, made Black workers even more susceptible to "the money-lending business which all foremen carry on at twenty-five cents interest on the dollar." To keep their jobs in some camps, many found "it was necessary to pay a portion of one's wages to the local employer, each pay day. Those who did not, were laid off without explanation." These practices happened with regularity throughout the camps. While riding along, an acquaintance expressed to Wilkins "the almost universal sentiment: 'These white folks don't do us right. They's something crooked going on and I wouldn't be the one to say whose doing it, though I got my ideas. We works too hard and too long for the little money we gets. But I say this, they is two things I won't stand for. One is cursing me and calling me 'nigger' and the other is not paying off. I want my money and I don't want nobody calling me names.'"[50]

The NAACP made sure that the War Department, which was "responsible for the flood control project, the contractors and conditions in their camps," knew full well what was going on in the encampments.[51] War Department officials had received Boardman's investigative report as well as references to the AFL report. The charges of exploitation and brutality received a staunch rebuke from Maj. Gen. Lytle Brown, chief of the Corps of Engineers. He challenged the accuracy of the charges and pointed to a lack of specificity.[52] Despite Brown's testimony before the House Committee on Labor rebuking the NAACP's charges, Wilkins wrote, "War department knows all about this exploitation on the river. . . . In every camp there lives a War department engineer. The flag of the United States floats above his tent and over the sweating backs of the 'free' black citizens who swear allegiance to it."[53] Although the War Department may not have been directly to blame for instituting labor repression within the camps, the NAACP believed that it was still culpable. Walter White made it clear that we "are not alleging that the War Department originated the slavery system that still prevails there. We do charge [however,] that the War Department through the contract system now in use, is conniving at and helping to maintain this human bondage."[54]

Money was the issue, and for African American workers plenty of it had gone missing. Roy Wilkins suggested "that a minimum sum of five millions of dollars a year would be added to the wages of Negroes on the flood control project if they were paid a decent scale." Maximum estimates, however, suggested an annual loss of $10 million. Wilkins quickly pointed out that, considering the fact that the "project is a ten-year proposition," then "between fifty and one hundred millions of dollars would go into the pockets of Negro workers in the next ten years if proper hours and wages were the rule on the levee jobs." The NAACP worked to achieve three key things associated with the labor exploitation of African Americans: a Senate investigation, which would officially record labor conditions on the levees; to get levee construction work "placed within the provisions of the eight-hour law"; and finally, to "secure the prevailing rate of wage scale for levee workers."[55]

The investigations and political challenges the NAACP conducted eventually produced results during the New Deal. On October 14, 1933, the *Chicago Defender* reported Secretary of War George H. Dern's announcement that "thousands of unskilled workers in the levee camps along the lower Mississippi river will have their pay raised and their hours shortened by recent regulations of the public works administration and the war department." Unskilled workers on contracts funded by the Public Works Administration in the South would get forty cents per hour and work "a 30-hour week." The *Chicago Defender* further reported that Dern, in a letter to Roy Wilkins, had informed him that employment "on flood control projects to be prosecuted by contract with funds provided under the national industrial recovery act . . . which provide[s] for a 30-hour week, specified minimum rates of labor and other protective measures."[56] These economic changes, although far from perfect as African Americans still faced financial exploitation, resulted partly from the pressure Black workers and community folk had placed on the NAACP to fight on their behalf.[57]

The improved labor conditions were also the result of consistent pressures African Americans exerted upon President Roosevelt to exact change and for New Deal programs to address the needs of African Americans. The 1930s witnessed a more militant NAACP in response to Herbert Hoover's conservative approaches to addressing needs generated by both the Mississippi Flood and the Great Depression. Both catastrophes profoundly compelled the federal government to assist its citizens. The NAACP quickly recognized the potential for sociopolitical change this political and economic climate presented and thus intensified its advocacy toward governmental agencies. Hoover's failure to fully utilize governmental resources to assist those in need caused rifts within his support base—ones the NAACP took advantage of by publicizing Hoover's shortcomings. Walter White, referring to Hoover, exclaimed that "'The Great Engineer' sat stolidly in the White House, refusing bluntly to receive Negro citizens who wished to lay before him the facts of their steadily worsening plight or to consider any remedial legislation or governmental action."[58]

Shortly before the 1932 presidential election, W. E. B. Du Bois, NAACP director of publicity and research, openly castigated Hoover regarding his record on race and lack of real assistance to Negro flood sufferers:

> Mr. Hoover has permitted and ordered outrageous discrimination based on color. . . . He was begged to stop open discrimination against Negroes in Red Cross relief, following the Mississippi flood in 1927; he first denied the facts, and when

they were confirmed by his own committee, he suppressed their report and never applied adequate remedies.

In the same way, he is today allowing the War Department to whitewash the equally unjustifiable discrimination against Negroes and bad treatment of workers in the government contracts in flood control. . . . No one in our day has helped disfranchisement and race hatred more than Herbert Hoover by his "Lily-White" policy[,] his appointments to office, and his failure to recognize or appreciate the plight of the Forgotten Black Man.[59]

The 1932 election proved important for Black political empowerment. Walter White noted that "1932 marked the emergence of the Negro voter as a force which no political party could longer ignore or flout." The NAACP sent both Hoover and Roosevelt questionnaires "asking for a 'plain and unequivocal declaration on the subject of race relations.'" Neither presidential candidate responded, but the NAACP's purpose was to establish "a yardstick by which Negro voters could measure the records of both candidates" and hold them accountable.[60] In his speech before the Democratic National Convention on July 2, 1932, Roosevelt pledged "a new deal for the American people." He also advocated "a call to arms . . . to restore America to its own people." Roosevelt won the election by a landslide and in his inaugural address the following year, announced that our "greatest primary task is to put people to work."[61]

Roosevelt's large-scale relief and reform work programs, however, were susceptible to racists and corrupt practices. As a result, the NAACP positioned itself as a watchdog organization protecting the rights of Black workers and the economic gains they had already achieved. In 1933, White announced that the NAACP "is continuing its efforts to see that the contractors' code, now being considered by the NRA [National Recovery Administration], does not exclude the flood control workers. . . . Our next task is to check up in the flood control camps themselves to see whether the men are actually being paid the wages they are supposed to be paid. . . . We know the many tricks used to cheat our workers both in the old days and under the NRA, and the N.A.A.C.P. will not be satisfied until we know the workers are really getting the wages and working the hours ordered for them by the government." The NAACP leadership also wrote Secretary of War George Dern informing him that public assurances on his part "of better wages and shorter hours for the levee workers will revive the faith of colored people in the New Deal."[62]

African Americans demanded that the arbiters of the New Deal not only address their economic oppression but also join in the fight to destroy Jim Crow. As a strategy, "Negroes" utilized their newfound voting power and secured positions within New Deal programs to advocate for a Black agenda. Reporter Lewis Caldwell, Jr., writing for the *Chicago Defender*, pointed out such notable "Negro" leadership:

> In the department of commerce is Eugene Kinckle Jones as advisor on Negro affairs and Henry Hunt occupies a similar position . . . in the department of agriculture. William Hastie is in the interior department. Dr. Abraham Harris is a member of the consumers board of the NRA and Dr. Murchison is on the subsistence homesteads board. Dr. Robert Weaver and Dr. [Joseph] Johnson are assistants to Clark Foreman, special advisor on Negro affairs. Forrester Washington is an assistant director of CWA [Civil Works Administration] and Earl Moses holds a position in the research department of the same administration. Lieutenant [Lawrence] Oxley is in the department of labor and Robert L. Vann is a special assistant district attorney in the same department. This group of men are doing everything within their power to see that the rights of black America are protected.[63]

The NAACP, when it came to Black people, was under no illusion regarding the shortcomings of both Roosevelt and his New Deal programs, and Wilkins expressed as much:

> I have always felt that F.D.R. was overrated as a champion of the Negro. He was a New York patrician, distant, aloof, with no natural feel for the sensibilities of black people, no compelling inner commitment to their cause. The New Deal, of course, was designed to help poor people, and some of the benefits were bound to spill over to blacks, the poorest of the poor. For that Negroes were grateful; but it wasn't as if F.D.R. and his brain trust had worked out a program for uplifting the country's Negroes from generations of neglect and centuries of servitude. In practice, the effect of F.D.R.'s alphabet agencies was often quite different. Checks from the Agricultural Adjustment Administration often wound up in the hands of white landholders, who withheld them from black tenant farmers and sharecroppers. The Public Works Administration set no minimum wage for Negroes and offered too few jobs. The National Recovery Administration

countenanced differential wage scales. . . . To get the Cotton Textile Code passed, F.D.R. threw Negroes to the wolves, exempting them from its provisions. When Social Security was passed, it left out farmers, domestics, and casual labor—and millions of black people. For rallying the country during the Depression and for leading it through World War II, black Americans, like all other Americans, could be profoundly grateful to F.D.R., but as a patron saint for Negroes, he had plenty of red clay on his feet.[64]

Black men and women applied pressure from all sides to force the architects of the New Deal to address their concerns and to side with them over powerful Delta patricians. They also made it clear that they would hold the Roosevelt administration accountable when failing to address their economic grievances or protect the sociopolitical rights of its Black citizenry.

Both the Mississippi Flood of 1927 and the Great Depression helped intensify the fight for political and labor rights that Black men and women engaged daily. They also underscored their continued commitment to attacking white supremacy and labor oppression on all fronts and demanding governmental accountability. For African Americans, attaining full citizenship rights and fair play were always the objective. Rosie Smith, who sharecropped with her husband Charlie in the Mississippi Delta, spoke to issues of fairness, humanity, and respect: "As far as regarding the white folks, I have always seed them as human beings and . . . I've always respected them as I would want them to respect me. Treat me nice and give me all I am due just like I'd do them. And if I work pay me for my work."[65] Her words represented the protracted fight African Americans waged against labor exploitation, white violence, white supremacist dogma, and discrimination in order to be seen and treated as human beings. Yet they also serve as blatant reminders of everything whites systematically fought tooth and nail to deny them and why the Black Freedom struggle continues.

CHAPTER 7

"Boss Man Tell Us to Get North"

Mexican Labor and Black Migration in Lincoln County, Arkansas, 1948–1955

MICHAEL PIERCE

> We don't like it, we don't like it, but we can't com-
> plain. Boss man tell us to get North if we say any-
> thing about them Mexicans.
>
> —Elderly African American man chopping
> cotton in the Arkansas Delta in 1957[1]

IN NOVEMBER 1951, Ethel Dawson, the National Council of Churches'
(NCC's) social worker assigned to alleviate poverty among African
American sharecroppers and tenant farmers in the cotton fields of
Lincoln County, Arkansas, sent her supervisors a newspaper clipping
detailing the increasing use of Mexican contract workers, commonly
called braceros, in the Arkansas Delta. She explained that the clipping
"offers further proof" of the "evils of exploitation, intimidation, and brutality" that planters were inflicting on agricultural workers in Lincoln
County, almost all of whom were African American.[2] Over the next five
years, Dawson witnessed planters using threats, violence, and braceros
in a concerted effort to push African American laborers—made redun-
dant for much of the year by mechanization—off the land and out of the
region. These efforts climaxed in the spring of 1955, when planters precipitated a showdown with Black agricultural day workers by demanding
that they chop cotton at twenty-five cents per hour, half the rate paid
to braceros and just one-quarter of what was paid to those who qualified for the federal minimum wage. County officials then cut off federal

welfare assistance—Aid to Dependent Children and food from the surplus commodities program—to pressure the domestic agricultural workers to either accept the low rate or leave the region. Unable to survive,
large numbers of African American laborers had little choice but to leave
Lincoln County. The transition of Lincoln County from a Black majority county in 1950 to a white majority county in 1960 was not simply a
function of the pull of urban prosperity.[3] The increasing availability of
braceros provided planters the opportunity to rid Lincoln County of the
African American laborers they no longer needed and had long denigrated as threats to the community.[4]

This essay uses Ethel Dawson's unsuccessful efforts to curtail the
employment of Mexican labor in Lincoln County to document not only
the ways that the planters' use of braceros allowed them to push out a
portion of the Black residents, but also the ways that African American
activists like Dawson responded to the introduction of Mexicans into the
traditional white–Black racial binary. Dawson placed the blame for the
use of Mexican labor, the increasing impoverishment of Black workers,
and their migration solely on the planters' shoulders. She would have
agreed with the unemployed agricultural laborer from Poinsett County
who in 1956 told Sen. J. William Fulbright that it was the "high up land
lords [who] choose to deprive us of our rights to earn a living" and "not
the Mexicans['] fault . . . you can't blame them." Dawson clearly understood the power structure in the Arkansas Delta and rooted the causes
of African American economic hardships in the actions of the plantation
elite rather than the newly arrived Mexican competitors.[5]

To check the power of the planters, Dawson first tried to enlist religious organizations. But leading ministers and churchwomen—often
tied to the planter elite through economic and familial bonds—proved
unwilling or unable to challenge seriously either the abuses of plantation agriculture or the prerogatives of the state's economic elite. Dawson
sought social and economic justice, but white church leaders counseled
her to work to improve race relations by promoting education and
mutual understanding. Out of frustration, Dawson then turned to trade
union activists to help limit the number of braceros coming into Lincoln
County, working with representatives from the Congress of Industrial
Organization's Political Action Committee (CIO PAC) and the United
Automobile Workers (UAW) to pressure local, state, and federal officials to reform the bracero program so that it would not harm domestic
workers. This cooperation between Black activists like Dawson and trade

union leaders was part of a larger class-based effort to reform the state that would bear fruit in the 1960s and 1970s. In the shorter term, though, Dawson and her allies failed to prevent planters from pushing Black labor out of Lincoln County.

Dawson's fight against the widespread employment of unfree Mexican labor in Lincoln County challenges the historiography of the bracero program in Arkansas and the Jim Crow South. This historiography, most significantly the work of Julie Weise, is rooted in the neoliberal globalist idea that the movement of workers across borders improves the lives of both the migrants and those already there.[6] Weise insists that the arrival of Mexican workers into the Arkansas Delta helped loosen the rigid white–Black racial binary and forced white conservatives to "compromise in the area of racial segregation." However, Weise uncritically accepts the planters' claims that there was a labor shortage in the Arkansas Delta and constructs her argument around the premise that African American outmigration had already left the cotton fields bereft of labor. This allows her to ignore the effects of the bracero program on the region's African American workers. She insists, without providing any evidence, that "most of the Arkansas Delta's African Americans envisioned a future away from the cotton fields and did not begrudge Mexicans' arrival" and even dismisses an unnamed Lincoln County critic of the bracero program as representing "a rapidly shrinking number of Black Arkansans who sought futures in agriculture." This acceptance of planters' claims of a labor shortage and silencing of African Americans who suggest otherwise allow Weise to conclude that the operation of the bracero program "abetted both strands of the liberal agenda: economic security and an end to de jure discrimination."[7] But, according to Ethel Dawson, there was no shortage of African Americans willing to work the Arkansas Delta's cotton fields, and planters employed braceros to lower domestic wages, stifle worker protests, rid Lincoln County of Black people they had long considered dangerous, and maintain near absolute power at a time when pressure to end Jim Crow was building.

Dawson began working for the NCC's predecessor in Lincoln County in 1946, after spending a decade teaching school and serving as a home demonstration agent in the area. Her employment with the NCC freed her from dependency on local potentates and afforded her the rare ability to speak frankly about conditions in the Delta. She also realized that her gender allowed her to express economic and racial grievances in ways that Black men could not. Although she was born and raised in

Lincoln County and took her undergraduate degree in nearby Pine Bluff at Arkansas Agricultural, Mechanical & Normal College (now part of the University of Arkansas System), Dawson spent portions of her early adult life in the urban North, taking graduate courses at the University of Chicago, Columbia University, and Northwestern University. Her decision to return to Lincoln County—where she realized "every phase of the Negro's life . . . is overshadowed by discrimination and injustice" rooted in the plantation system—was a choice motivated by her love of the region: "I don't care for large cities because every time you step outside you put your feet on concrete. I was born and reared on the farm. I like open spaces. I like farm life." Like countless other African Americans from the Delta, she did not see migration as the only (or even best) response to Jim Crow and economic exploitation. Rather she intended to reform the rural South, especially the plantation system, to make it a place in which African Americans could flourish.[8]

Although the bracero program began during World War II as a binational agreement between Mexico and the United States to place Mexican workers on farms and plantations suffering from war-related labor shortages, the program did not take off in Arkansas until 1948. That year, 13,048 braceros picked Arkansas cotton. The program expanded rapidly; just three years later, about 7,600 braceros arrived for the early summer chopping season and an additional 31,200 in the late summer for harvesting. The numbers fluctuated throughout the 1950s with the annual arrival of between 25,000 and 38,000 Mexican choppers and pickers. It is unclear exactly how many braceros made their way to Lincoln County as those numbers were aggregated with the figures for the braceros contracted for all southeast Arkansas through the state's Employment Security Division office in Pine Bluff. There is little reason to believe, however, that Lincoln County was much different from the Arkansas Delta as a whole, where braceros comprised about one-third of the agricultural workforce. Arkansas officials and the state's congressional delegation justified the program and its expansion as a response to shortages caused by the migration of agricultural laborers to urban and industrial centers. Braceros arrived, officials explained, simply to make sure that there was sufficient labor to harvest the cotton crop, and care was taken to ensure that their presence in the labor force did not harm Arkansas workers. Explaining the origins of the bracero program, Senator Fulbright assured a day laborer in Poinsett County that Mexican workers could only be employed "when there was a shortage of local workers to such an extent that the crops could not be taken care of properly. It was never intended to bring about direct competition between the two." But officials like Fulbright, who, like nearly all politicians running statewide in Arkansas, depended on the votes that planters supplied by the hundreds, never looked too closely at labor conditions on the ground.[9]

For Dawson, the use of braceros was just another tool planters used in the effort to wring as much profit as possible from the work of others. She likened plantation owners to "the parasitic insect which will suck blood as long as there is man or beast around for him to feed" and cataloged their methods of exploiting the African Americans who picked, chopped, and harvested cotton in Lincoln County. In Dawson's telling, the whole plantation system, especially the relationship between landowners and Black workers, was built upon the ability of planters to employ violence and threats with no fear of legal repercussions. Planters visited workers in the fields with "guns on their hips," and when it came time to settle accounts at the end of the year, "a pistol is usually within reach." They also had the county sheriff, Tebo Cogbill, at their beck and call. Cogbill would arrest Black men considered troublesome on petty charges and then send them either to local plantations to work off their fines or the state prison farm (located in Lincoln County) where they could be "loaned" to planters. The terror that planters instilled allowed them to refuse written contracts, cheat sharecroppers and day laborers, ignore calls to improve Black schools, maintain political control, and keep African Americans from banding together to improve their lots.[10]

Ideally, Dawson wanted the federal government to end the plantation system altogether. She explained that all it would take would be the withdrawal of federal subsidies to planters. This, she explained, would drive planters, who were already highly indebted, into bankruptcy and force them to liquidate their holdings. The federal government then could buy the agricultural land on the cheap and offer it to those who actually worked it with low-interest mortgages. She pointed to the Farm Security Administration as a model for her plan. Dawson realized that her preferred solution did not have political support, and she devoted most her time as a social worker to addressing the symptoms of poverty rather than the underlying cause—enforcing contracts, improving schools, increasing Black suffrage, strengthening Black institutions, and, most important for the purposes here, preventing the use of braceros.[11]

In the early 1950s, Dawson's main complaint about the bracero program was that there was no shortage of domestic agricultural workers in

Lincoln County, and the addition of Mexican workers only added to the hardships of those already on the ground. Lincoln County (and the rest of the Arkansas Delta), she insisted, was experiencing a period of increased unemployment and underemployment of African American agricultural laborers, who already lived in grinding poverty. Mechanization, crop diversification, and federally mandated reductions in cotton acreage were taking their toll on the overwhelmingly Black domestic workforce, and the importation of more workers into this environment only added to the misery. Dawson told the state officials running the bracero program that their primary concern should not be helping planters import additional labor or solving the problems facing Mexican workers in an alien land but rather aiding Black agricultural laborers in places like Lincoln County: "There is no work available for the majority of them and they are asking what will we do to make a living."[12]

There is plenty of evidence to back up Dawson's claims of a labor surplus. Like elsewhere in the cotton South, the demand for agricultural labor in Lincoln County fell rapidly in the years after World War II, mostly because agriculture became mechanized. Mechanization was never a smooth process but one of fits and starts. The first stage started before World War II with the introduction of tractors that began replacing the mules long used to pull cultivators and plows. Adoption started slow but picked up at the end of the war. Between 1945 and 1952, the number of tractors in the county increased by 150 percent. The second stage, the use of mechanical pickers to harvest the crop, began in the late 1940s with the development of dependable pickers and the alteration of gins so that they could process machine-picked lint. By 1954, 40 percent of the cotton in Lincoln County was picked by machine. This placed the county well ahead of the rest of the state, which overall had 25 percent of the crop mechanically picked. The third and final stage of mechanization began about 1950 with the introduction of chemicals that eliminated much of the labor devoted to chopping and weeding. In 1954, the Lincoln County Agricultural Planning Board reported that the increasing use of "numerous insecticides, pre-emergence and post-emergence [herbicides] and flame cultivation for weed control" had lessened the need for workers with hoes. Surveying the effects of mechanization, a Pine Bluff journalist reported that between 1945 and 1955 the amount of labor needed to plant, cultivate, and harvest an acre of cotton in that city's agricultural hinterlands—an area that included Lincoln County—fell by 75 percent from 160 hours to 40 hours.[13]

The effects of mechanization were aggravated by a steep reduction in cotton acreage planted in Lincoln County after 1949. Like elsewhere throughout the cotton South, the county had seen a dramatic uptick in the amount of land devoted to cotton production in the years immediately after World War II, from 38,000 acres in 1945 to 64,000 acres in 1949. This expansion, along with higher yields, glutted the cotton market; prices declined, stockpiles of unsold bales increased, and parity payments grew. In 1950, the U.S. Department of Agriculture—with the approval of cotton planters but no consultation with laborers—mandated the first of a series of nationwide acreage reductions that sought to bring production more in line with consumption. In 1953, Lincoln County devoted 45,000 acres to cotton production; two years later, that fell to 35,800 acres. So, between 1949 and 1955, the number of Lincoln County acres planted with cotton dropped by more than 44 percent. Planters devoted the acreage taken out of cotton production to substantially less labor-intensive uses, mostly rice, corn, and cattle.[14]

Mechanization and acreage reduction combined to cause the aggregate demand for agricultural labor to fall like a rock in Lincoln County in the decade after World War II. In 1945, Lincoln County's cotton production required approximately 6,080,000 hours of labor (38,000 acres at 160 hours/acre). By 1955, the county's demand for cotton labor fell to 1,432,000 hours (35,800 acres at 40 hours/acre), a 76 percent drop from the 1945 level. The decline, though, was not linear, with almost all of it coming after 1949 when the number of cotton acres peaked at 64,000 and the adoption of dependable mechanical pickers began.[15]

While significant numbers of Black laborers—estimates run as high as 35 percent—left Arkansas Delta counties in the ten years after World War II, the demand for labor was falling much faster than the supply.[16] In 1954, Lincoln County had 4,843 Black farm laborers, according to the Arkansas Cooperative Extension Service. Although the vast majority of these laborers worked the cotton fields, the precise percentage is unknown. But if just half of them worked fifty hours each week during the sixteen weeks of the chopping and harvesting seasons, they could supply 1,937,200 hours of labor, more than enough to bring in the cotton crop.[17] While Lincoln County might have had a shortage of agricultural workers immediately after World War II, it was experiencing a surplus by the early 1950s, when Dawson began protesting the arrival of Mexican workers.

Dawson's insistence that there was a surplus of Black farm laborers in Lincoln County is consistent with the findings of economic historians who have looked closely at the cotton labor market elsewhere in the Delta. In his detailed study of a cotton-growing region in Mississippi that resembled Lincoln County, Richard Day concludes that the labor market tipped from shortage to surplus in 1949 and that the surplus quickly grew over the course of the 1950s. But even the earlier claims of labor shortages must be put into context. As economic geographer Charles Aiken explains, "Planters who complained of labor scarcity . . . meant lack of cheap, abundant labor, not lack of workers. . . . no attempt was made to hold or recruit agricultural workers by increasing wages or the percentage of the cotton crop given to tenants."[18]

Black agricultural laborers understood quite well that the planters' increasing use of braceros was not a response to a labor shortage but rather a choice. George Stith, a National Farm Labor Union activist in Lincoln County, testified before the U.S. Senate in 1952 that he saw a planter telling a group of African Americans eager for work, "Sorry boys, would like to have you but I got these Mexicans." Stith also told the legislators that it had become standard practice that once a gang of braceros had finished at one plantation it would be moved onto the next and "[i]f there were some local workers picking cotton on the plantation they would be fired so the Mexicans could be employed." An *Arkansas Gazette* story on the abject poverty of those who chopped and harvested cotton in the Arkansas Delta asked "Who's the Villain in Cotton Country? The Mexican, the Machine or Dirt," and unemployed cotton pickers in Poinsett County were unanimous in blaming the planters' preference for braceros for their woes: "They don't want us. They would rather hire Mexicans"; "Mexican labor cheated us out of work last fall"; and "If them Mexicans come back next year, I don't know what is going to happen. It might be bad."[19]

When not speaking to Labor Department officials overseeing the bracero program, Delta planters readily admitted that their employment of braceros was a choice rather than a function of a "labor shortage." A Mississippi County plantation operator, for instance, told an *Arkansas Gazette* reporter in early 1955 that he would employ as many braceros as he could during the upcoming season even though there would be domestic laborers desperate for work: "The Mexicans are better workers. A Mexican is worth $2 a day more than our native labor." The planter explained that the braceros were all able-bodied men in the primes of their lives, while the domestic workforce included women, children, and the elderly. An Arkansas Department of Public Welfare official, who insisted that the bracero program was necessary, conceded in 1956 that there was sufficient domestic labor to chop and harvest the state's cotton crop. Planters needed braceros, he said, because they were better workers and would speed the harvest.[20]

But there was more to the planter preference for braceros than just simple workplace economics. Mechanization and the federally mandated acreage reduction hastened the demise of sharecropping, a labor system that planters had long justified as necessary to control the social, economic, and political activities of potentially dangerous Black populations. Dawson dated the final end of sharecropping in Lincoln County to the mid-1950s, and by then the former sharecroppers had become day laborers who worked the gaps in cultivation left by the machines and chemicals. This transition lessened planter control over the lives of Black workers while increasing their autonomy. Day laborers certainly lived more economically precarious lives than sharecroppers, but they were paid in cash, could spend it as they wished, and had more time on their hands. The six-week chopping season and ten-week harvesting season meant that for the remaining thirty-six weeks Black workers had to find casual employment or were unemployed. The existence of a pool of mostly idle, unsupervised, landless, and impoverished African Americans surely worried Lincoln County's planter class. The bracero program made it possible for planters to push this population out of the county and replace it with workers who would be trucked back to Mexico as soon as the crop was picked.[21]

Similarly, sharecropping's demise threatened the planters' political control, raising the possibility that whites would be outvoted in Black-majority areas such as Lincoln County. Unlike in neighboring Mississippi, where cotton planters employed significantly fewer braceros, Black Arkansans began casting free ballots in 1946. This expansion of Black suffrage first occurred in cities, where Black workers were paid in cash and thus able to pay their poll taxes. In the Arkansas Delta, though, the sharecropping system continued to stifle free Black voting. In fact, it had long been the practice for planters to "vote" their sharecroppers—that is, purchase poll tax receipts in the names of sharecroppers and tenants, and then vote them on election day. Black civil rights attorney Wiley Branton recalled how the system worked in the areas around Pine Bluff in the late 1940s: "These plantation owners and others would line them [tenants and sharecroppers] up on election day and have them go through the little voting place without doing anything and they'd just check them off and the clerks would vote for them." The demise of sharecropping not only made it more difficult for planters to "vote" their workers but also increased the possibility that African Americans would pay their own poll taxes and vote freely.[22]

Dawson-led efforts to get Blacks to cast free ballots in Lincoln County grew more insistent in the early 1950s, the very time that planters began relying on braceros. The suffrage campaign in Lincoln County began in the wake of the U.S. Supreme Court's 1944 *Smith v. Allwright* decision abolishing the all-white Democratic primary. Black leaders, including Dawson, organized a civic league to qualify African American voters. The effort provoked an immediate response from the county's leadership. Dawson recalled that Sheriff Tebo Cogbill visited the league's leaders, told them that "no niggers will ever vote in Lincoln County," and flashed his gun and blackjack to emphasize the point. Cogbill's threat scared off most potential voters, but efforts picked up again in the early 1950s with Dawson leading the way. She helped form several local groups—Progressive Women Voters Association of Lincoln County, Lincoln County Civic Association, Gould Citizens' Association, and the Community Civic Club—to "encourage people to pay their poll taxes and vote." Such activities gave planters another reason to push Black workers out of the county and favor braceros.[23]

The labor surplus and preference for braceros made life increasingly precarious for Black cotton laborers in Lincoln County. As George Stith testified before the U.S. Senate in 1952, "Cotton picking wages in my section were good. We were getting $4 per 100 pounds for picking. As soon as the Mexicans were brought in wages started falling. Wages were cut to $3.25 and $3 per 100 pounds." By 1954, the Labor Department reported that the prevailing wage for picking cotton in Lincoln County had settled somewhere between $2.00 and $2.50 per 100 pounds. Similarly, wages during chopping season fell across the entire Arkansas Delta from an average of fifty cents per hour in 1948 to thirty cents per hour in 1956. It is little wonder that in 1954 Lincoln County had the lowest per capita income in the state at $359, a figure that was just 15.3 percent of the national per capita income of $2,341.[24]

These conditions pushed many in Lincoln County's Black workforce to seek futures elsewhere. Dawson recounted a meeting with H. Y. Gordon, a Baptist preacher and cotton picker, who had long been determined to remain in Lincoln County to improve conditions and minister to his people. In 1953, Gordon explained to Dawson that he was giving up: "Everyone can see that machines, Mexicans, livestock and various crops are rapidly displacing Negro farm laborers, sharecroppers, and renters. In the next three to five years, I believe that all of the remaining colored people in these groups will be gone." Convinced that Black agricultural laborers had no future in Lincoln County, Gordon told Dawson that he would be heading to California. A special investigation into the effects of braceros on domestic workers commissioned by the United States secretary of labor suggested that Gordon's experience was hardly unique. The introduction of braceros into cotton-growing regions, the commission's 1959 report concluded, had pushed domestic agricultural workers "to migrate to other areas."[25]

Not all Black agricultural laborers in Lincoln County, though, chose to leave the cotton fields for urban life. As late as 1960, more than 25 percent of Black wage earners across the entire state were still classified as agricultural laborers, and in Lincoln and other Delta counties the percentage was much higher. Some, like Dawson, worked to make their communities more hospitable for those who did not want to leave their homes. When officials with the Arkansas Employment Security Division, which oversaw the bracero program in the state, appeared at a 1954 forum put together by Dawson and the Arkansas Council of Churches, a couple dozen Lincoln County agricultural laborers demanded to know "why did they permit Mexican Nationals to come into the state to do farm work when there were farm people here wanting work?" These men, though destitute, wanted to remain in Lincoln County and saw braceros as obstacles to that future.[26]

Dawson's outspoken criticisms of the bracero program and the broader plantation system so angered the leaders of the white Arkansas Council of Church Women (ACCW) that they contacted the NCC in the early 1950s to have her fired. These efforts were led by ACCW president Olivia Draper and Ernestine Henderson, the chair of the ACCW's Christian Social Relations Committee. At the heart of this conflict were differing understandings of the character and origins of racial problems in the state. Draper, Henderson, and the ACCW leadership worked to improve "race relations." They thought that misunderstandings, distrust, inadequate schools, and failures to grasp the teachings of Christ—rather than the plantation system and exploitative economic structures—were the root causes of racial discord and black poverty. Race problems, they asserted, should be addressed through dialogue and trust-building workshops, like having white and African American young people from all over the state get to know one another at special dinners, church-sponsored youth events, and lectures by religious speakers. Henderson told officials at the NCC that Dawson's rejection of such approaches and her eagerness to accuse plantation owners of misdeeds had "set back the whole cause of race relations in the area as much as fifteen years."[27]

Dawson saved her job by doubling down. She told her supervisors that the ACCW leaders were complicit in the exploitation of the state's rural African Americans: "Mrs. Draper, President of Arkansas Council of Church Women, is the wife of a plantation owner at Forrest City. . . . Mrs. Henderson told me in 1948 that she has an uncle who is a plantation owner, and other officers of the Council of Church Women in this state are wives or relatives of plantation owners." Dawson's implication was clear: these women's class positions had rendered them unwilling or unable to understand the structural and economic underpinnings of Black poverty and exploitation. Their emphasis on "race relations" allowed them to show concern about the fate of the state's African Americans while doing nothing that addressed the underlying causes or threatened their own economic status.[28]

The NCC's leaders backed Dawson in her conflict with the white Arkansas church women, but she put them in a bind. The Council could hardly ignore the white Protestant denominations and groups of church women that it had to work with and who contributed to its mission. Dawson's supervisor, Don Pielstick, shared her understandings of the problems associated with the plantation system and protected her for the next five years, even though he considered her to be needlessly blunt and outspoken. Pielstick, though, could do little more than defend Dawson, admitting that the NCC did not have the means or the ability to improve the lot of agricultural workers in places like the Arkansas Delta. He considered the problems in Lincoln County to be "almost unsolvable according to our present social system."[29]

Disaffected by church-based reformers who were either openly hostile or unable to conceive of ways to help, Dawson turned to the labor movement in early 1955. That year, she began working with Philip Weightman, the CIO PAC's top African American political organizer. Weightman had initially ventured into the state in 1953 as part of an effort to qualify Black voters in the hopes that they would go to the polls to help defeat the state's senior U.S. senator, John McClellan, in his 1954 reelection bid. Weightman's 1955 return focused on getting 100,000 Black Arkansans qualified to vote for the following year, when a labor-sponsored state constitutional amendment to abolish the poll tax was slated to appear on the ballot. Weightman sent Dawson a mimeograph machine and supplies to help her mobilize Black voters and agreed to visit Lincoln County to aid the effort. These activities alarmed Dawson's supervisors at the NCC. Pielstick was fine with Dawson mobilizing voters but insisted that her efforts not be "so closely tied to the CIO-PAC." He concluded with a veiled warning: "I certainly would not be in favor of your becoming an organizer for the CIO, at least not as long as you are on our staff."[30]

Dawson ignored Pielstick's warning, and her continued work with Weightman led to a concerted effort to curtail the use of braceros in Lincoln County. Dawson scheduled Weightman to speak on "the advantages of our paying poll tax, voting, and cooperating with organized labor movements" at the Rural Life Improvement Institute that Dawson had organized to be held May 21, 1955, at the Damascus Baptist Church near Grady in northern Lincoln County. But he had to cancel his appearance. In his stead, he sent Paul Sifton, the UAW's chief lobbyist and speechwriter for Walter Reuther, who was in the state on other business, along with Ed Stone, the state's CIO director.[31] Sifton, a white man, was one of the nation's leading Cold War liberals. In the 1930s, he joined President Franklin Roosevelt's "Brains Trust," working at the Department of Labor to enforce the Fair Labor Standards Act. He then became the director of the Union for Democratic Action, the forerunner of Americans for Democratic Action, and served as a lobbyist/public relations director for both the National Farmers' Union and the National Council for a Permanent FEPC (Fair Employment Practice Committee). After World War II, he joined his friend Walter Reuther at the United Automobile Workers.[32]

Even before his arrival in Lincoln County, Sifton had been an outspoken critic of the bracero program. During the Senate's 1952 hearings on the "Mexican Labor Bill," Sifton drew on his experience with the Farmers' Union and testified on behalf of the UAW. He explained that the program would not be needed if southern cotton planters and western growers would simply pay fair wages to U.S. workers. Rather than allowing unfree Mexican workers to drive down the wages of American workers, he thought Congress should mandate a minimum wage and better working conditions for domestic agricultural laborers.[33]

Sifton was stunned at what he learned at that church near Grady in 1955. In a report to Roy Reuther, the head of the UAW's Political Action

Committee, he detailed the "shocking set of facts" that were converging in Lincoln County to create unprecedented levels of misery among African American farm workers. First, the state was allowing planters to employ increasing numbers of braceros for the summer chopping season—10,380 as compared to 7,400 for the previous year—even though there was a surplus of Black farm laborers desperate for work. Second, local planters were offering African American farm workers hourly rates of pay that were half of what was being given to braceros—twenty-five cents versus fifty cents. Sifton explained that "the principal consideration of the Negro farm workers in the meeting, as stated over and over again," was how to get the same rate as braceros and that there was a general unwillingness among the Black workers to accept the lower rate. Third, county authorities had cut off all federal welfare payments, including Aid to Dependent Children and food from the surplus commodity program, as part of an effort to force the Black workers to either accept the lower wages or leave the county. Sifton concluded by noting the gross injustice of the federal government's facilitating the importation of low-wage contract workers into one of the nation's poorest counties.[34]

Dawson, Sifton, Weightman, and Stone agreed to launch a campaign to protect African American farm workers from competition from braceros and ensure that those in Lincoln County had enough work and food to survive. Sifton worked at the national level, mobilizing allies in the labor movement and lobbying members of Congress. He visited Senator Fulbright's Capitol Hill office in June 1955 to ask for help in addressing the situation in Lincoln County. Fulbright's staff expressed concern and promised to do whatever possible to help the county's Black farm workers, but his office took no discernable action. In fact, Fulbright's staff continued its long-standing practice of helping planters navigate the bureaucratic process of securing Mexican workers. For Fulbright, the planters—who could still deliver the votes of agricultural workers by the hundreds and were often integral parts of county political machines that controlled thousands of votes—were a much more important constituency than rural African Americans or the labor movement. When an agricultural worker from Lepanto asked the senator the following year "to help get those Mexicans out of here and give the labor back to our people so we can make a living for our children like we should be allowed to do," Fulbright expressed sympathy but told her that there was nothing that he could do.[35]

Sifton, though, devoted most of his energy to lobbying Congress to amend the "Mexican Labor Bill" (HB 3822) that was making its way through the House of Representatives. Mobilizing the support of other labor lobbyists, he pushed for two specific changes. The first would require public hearings before state and federal officials could certify that there was a farm labor shortage that necessitated the importation of Mexican workers. The second would prohibit planters from putting braceros to work until after all local residents had been offered positions at the rate stipulated in the agreement with the Mexican government. The House Agriculture Committee approved the second change, but the provision was stripped from the bill on the House floor at the behest of a coalition led by Rep. E. C. "Took" Gathings, who represented the northern portion of the Arkansas Delta. The provision, Gathings insisted, would transform the Mexican government into the "bargaining agent for the domestic American workers," and it was unfair to Arkansas's planters that a foreign government could set wages paid to their American workers. In the end, neither provision was added.[36]

Meanwhile Weightman and Stone worked in Little Rock, trying to convince the governor to reduce the number of braceros coming into the state. The CIO officials had good reason to believe that Gov. Orval Faubus would be responsive. Both organized labor and African Americans were important constituencies. Right after taking office a few months earlier, Faubus had publicly credited the CIO for his victory the previous summer. Stone reported that the meeting with the governor was productive. Faubus agreed to cut the number of braceros coming into the state by half that fall and to work with labor on the issue moving forward.[37] But he did not keep his promises. Like Fulbright, Faubus would not alienate politically powerful planters and kept Mexican labor flowing into the Delta. For the fall 1955 harvesting season, 29,145 braceros came to the state, up from 21,673 the year before. As the state director of the Employment Security Division bragged that fall, "There is an abundance of Mexican Nationals in the state."[38]

Dawson managed efforts in Lincoln County. She and a committee of the agricultural workers formed at the May 21 meeting visited the Lincoln County judge (the county's chief executive) to plead for the resumption of welfare payments and the distribution of food through the surplus commodity program. Without this aid, Dawson explained, Lincoln County families could not survive on the wages being offered and would be forced to migrate. The judge, G. J. Matthews, told Dawson that the surplus food program, which had provided commodities to about 1,650 families at the beginning of the year, had been discontinued because the county did not have access to adequate refrigeration for the cheese and shortening and could not afford the $2,000 needed to construct such a facility. But Dawson did not believe Matthews' story: "We know that Lincoln County is free of debt and has a large surplus of cash according to reports made in the newspapers. One official reported that $15,000 had been appropriated by the quorum court (county legislature) to finance the annual livestock show. It appears that cows and hogs are more important than human beings." Dawson realized that county officials envisioned a future with a much smaller Black population.[39]

In the end, the efforts of Sifton, Weightman, Stone, and Dawson to curtail the use of braceros in Lincoln County and prevent the displacement of African American families amounted to little. But they had been expecting this. As Weightman warned Dawson at the start of the effort, "Don't hold out too much hope for immediate relief from this condition. We need many more voters before we can command attention." Lincoln County's domestic workforce did not have the luxury of time, though. Without adequate wages or welfare assistance to sustain them, large numbers of them had little choice but to leave. The use of braceros gave planters the ability to rid the county of the people they no longer depended on for labor, they had long derided as threats to the community, they no longer controlled through the sharecropping system, and they feared were mobilizing politically.[40]

Not long after Dawson began working with Weightman, Sifton, and Stone, the NCC fired her. The reasons were many. She had continued to work with the CIO PAC even after being warned against it. She originally had been hired to address the needs of sharecroppers and tenants, but the sharecroppers and tenants were all gone, replaced by machines, chemicals, and day labor. The man who had long protected her at the NCC, Don Pielstick, died unexpectedly in the summer of 1955. Pielstick's replacement tried to convince Dawson to refocus her work on a new initiative to help braceros adapt to life in Arkansas, but she refused. So, in January 1956, the NCC gave Dawson her notice. Dawson's activism, though, continued after she was fired. In the early 1960s, she worked closely with the Student Nonviolent Coordinating Committee (SNCC) when it arrived in Pine Bluff.[41]

As the NCC was firing Dawson and abandoning its only mission to African American sharecroppers and tenants, it began working with white Arkansas church groups to open centers in Blytheville, Helena, and Forrest City to help braceros adjust to life in the state and improve relations between the Mexican workers and white Arkansans. The same women who championed "race relations" and had tried to get Dawson fired in the early 1950s led these projects. For instance, Olivia Draper, who Dawson had noted was a planter's wife, oversaw the center in Forrest City. Draper boasted to NCC officials that the area's ministers, professionals, law enforcement officers, and public officials had welcomed the braceros with open arms: "The Christian people of our town co-operated as never before." Draper hoped that the opening of the center would mark a new era for the Arkansas Delta, one of increased racial tolerance and cultural understanding. But, of course, the "Christian people of our town" did not include Black folk, and those she later called "our Mexicans" were expected to celebrate their white benefactors. Braceros thus allowed white church women like Draper the opportunity to perform their racial enlightenment in ways that sustained the plantation system while imagining a future without African Americans.[42]

Organized labor in Arkansas continued to work for changes in the bracero program that would protect the livelihoods of cotton laborers, regardless of race or nationality. At 1962 hearings in West Memphis on a U.S. Department of Labor proposal to increase wages paid to braceros, J. Bill Becker, the Arkansas AFL-CIO's secretary-treasurer, detailed the miserable conditions of agricultural workers in the Arkansas Delta, the outmigration of African American workers, and how the employment of braceros had "contributed substantially to this population loss." To solve these problems, Becker, who was white, called for federal labor protections, including collective bargaining rights, the minimum wage, and the forty-hour week, to be extended to domestic agricultural workers and for the wages of braceros to be raised to the federal minimum of one dollar an hour, twice what planters had been paying.[43]

If the employment of braceros helped loosen Jim Crow and undermine white supremacy in the Arkansas Delta, as Weise would have her readers believe, that was not apparent to the SNCC workers who arrived in Lincoln County in 1964, just as the bracero program came to an end. SNCC worker Laura Foner described Gould, in the heart of the Delta portion of Lincoln County, as a town run by one of the state's largest cotton planters, dominated by white supremacy, devoid of any meaningful Black suffrage, overwhelmed by racialized poverty, bereft of economic opportunity for African Americans, and rigidly segregated by threats and violence. As far as Foner could tell, not much had changed over the course of the twentieth century.[44]

The literature on the bracero program in the Arkansas Delta echoes the neoliberal position that the arrival of migrants benefits the entire community, including the domestic labor force, and any opposition to this migration is irrational and bigoted. There are certainly plenty of economic and humanitarian reasons to welcome immigrants into the country, but when supporters of immigration insist that new arrivals do no harm to domestic workers, they are flat wrong. The bromide used to justify both the bracero program and more recent immigration—that newcomers are only doing the jobs that domestic workers refuse to take up—obscures the ways that migration increases competition for jobs, depresses wages, and robs domestic workers of leverage necessary to improve their conditions. While neoliberals discount these valid concerns, conservatives exploit them, fanning the flames of nativism and bigotry for electoral gain. The nation would be better served following the approach of Ethel Dawson, Paul Sifton, Phil Weightman, and, later, Bill Becker. These activists recognized the harm that the arrival of braceros was doing to domestic workers, but they did not blame the Mexican workers or even call for a complete end of the bracero program. They simply demanded that the federal government—which sustained planters through extensive subsidies and insulated them from market forces—take steps to ensure that those who chopped and picked cotton could earn decent wages, regardless of race or immigration status.

CHAPTER 8

Sweet Willie Wine's 1969 Walk against Fear

*Black Activism and White Response in East
Arkansas Fifty Years after the Elaine Massacre*

JOHN A. KIRK

FOR FIVE DAYS IN AUGUST 1969, Lance Watson (alias Sweet Willie
Wine), the leader of Memphis Black power group the Invaders, led a
"walk against fear" across east Arkansas. The walk became an iconic episode in the state's civil rights history and the stuff of local folklore. It even
inspired Arkansas-born poet C. D. Wright's acclaimed 2010 long-form
poem *One with Others [a little book of her days]*.[1] Watson's walk echoed
an earlier protest by James Meredith, who integrated the University of
Mississippi in Oxford amid great controversy and conflict in 1962.[2] In
1966, Meredith set off on a one-man "march against fear" across rural
Mississippi from Memphis to Jackson. Soon after setting off, Meredith was
shot and wounded. Major national civil rights organizations continued
the march while Meredith lay in his hospital bed. The march is perhaps
best remembered for Stokely Carmichael, chair of the Student Nonviolent
Coordinating Committee, popularizing the slogan of "Black power" that
quickly became the clarion call for a new Black youth movement.[3]

This essay explores the significance of Watson's walk against fear by
using that demonstration as a counterpoint to compare with the events
that unfolded during the Elaine Massacre fifty years earlier.[4] It examines
what those two civil rights episodes from different eras tell us about the
continuities and discontinuities in Black activism and white responses
to it. The two episodes point toward a continuity in Black activism and
assertiveness, while illustrating a fundamental discontinuity in white
responses. They suggest that white mob violence steadily declined in east

Arkansas in the post–World War II era to be replaced by a reliance on law enforcement authorities to police the color line.

There is a relative dearth of works examining and theorizing the demise of white mob violence in the post–World War II South. Most surveys chart developments in the first half of the twentieth century, a literature that has flourished and expanded in recent years.[5] Although there have been numerous accounts of individual episodes of white mob violence in the second half of the twentieth century, the literature for this period lacks a coherent and comprehensive survey that assesses how and why its role changed during that era, and why overall it declined. There is, for example, no equivalent to Herbert Shapiro's bold, imaginative, and provocative study *White Violence and Black Response: From Reconstruction to Montgomery*, which provides an overview of racial violence from the late nineteenth to the mid-twentieth centuries.[6]

Two scholars have provided notable tentative theses about the decline in white mob violence in the postwar era. For constitutional historian Michael R. Belknap, writing in *Federal Law and Southern Order: Racial Violence and Constitutional Conflict in the Post-Brown South*, the mid- to late 1960s were a pivotal moment that witnessed a sharp decline in such violence in the South. Belknap identifies the 1964 Freedom Summer in Mississippi, which saw an "orgy of burning, bombing, beating and killing" of civil rights targets, as the turning point. Such violence, Belknap argues, finally convinced civic, political, and economic leaders in the South that law and order was more broadly threatened by white mob violence and that the region faced a descent into anarchy. Southern newspapers echoed these concerns. "Fearful of a breakdown of law and order in their communities," Belknap writes, "southerners . . . themselves assumed responsibility for controlling and punishing racist violence." He concludes that "by 1969"—the year of Watson's walk against fear—"in most of the South it was apparent that those responsible for enforcing the law had committed themselves to suppressing racial violence."[7] Belknap's thesis could certainly use greater expansion and elaboration, although the main purpose of his book is to demonstrate how the lack of federal action on white mob violence generally slowed rather than hastened the South's moves toward self-regulation. Nevertheless, it offers one useful perspective to help understand the events surrounding Watson's 1969 walk against fear.

Historian Gail Williams O'Brien's *The Color of the Law: Race, Violence, and Justice in the Post–World War II South* uses an averted 1946 lynching in Columbia, Tennessee, to develop a much broader thesis about the decline in white mob violence in the postwar South than Belknap's account. O'Brien pinpoints World War II as the defining moment in the decline of such violence because "Blacks, as well as whites, fought in the armed forces, migrated in large numbers within and outside the region, switched jobs, joined unions, and sometimes improved their living standard." The result was a new set of expectations and patterns in race relations. Blacks, emboldened by the changes that had taken place, demanded better treatment for the role they had played in the war effort at home and overseas, and in urban areas they formed a stronger collective base (and in the North, with voting rights) to challenge white supremacy. Although there was an upturn in racial violence after the war, it quickly dissipated, O'Brien asserts, because an urbanized (and, it might be added, ever more suburbanized) and more affluent white population increasingly eschewed using mob violence in race relations. Such violence, O'Brien claims, was more likely to be used to enforce the color line in rural communities and far less likely to be used in the growing, segregated, and purportedly more respectable postwar white suburbs. Moreover, in embracing middle-class respectability, larger numbers of white suburbanites were far less likely to resort to or to endorse white mob violence, which they equated with lower-class incivility. Rather, O'Brien says, policing race relations was left ever more to law enforcement authorities. In this transition of responsibility, O'Brien sees the foundations of the problematic relationship between race and the criminal justice system that exists today.[8] Neither Belknap nor O'Brien suggests that white mob violence disappeared entirely, but they do both insist, if for different reasons, that there was a palpable relative decline in such violence by the end of the 1960s.

With some modifications and additions from other areas of civil rights historiography, Belknap's and O'Brien's theses provide helpful starting points in understanding the similarities and differences between the 1969 walk against fear and the 1919 Elaine Massacre. One of the themes that strongly links the two events is the continuities in Black activism in east Arkansas. Historian Jaquelyn Dowd Hall has outlined the idea of a "long" Civil Rights Movement.[9] This concept seeks to extend the chronology of the Civil Rights Movement beyond what Black activist Bayard Rustin termed its "classic" phase in the 1950s and 1960s. This phase comprised what have become familiar and recognizable events beginning in the mid-1950s with the U.S. Supreme Court's 1954 *Brown v. Board of Education* school desegregation decision, the 1955 murder of Emmett Till, and the 1955–56 Montgomery bus boycott, and ending with Martin Luther King Jr.'s 1968 assassination in Memphis.[10]

The better-known events of the 1950s and 1960s, proponents of the long Civil Rights Movement argue, often have lesser-known origins in the decades that preceded them, and they built upon this past, largely unheralded Black activism. Equally, civil rights struggles in the classic era also have long-lasting legacies that continue to shape society today. By stretching the chronology of the Civil Rights Movement back before the 1950s, and forward after the 1960s, we can view the classic phase of the Civil Rights Movement that unfolded in those decades as forming part of a much longer Black struggle for freedom and equality. Both the efforts of Black sharecroppers to unionize in east Arkansas for better conditions in 1919 and Watson's struggle to have Black demands heard in east Arkansas in 1969 belong to such an ongoing struggle. They bear witness to a long tradition of insistent Black activism that refused to accept the limits and strictures of white supremacy. Many other Black people, organizations, and events connect the historical threads that link Watson to Elaine, some of which have been documented and some not. Each of these building blocks of Black activism reinforced the others to pave the way for Black advancement in the region.[11]

Hall is equally insistent that a long history of white resistance runs parallel to the long Civil Rights Movement.[12] Yet in contrast to the continuities in Black activism between Watson's walk against fear and the Elaine Massacre, what is striking about white responses to those events are the marked discontinuities. To be sure, Watson's walk indicated the ever-present possibility of mobilizing white mob violence to suppress Black activism that continued to exist in east Arkansas and elsewhere. And yet the very different outcomes—Watson completing his demonstration relatively unscathed, while Black people in Elaine and surrounding areas were massacred in the hundreds for seeking to unionize—speak powerfully to a profoundly changed environment in race relations.

Clearly, the historical context in 1969 was very different from that in 1919. The Red Summer of 1919, when the Elaine Massacre was one of a number of episodes of deadly force deployed by whites against Black citizens, occurred in a pervasive climate of racial violence in the United States.[13] In the 1920s, the Ku Klux Klan reached the height of its influence, winning political offices not only in southern states like Arkansas but nationwide.[14] Yet in the 1930s a number of seismic changes began to lay the foundations for the emergence of the modern Civil Rights Movement. Space here allows only the most perfunctory thumbnail sketches to indicate these changes, although there exists a rich and extensive literature to learn more about them, as the footnotes of this essay indicate.

The New Deal, composed of programs and policies implemented by Democratic president Franklin D. Roosevelt's administration that were geared toward addressing the country's economic collapse, transformed government and politics in the United States, enlarging the scope of federal responsibility and activism that was a necessary precondition to challenging segregation, disfranchisement, and racial discrimination. New Deal policies also had profound demographic implications: the collectivization and mechanization of agriculture heralded the demise of sharecropping and tenant farming in the South. Though it is generally acknowledged that the New Deal did far too little to protect African Americans, especially agricultural workers, it did prompt the increasing urbanization of Black populations that made them less isolated and less vulnerable to white attacks, and more capable of collective mobilization and action against white supremacy.[15]

As O'Brien suggests, World War II catalyzed further urbanization, swelling Black populations in cities outside of the South and forming a growing base for exercising Black political power beyond the bounds of southern disfranchisement. The Black press championed the "double V" for victory—a victory abroad against fascism and a victory at home against racism. Labor leader A. Philip Randolph threatened a mass march on Washington, DC, that persuaded President Roosevelt to address discrimination in federal employment. Membership in the National Association for the Advancement of Colored People (NAACP) grew tenfold, with many of its new members joining burgeoning southern branches.[16]

America's plunge into the Cold War after 1945 made how it treated people of color an issue in foreign policy and international relations. The United States' claims to be the leader of the free world rang hollow while white mob violence against Black folk ran rampant in its own backyard. The Soviet Union criticized the United States' human rights record and asked people of color to decide which country they believed truly held their best interests at heart. Consequently, America became far more sensitive to the impact of domestic race relations on international relations. Postwar anticolonial struggles for independence by people of color around the globe provided Black Americans with hope and inspiration for liberation in their own country.[17]

All these developments, along with many others, contributed to a transformation in southern race relations. Notably, there was a decline in occurrences of white mob violence such as witnessed in the Elaine Massacre. Instead, law enforcement authorities took greater responsibility for intervening in racial matters. This was characterized by efforts to uphold law and order rather than allowing rampant mob chaos. In Arkansas, for example, Gov. Winthrop Rockefeller's role in the 1969 walk against fear stands in stark contrast to Gov. Charles Brough's role in the 1919 Elaine Massacre. In 1919, Brough acceded to requests from local whites to help put down what they termed a Black insurrection in Phillips County by requesting federal troops from Little Rock's Camp Pike. Some historians believe that this escalated the mob violence in Elaine.[18] In 1969, Rockefeller sought to defuse rather than aggravate racial tensions in east Arkansas, and he mobilized the Arkansas National Guard to prevent harm from being perpetrated on Watson and other Black activists.

Rockefeller's role reflected a relatively recent sea change in Arkansas politics, which Belknap suggests was also occurring in other southern states.[19] In 1957, Governor Faubus had used the Arkansas National Guard to prevent the desegregation of Central High School, bringing national and international attention to the state. In many ways, Faubus's actions represented a transition point in policing the color line in Arkansas: he used the National Guard in the name of preserving the peace against potential white mob violence while simultaneously deploying state soldiers as defenders of segregation.[20] After Faubus declined to run for reelection in 1966, following a record-breaking six consecutive terms in office, the gubernatorial election that year offered a clear choice forward to voters. The Democratic Party of Arkansas nominated James D. Johnson, former head of the Associated White Citizens' Councils of Arkansas, an organization that had led school-desegregation resistance efforts in the state, and who was an even more rabid segregationist than Faubus. The Republican Party of Arkansas nominated Rockefeller, the grandson of John D. Rockefeller Sr., founder of the Standard Oil Company. Rockefeller, who had moved to the state in 1953, was a racial moderate who had served on the board of trustees of the civil rights organization the National Urban League from 1940 to 1964.

Civil rights proved an important issue on the campaign trail; Johnson refused to shake hands with Black voters, saying that he "did not campaign in their community."[21] Although many white Arkansans shared Johnson's segregationist sentiments, they were concerned about his ability to handle racial incidents responsibly, with polls revealing that in this respect they trusted Rockefeller over Johnson by three to one. As Rockefeller noted, "The reckless course of white supremacy at any cost was running out of appeal; it was losing its credibility with the people."[22] Rockefeller won election in 1966 as the first Republican governor of the state in ninety-four years, and he was reelected in 1968, both times with overwhelming Black support. In office, Rockefeller appointed more Black Arkansans to state jobs and to state government committees than ever before, and he held true to his promise, as the walk against fear demonstrates, to take a more moderate approach to race relations.[23]

Watson's 1969 walk against fear, and white responses to it, were shaped by many of the far-reaching developments that had occurred in east Arkansas, the South, and the United States in the years since the 1919 Elaine Massacre. Watson's own life had unfolded during these changes. Born in 1938 and raised in Memphis, Watson joined the U.S. Army at age seventeen. After receiving a discharge, he fell into a life of crime, accumulating a long record of arrests and convictions that included a pair of two-year stretches in jail.[24] Upon his second release, Watson became involved in the civil rights and Black power movements. He was in Memphis when Martin Luther King Jr. was assassinated in April 1968, and close enough to the Lorraine Motel to hear the gunshot. Later that year, Watson joined the Invaders in organizing a caravan of protesters on a journey to Washington, DC, as part of the Poor People's Campaign run by the Southern Christian Leadership Conference (SCLC). Watson and the Invaders helped to run security at Resurrection City, an encampment constructed on the National Mall as part of the campaign.[25]

Watson's walk against fear in Arkansas grew out of his involvement with civil rights struggles in Forrest City—a place named after the first grand wizard of the Ku Klux Klan, Nathan Bedford Forrest—that were orchestrated by local leaders Rev. James F. Cooley and factory worker Cato Brooks Jr. Cooley and Brooks were campaigning for speedier school desegregation and more job opportunities for Black residents.[26] After escalating conflict in Forrest City demonstrations, Cooley threatened to hold his own "poor people's march," along the lines of the SCLC's demonstration the previous year, from West Memphis to Little Rock to place pressure on the white business community to implement changes. This brought the intervention of Gov. Winthrop Rockefeller at the request of local white leaders who felt that such a march would only lead to more conflict. Rockefeller established a committee, chaired by Ralph Barnhart, dean of the University of Arkansas Law School, to investigate. The investigation, which included a dialogue with Black and white communities in Forrest City, resulted in an agreement on several action points to improve race relations. Satisfied with the agreement, Cooley and Brooks postponed the threatened march for thirty days to await the results.[27]

Within hours of Cooley and Brooks postponing the poor people's march, Watson announced that he would forge ahead with his own walk against fear from West Memphis to Little Rock. Watson and the Invaders had been working with Cooley and Brooks at the local leaders' invitation since April 1969. Although he refrained from criticizing the two directly, Watson insisted that the momentum of recent demonstrations must be continued.[28]

Watson began his 135-mile walk to Little Rock along U.S. Highway 70 on Wednesday, August 20, the day after his thirty-first birthday, starting in West Memphis—just seventy miles northeast of Elaine—bright and early at 8:07 a.m.[29] He was joined by three other Invaders, Kenny Baker, age 28, and Joe Calhoun and Wilbur T. C. James, both age 20; and two Forrest City residents, Dorsey Melvin Hill II, age 20, and Cleveland Johnson, age 16.[30] Five Arkansas state police cars and a dozen reporters and photographers accompanied them. The state police cars contained seven Criminal Investigation Division men, led by Capt. W. A. Tudor, who told reporters that he and his colleagues were there "to prevent any incidents." Throughout the day, the police took down the license numbers of vehicles joining the walkers.[31]

At a sidewalk press conference in front of West Memphis City Hall, Watson told reporters, "We're going to see if Black people can walk in Arkansas." He asserted that the walk was "to keep people from thinking there's been a sellout," because of the cancellation of the poor people's march by Brooks. Additionally, the walk was intended as a memorial to a "Black brother," nineteen-year-old Lee Williams, who had been killed in Benton, Arkansas, the previous Sunday after being shot and run over in a racial incident there.[32] Watson emphasized that neither he nor anyone else in the group were carrying weapons and that he expected the walk to be peaceful. He said that the walk would average thirty to forty miles a day, and that it would take place from 8:00 a.m. until between 6:00 p.m. and 7:00 p.m. "If people can stay in the cotton field until 6 or 7 p.m., we can walk that long," he insisted.[33]

The fact that Watson's walk against fear began with a press conference indicates the important role that the media played in covering the Civil

Rights Movement in the 1960s. In 1919, Elaine and east Arkansas were far removed from the rest of the world in terms of news and communications, which made events there out of sight and out of mind for large numbers of Americans. The newsworthiness of the Civil Rights Movement in the 1960s, and the seemingly ever-present media coverage of it, provided a layer of protection for Black activists and a layer of accountability for whites that had been largely absent in the past.[34]

Following a morning rain shower, the temperature quickly reached the sultry mid-nineties. Five miles outside West Memphis, eight Black people from Earle and Parkin joined the walk for about ten miles.[35] Others participated at various points. Wide Boone, age 28, from Forrest City, walked for four miles, despite suffering curvature of the spine. He told reporters that he was there "to dramatize poverty by marching." At Shearerville, two brothers, Roy Gaines, age 18, and Donnell Gaines, age 17, joined the walkers. They said they did not know Watson but that they "believed in the purpose of the march." [36] The only Black woman to join the walkers was Matilda Williams, age 34, from Forrest City, who stepped along in solidarity for four miles.[37]

The walkers attracted curiosity along the way from both Black and white bystanders, who "watched silently from country stores, sharecropper shacks, front porches and the roadside." The walking column saluted Black drivers with Black power clenched fists that were often returned through car windows. At one point, a farm laborer brought his eight children to the highway to watch the procession. He told reporters that one of his children had asked to attend since "they have never seen anything like this before." At one point there were nineteen walkers, although sometimes that number dropped to as low as three, as members of the Invaders alternated between walking and riding the route.[38]

A caravan of cars followed them. One was a station wagon driven by Peggy Vittitow, age 36, a white woman from Forrest City who had supported civil rights demonstrations there over the summer.[39] A mother of seven children, and the wife of a television and radio storeowner, Vittitow said that she had "decided a few months ago to help Forrest City Negroes find a better way of life." This had led to social ostracism in her hometown: there were no more invitations to bridge parties, she was shunned by former white friends and acquaintances, and her husband suffered an economic boycott of his business. Vittitow had, in turn, she told reporters, "dissociated myself from the white community."[40] Vittitow carried supplies for the walkers, including water, soft drinks, and sandwiches. Other cars went ahead of the walkers to keep an eye out for potential trouble spots.[41]

Alongside the civil rights caravan, there was also a train of police vehicles. Some police cars drove along Interstate 40, which ran parallel to Highway 70. Others drove along Highway 70 with the walkers. Rev. Harold Scott, from Monticello and the chaplain for the state police, transported sustenance, including coffee, water, and other refreshments, for law officers in a trailer behind his car. No resistance was reported along the route, save a white man at Black Fish Lake who cursed out reporters for covering the walk.[42]

Seventeen miles into the walk, Watson was beginning to feel the strain and his feet were hurting. When a reporter asked him how he felt, Watson replied, "I just wish we had started this thing three or four years ago." After five-and-a-half hours of walking, Watson dropped out of the group and got into a car, which drove to a rest stop. There, Watson took off his sandals—not the most appropriate footwear for a long walk on a hot asphalt road—and rested his feet for a while. After resuming the walk, Watson learned that deputized men in Hazen, two days' walk away down Highway 70, were forming roadblocks to halt them. When asked by the press what the walkers intended to do when they arrived there, Watson insisted, "We're going to Little Rock."[43]

At 7:00 p.m. that evening, which ended the day as it had begun with a rain shower, the walkers reached their destination of Forrest City. Arkansas national guardsmen had been deployed to prevent any trouble.[44] Later, Governor Rockefeller revealed that a group of white Forrest City leaders wanted to jail Watson upon arrival, but he had vetoed that suggestion. The following day, the governor was due to speak in Searcy and Beebe, and he was, he said, "interested to see what reaction I get [to the handling of the march]. I think most people are glad we are not faced with a confrontation. But there are those who will always take an attitude that I shouldn't have compromised." Asked what he intended to do upon Watson's arrival in the state capital, Rockefeller deflected with, "If his legs continue to hurt, he might not reach Little Rock."[45]

Meanwhile, in Hazen, a town of approximately 1,500 residents, white citizens spent the day readying themselves for the arrival of Watson and his fellow walkers. Mayor Jerry J. Screeton, a former state senator, led the resistance. As *Arkansas Gazette* reporter Matilda Tuohey described the scene, "at every entrance to the city, except the highways, and at the intersection of every city street with Highway 70 were large rice combines and barricades manned by lone men or groups of men, all carrying shotguns and wearing white helmets and hunting vests crammed with bullets."[46]

The community had seemingly come to a standstill, with all businesses closed, and no women or children in sight. A few stray dogs wandered the emptied downtown streets. Mayor Screeton ordered a curfew at 11:00 a.m. while calling into duty 125 of the city's auxiliary police. "With his [Watson's] twisted, diseased mind, you don't know what he's going to do," Screeton told reporters. He assured them that the auxiliary police were "not a killer organization," but rather, "purely a law and order organization that has one purpose—to make our homes secure." The auxiliary police, which included three ministers, two lawyers, a dentist, and several businessmen and farmers, had been formed over a year ago. Talk of possible marches and demonstrations had recently swelled its ranks. "What's so unusual about mobilizing your people and your resources to protect your homes?" Screeton demanded to know. He added that nothing would happen if the walkers were peaceful, or even if they "shout obscenities" or "threw a rock at a store front." But, he added, "burning or looting will not be tolerated." Screeton insisted that Hazen was a respectable city with no Ku Klux Klan, no White Citizens' Council, and no John Birch Society. "You don't see any Confederate flags flying around here," he said.[47]

On Thursday, August 21, the walkers completed their second leg of the journey, twenty-three miles from Forrest City to Brinkley. The ill effects of the walk were already becoming evident. Two of the five walkers from the previous day, Kenny Baker and Joe Calhoun, rested up with leg cramps, while Watson alternately hobbled and rode along the highway.[48] That morning, eleven people, including five women from Forrest City, started the day's walk.[49] The size of the walking column varied from twenty to two as the rain steadily came down.[50] Another person who joined them was veteran Arkansas civil rights activist Ozell Sutton. Sutton worked with the Community Relations Service of the Department of Justice, which had been created by the Civil Rights Act of 1964. "I will be in and out until this is completed," Sutton explained to reporters. "I am only an official observer. I am interested in seeing that no harm is done to these marchers."[51] The presence of a federal representative on the ground added a further restraint on the use of white mob violence.

There were several minor incidents along the way. In Goodwin, a white grocer closed his door to Peggy Vittitow who was trying to restock supplies. Two white women threatened Vittitow if she did not move along. Capt. Dwight Galloway, commander of the Forrest City Division of the State Police, stepped in to ease the situation. Five miles further up the highway at Wheatley, three grocery stores also closed to avoid the patronage of the walkers. Between 100 and 150 people watched the walkers pass through town, with thirteen state policemen lining the route to make sure that no trouble occurred.[52]

At the end of the day, fifty Black residents in Brinkley were waiting to welcome Watson and his fellow walkers into the city. The group assembled at City Park alongside the Cotton Belt Route railroad tracks in downtown Brinkley. There, the walkers sat on the grass eating neckbones and black-eyed peas, sipping sodas, and singing. Watson told the group that the low number of walkers who had joined him was proof that a climate of fear still existed in Arkansas. "We are marching to get this fear out of your hearts," he told them. "You must remember the white man puts his pants on the same way you do, one leg at a time. You first got to get fear out of your heart. . . . I don't preach no violence but I say take care of yourself anyway you feel possible—with a sling shot, a bow and arrow and spitball." Watson told the press that, despite his sore feet and aching legs, he intended to walk the full twenty-two miles to Hazen the following day. "It'll take about 20 minutes to walk through that little town," Watson said. "I don't see why he [Mayor Screeton] should go to all that trouble." At the conclusion of the Brinkley rally, Watson and his fellow walkers returned to Forrest City to stay the night.[53]

On Friday, August 22, Watson returned to an overcast Brinkley at 8:00 a.m. to head to Hazen.[54] He and twenty-five other Black protestors set off from City Park at 8:50 a.m. They traveled through Biscoe and DeValls Bluff before arriving at their destination.[55] Prairie County sheriff F. E. Grady and ten uniformed members of the Prairie County Radio Control greeted Watson and the group of walkers when they reached the Prairie County line at the Cache River. "Willie, are your feet getting sore?" asked Grady good-naturedly. "Yes, sir. How are you today?" Watson replied. Grady told Watson that he and his son, the only two law officers in the county, had called out the radio patrol and another twenty-nine men to assist in the safe passage of the walkers. As they entered Hazen, sixteen uniformed state troopers and five members of the Criminal Investigation Division joined them.[56]

The walkers encountered less resistance in Hazen than expected. The previous day, Mayor Screeton had sheepishly withdrawn the armed guard and blockades from the city. He had also lifted the curfew, claiming that he had "been misled by news accounts of the number that would come through the town on the walk."[57] Watson, with sore, blistered, and taped feet, along with Mareva Brown, age 59, Ida Mae Hampton, age 44, and Matilda Williams, age 33, all from Forrest City, formed the main walking party into town. As she passed through Hazen, Hampton held up a red Bible high in front of her face and recited Psalm 23, "Yea, though I walk through the Valley of the Shadow of Death, I will fear no evil."[58]

The walkers drew a crowd of curious Black and white onlookers. Some watched from the side of the road, some sat on their car hoods, some remained inside their locked vehicles, and some peered out from behind store windows. Several local Black residents occasionally joined the walkers, but more as curious bystanders than actual participants. Watson variously waved, flashed peace "V" signs, and held aloft his arm in a Black power clenched-fist salute as he strode through town. These gestures were returned by fifty or so white teenagers enjoying the spectacle alongside members of the local Black community.[59] "You don't look so dangerous," one of the white teenagers told Watson. "We think our mayor was crazy to arm out town like this."[60]

Watson seemingly had a whale of a time. "Now, I see this fear has been broken by the reception we've received," a waving Watson told reporters. "This is one of the better things that has happened to Hazen—Hazen itself being challenged." Mayor Screeton scowled in the doorway of the Prairie County Bank, of which he was president, as the walkers passed right by him. Screeton had sent his employees home, but he had left the doors of the bank open with a shotgun inside. Afterward, Watson had nothing but praise for the Arkansas State Police and the protection that they had offered the walkers. "If police were like them all across the United States, we wouldn't have any police brutality," he told reporters. He credited the brown rubber shrunken voodoo head that he wore hung around his neck for keeping the skies overcast and the temperatures down. "I came and saw and walked through Hazen," he triumphantly declared.[61]

On Saturday, August 23, walkers set out at 9:00 a.m. from east of Carlisle after again spending the night in Forrest City. From fifty to four people variously participated as they strolled onward to North Little Rock, around thirty miles away. The walk even picked up some more white participants. Tom Flower of San Antonio, who was the peace education secretary for the regional division of the Quaker organization the American Friends Service Committee, accompanied the walkers. So too did Clare Flower, his eight-year-old daughter, and Christopher Flower, his ten-year-old son. They were joined by Rev. Joe O'Rourke, a Jesuit priest.

O'Rourke taught moral theology in Baltimore, Maryland, and he was on a speaking tour when he had read about the walk against fear in the *Arkansas Gazette*. Other walkers joined along the way, though most of them only for a mile or two at a time.[62]

The largest number of reinforcements arrived in Lonoke. Two Black men, Frank Townsend and Ben Jackson, traveled from El Dorado, Arkansas, to participate. Two civil rights activists from Memphis, O. W. Pickett and Cornelia Crenshaw, the cofounders of Citizens Opposed to Starvation Taxes, also joined.[63] They had been picketing in their home city against a $2.50 sewer and garbage charge imposed upon residents the previous year. In the final few miles before reaching North Little Rock, Joseph Crittenden, a member of the board of directors of the Memphis NAACP branch and a staff member of the SCLC, also joined the walkers. "These people are coming out to demonstrate against fear," Watson told reporters. "When they go back to their communities maybe they will be ready to help make constructive changes." He said that he was heartened by the response of whites to the walk: "Many of them waved at me. Fear is leaving them too." Watson was pleased that they "recognize me not for my prison record or think I'm supposed to be a hoodlum, but recognized me for my convictions."[64] Meanwhile, rumors circulated that the walk was under constant surveillance by a white supremacist group called COBRA: the Congress Opposing Belligerent Revolutionary Action.[65]

Four miles east of North Little Rock, at Galloway, Watson went into a closed fifteen-minute meeting with Bobby Brown, president of Little Rock's Black United Youth (BUY). Brown was the younger brother of Minnijean Brown, one of the Little Rock Nine students who desegregated Central High School in 1957, and he had arrived with twenty-five cars containing fifty BUY members.[66] When Watson and Brown emerged from their meeting, Watson said that the two had discussed overnight accommodations for the walkers in the Little Rock area. Drinking from a glass jar, Bobby Brown accompanied the walkers for a couple of miles, dropping out just before they reached North Little Rock. Eventually, more than thirty marchers clapping their hands and singing freedom songs walked into North Little Rock at 6:30 p.m. "It was beautiful," said Watson of the walk. "It served its purpose."[67]

On Sunday, August 24, the walkers set off at 10:45 a.m. from outside First American Bank's Prothro Junction branch on the outskirts of North Little Rock. It was a relatively short six-mile walk from there to the steps of the Arkansas State Capitol, where a final rally was planned.[68] Forty-three people started the walk on foot, with about as many again traveling along by car. Fifteen state police, Pulaski County sheriff's deputies, and North Little Rock and Little Rock police, as well as Gene Young, a member of Governor Rockefeller's personal security staff, were on hand to marshal. The walkers traveled along Highway 70 to Washington Avenue in North Little Rock, across Main Street Bridge into Little Rock, and then down Main Street to Capitol Avenue. They then headed west along Capitol Avenue to the Arkansas State Capitol building. Watson led the procession. More recruits joined along the way. By the time the walking column reached the Arkansas State Capitol, it was 150 people strong. Another 100 people waited on the Capitol steps to join them for the rally, which began shortly after 1:00 p.m. O. W. Pickett served as the master of ceremonies.[69]

Watson was the star attraction. "One thing the white folks are going to have to learn is that white folks don't pick the leaders for the Black folks no more," he told the crowd. Another speaker, Cornelia Crenshaw, criticized Forrest City leaders Cooley and Brooks for calling off their proposed poor people's march, labelling it a "sellout." Crenshaw said that she had been without electricity, water, or gas for seventy-two days because she refused to pay a city assessment that had been added after the 1968 Memphis sanitation workers' strike. She claimed that the beat-up Lincoln she had driven to Little Rock to attend the rally was the same one that the late Martin Luther King Jr. had ridden while he was in Memphis supporting the striking sanitation workers. "I came over here because I wanted to put this man [Watson] in the same seat where Martin Luther King rode," she said. BUY's Bobby Brown told the crowd that the demonstration was historic because it was the first time that Black people in the city had gathered at the Capitol "without asking permission."[70] Brown mocked the fact that white people had been terrified at the prospect of a few Black people walking across east Arkansas, joking that, "I bet even the [white] babies had .22s." Several people from Forrest City also spoke, including Benny Pinkston and Ida Mae Hampton. The penultimate speaker was Mildred Tennyson, vice president of the Little Rock NAACP, who complained that there were too few members of her organization present at the rally.[71]

Although Watson's walk against fear passed off with relatively little incident, once out of the media spotlight—an indication of just how useful that spotlight could be—he felt the full repercussions of his actions. Back in Forrest City, following the stabbing of a white grocery store owner, there were allegations against the Invaders of armed robbery and assault with intent to kill, and two allegations of rape, all of which inflamed community tensions.[72] On August 26, hundreds of whites began picketing City Hall demanding an end to demonstrations. The crowd attacked Watson, a local newspaper reporter, and a local radio announcer.[73]

In stark contrast to 1919, white leaders quickly appealed to the state for white mob violence to be quelled rather than asking for assistance to put down a presumed Black insurrection. Governor Rockefeller sent in the Arkansas National Guard.[74] The *Arkansas Democrat* editorialized, "Law and order must be maintained. We must have good policemen to keep hot-heads from playing into the hands of people like 'Sweet Willie Wine' and making them heroes."[75] The *New York Times* headlined, "Whites in Arkansas Town Cry for 'Law and Order.'"[76] Watson found himself back in Little Rock, this time in hospital with a broken elbow and various cuts and bruises.[77] He later pledged to return to Forrest City to hold a freedom rally on September 14.[78] Three hundred Black people turned up to the rally, but Watson was absent after being arrested in Little Rock on a warrant issued in Forrest City that charged him with being a "disorderly person."[79]

Soon after, the main protagonists in demonstrations left Forrest City: Cooley took up a teaching position at Shorter College in North Little Rock, Brooks moved to work on civil rights projects in other Arkansas towns, and Watson returned to Memphis. Although the demonstrations won some concessions, racial tensions continued to simmer in Forrest City.[80] Watson came back to Arkansas periodically over the years to join further protest efforts in the state. Today—now under the name of Minister Suhkara A. Yahweh—he remains active in Memphis community affairs. The memory of his walk still resonated in Arkansas fifty years later. In 2019, as commemorations were taking place for the centennial of the Elaine Massacre, Forrest City residents held several events that invited Yahweh back to remember, revisit, and commemorate the fiftieth anniversary of his 1969 walk against fear. Looking back on events, Watson still believes that the most important legacy of his walk was "to get the fear out of the mind" of Black people, and to encourage them to insist on being "treated like a human being."[81]

That Watson believed fear remained entrenched in the minds of Black people in east Arkansas in the 1960s speaks powerfully to the long shadow that the 1919 Elaine Massacre and the violence that accompanied it cast in the region. Watson's actions demonstrated a continuity in Black activism that was unwilling to surrender to that fear. The white response to Watson's challenge to their authority was noticeably different than it had been in Elaine fifty years earlier. Even though whites were still clearly ready to and capable of collectively and forcefully mobilizing to halt Black dissent—as events in Hazen and Forrest City vividly illustrated —the citizens there were now notably far more hesitant to do so and were restrained by the swift action of state and local law enforcement. Unlike 1919, the state, embodied in the actions of Governor Rockefeller, did not automatically side with the white population to stamp out Black activism. Rather, Rockefeller acted as a moderating force who was far more predisposed to use state power to protect Black activists than to support white mob violence.

To recall the observation of historians Michael Belknap and Gail O'Brien, by the late 1960s the responsibility for handling southern race relations had shifted decisively away from the use of white mob violence and toward state and local law enforcement. Although there were plenty of other controls in place to limit Black freedom and equality in many other ways, the use of white mob violence as a blunt instrument to regulate race relations had declined significantly. Changes at local, county, state, regional, national, and even international levels had discernibly shifted the dynamics of race relations in east Arkansas and would continue to do so. Historians of post–World War II southern—and indeed American—race relations still have much more to do in untangling and examining the multiple intersecting strands of these developments, particularly their influence on transforming how the color line was policed.

CHAPTER 9

"Sick and Sinister"

Intersections of Violence and the Struggle for Economic Justice in the Late Twentieth Century

GRETA DE JONG

AS THE ESSAYS IN this volume document extensively, violence was an integral part of Black workers' experience in the American South. From the colonial period through to the mid-twentieth century, plantation owners and other employers used physical punishments such as torture, mutilation, and lynching to terrorize African Americans and prevent them from demanding fair payment or humane conditions in exchange for their labor. In the 1960s, Congress finally passed legislation that restored Black southerners' access to political power and legal protections that had been denied to them in the Jim Crow era, undermining white people's ability to beat or murder African Americans without fear of punishment. Yet violence continued to shape developments in the region in the late twentieth century. Supporters of racial equality encountered three intersecting forms of violence as they carried the freedom struggle into projects aimed at securing economic justice, activities that were just as threatening to white supremacy as the fight for political and legal equality.

At the center of this story is the first form of violence, that of the market: an economic system based on presumed "laws" of supply and demand that assigns value to human beings in the same way it assigns value to sacks of potatoes. If the supply of workers exceeds the demand for their labor, their value decreases and they will find it hard to secure jobs that pay living wages, as was the case for thousands of former sharecroppers after the mechanization of southern agriculture in the mid-twentieth century. Most people saw the effects of this system only in the abstract, as statistics on unemployment and poverty, but workers who were left without jobs or income felt it in their bodies, suffering through the physical effects of hunger, cold, and illnesses brought on by the lack of adequate food and shelter. A second form of violence came in the form of harassment, intimidation, and threats to the physical safety of activists and participants in federal antipoverty projects that tried to address the problems caused by market failure. These attacks, often orchestrated by the same segregationists who had blocked progress toward racial equality in previous decades, continued the tactics of "massive resistance" deployed by the Ku Klux Klan, Citizens' Councils, and other white supremacist organizations. Meanwhile, the federal government undermined the "war on poverty" it had declared in 1964 by spending heavily on the Vietnam War and other military interventions, a third form of violence that pulled resources away from programs that addressed social problems at home. Analyzing how economic violence, racist violence, and military violence intersected and reinforced each other in these decades, through the eyes of social justice activists who opposed all three, broadens our conception of the freedom movement and its opponents while helping to explain the persistence of racial and economic inequality in the United States.

In 1966, a year after the Voting Rights Act was passed, a document prepared by the Freedom Information Service (FIS) described the dire conditions confronting displaced agricultural workers in Mississippi and drew attention to some problems that would take more than civil rights legislation to solve. No longer victims of the debt peonage and forced labor that prevailed in the Jim Crow era, many Black southerners instead faced new threats to their wellbeing from an economic system that had no place for them. Tractors, mechanical harvesters, chemical herbicides, and reduced cotton acreages had made their labor obsolete, pushing thousands of people off the plantations where they had lived and worked all their lives. The FIS noted that the state's political leaders had done little to address the unemployment crisis and sometimes seemed intent on making things worse. Strict eligibility requirements for public assistance programs and racial discrimination by administrators denied aid to large numbers of poor Black people who desperately needed help to secure food, clothing, and housing. Those who were lucky enough to qualify for assistance could barely survive on the meager amounts they received from the state, which set its maximum payments far below the levels that government economists deemed necessary to meet basic subsistence needs. As a result, an estimated 40 percent of people in Mississippi did not have enough to eat, 90 percent of its Black population lived in substandard housing, and the mortality rate for Black infants in their first year of life was twice the rate for white babies. For centuries, plantation owners had kept Black workers poor and dependent in order to maintain a stable and cheap labor force, using both physical violence and economic reprisals to discourage challenges to their power. Now that those workers were no longer needed, the FIS observed, white supremacists were implementing their "'final solution' to the race question." That solution was the forced migration of African Americans out of the South through policies that denied them jobs, income, food, and housing, leaving them with no alternative but to leave.[1]

By referring to the final solution, the FIS deliberately invoked the physical extermination of Jewish people in Nazi Germany during World War II, reflecting these activists' belief that economic violence was just as deadly as inflicting direct bodily harm. They were not alone in deploying this analogy to highlight the disregard for human life that seemed evident in the actions of employers and policy makers. After visiting Mississippi in May 1967 as part of a team of doctors sent to investigate reports of widespread hunger, Raymond Wheeler described the state as a "vast concentration camp, in which live a great group of poor uneducated, semi-starving people, from whom all but token public support has been withdrawn." Wheeler was convinced that those who held power in the state were engaged in "an unwritten but generally accepted inhumane plan . . . to eliminate the Negro Mississippian, either by driving him out or by starving him to death."[2] Social workers Alex Waites and Rollie Eubanks used similar language in a report they prepared for the National Association for the Advancement of Colored People (NAACP), arguing that immediate action was needed if Black Mississippians were to survive "the programmatic and systematic eradication that blatantly denies [them] the minimum basic necessities of life consistent with human dignity and survival."[3]

Some observers pointed out the connections between the neglect of human needs and the southern states' history of authoritarian, one-party rule. By restricting access to the vote and discouraging political participation by poor people, a small group of wealthy white families monopolized power and wielded it arbitrarily, using their control over vital resources to reward people who accepted the status quo and punish those who did not. Activists in Sunflower County, Mississippi, noted that white supremacists controlled government programs that were supposed to help unemployed and low-income people, enabling them to deny aid to African Americans who were involved in the Civil Rights Movement. "The county's white masters, led by Senator [James O.] Eastland, have the means of starving out the politically independent," they wrote.[4] A. D. Beittel of the American Friends Service Committee told the *Wall Street Journal* that economic reprisals were "far more powerful and common in the race issue than is violence. Violence is the one you read about occasionally, but economic intimidation is the thing these people live with every day."[5] A summary of obstacles to Black political participation prepared by the Washington Human Rights Project referred to such tactics as common knowledge among activists working in the South, stating, "There is no need to recount again how a whole vast array of weapons from physical violence to economic pressures and even including manipulation of federal funds for welfare and assistance programs have been used to disenfranchise Negroes."[6]

In their report to the Field Foundation, the doctors who visited Mississippi in 1967 explained that much of the money that the federal government spent on social welfare programs never reached the people who needed it because local administrators who controlled access to public assistance used it as a political tool rather than an antipoverty measure. "What is a human need, a human right, becomes a favor or a refusal," they wrote.[7] Raymond Wheeler found the situation horrifying—more in line with the world's most corrupt and brutal dictatorships than a democracy like the United States. Testifying before the Subcommittee on Employment, Manpower, and Poverty of the Senate Committee on Labor and Public Welfare, Wheeler described the psychological toll of simply observing conditions in the rural South. "From the moment of my arrival until the moment I left the impact of the poverty, the malnutrition, the illness, the hostility of white Mississippians toward Negroes and toward even the whites who are seeking to help them, the impact of this was simply overwhelming," he stated.[8]

Political leaders in the South adamantly denied that they were actively trying to drive poor people out of their states, arguing that the situation simply reflected an oversupply of agricultural workers for the number of jobs that were available.[9] But even without deliberate intent, the failures of the nation's capitalist economic system were ample cause for alarm. While free-market proponents attributed mass unemployment to the natural workings of the economy and opposed government intervention, other Americans pondered whether allowing people who lacked jobs or income to slowly starve to death was any better than killing them by more direct means. In their book *Black Power*, Stokely Carmichael and Charles Hamilton placed the church bombing that killed four Black children in Birmingham, Alabama, in 1963 alongside the deaths of hundreds of babies who died every year in the city from lack of food, shelter, and medical care, citing both as examples of racist violence that were equally unacceptable.[10] Organizers of the Poor People's Campaign made a similar argument when they brought a multiracial coalition from all over the United States to the nation's capital for six weeks of protest in 1968. At mass rallies and in meetings with lawmakers, participants demanded to know how the richest and most powerful country on earth could allow some thirty million of its people to languish in poverty and despair. On June 19, Coretta Scott King delivered a speech to her fellow protesters that asserted, "In this society violence against poor people and minority groups is routine. I remind you that starving a child is violence. Suppressing a culture is violence. Neglecting school children is violence. Punishing a mother and her child is violence. Discrimination against a working man is violence. Ghetto housing is violence. Ignoring medical needs is violence. Contempt for poverty is violence. Even the lack of will-power to help humanity is a sick and sinister form of violence."[11]

In rural areas where agricultural work was disappearing and there were not enough alternative jobs to employ displaced laborers, simply doing nothing led to unnecessary suffering and deaths. But violence took more obvious forms in these regions as well. Dozens of people lost their lives in the struggle for racial equality in the 1950s and 1960s, and racist violence continued against those who remained active in the freedom struggle after the passage of civil rights legislation. After 1964, staff and clients of federally funded programs set up under the War on Poverty were targeted along with activists who promoted Black political partic-ipation or desegregation. Opponents of racial equality understood that antipoverty initiatives would encourage Black southerners to remain in the region instead of migrating away, potentially creating Black voting majorities in counties where African Americans far outnumbered white people. The War on Poverty also threatened white people's control over economic resources by allowing local community groups to receive direct federal funding from the Office of Economic Opportunity (OEO) to operate Community Action Programs (CAPs) that employed and pro-vided needed services for poor people, such as job training programs, health centers, assistance for small farms and businesses, and the early childhood education program Head Start.[12] For these reasons, white supremacists attacked projects that aimed to create jobs and enhance economic opportunities in the region with the same methods they had used to block desegregation and Black voting rights. Both the freedom struggle and massive resistance to it continued in conflicts over federal intervention in the economy, and it often involved the same people on both sides.

The Citizens' Councils of America, founded by Mississippi segregationist Robert B. Patterson in 1954 to incite opposition to school desegregation, took a leading role in undermining antipoverty efforts as well. Throughout the late 1960s and 1970s, its magazine, the *Citizen*, carried articles denigrating all forms of government action that helped poor people. Programs aimed at alleviating economic inequality were portrayed as unwarranted federal meddling that just encouraged laziness and dependence, particularly among African Americans. In the December 1967 issue, South Carolina senator Strom Thurmond argued that the War on Poverty had failed, calling it "a series of projects intended to offer social training to those who have not met the demands of modern civilization" and stating that its only effect was "to train the recipients to expect even more government assistance." Even worse, he claimed, "poverty warriors" were using federal funds to "whip up hatred" and inspire rioting and looting by Black people.[13] In a June 1972 commentary that echoed the views of Nazi eugenicists, Anthony Harrigan attributed poverty to the genetic deficiencies of poor people and expressed concerns that they were outbreeding the nation's more "able, productive citizens." The article was illustrated by photographs of Black welfare rights activists who had recently marched on Washington to (according to the captions) "demand larger welfare checks, greater amounts of free food, new childcare programs and more free medical care" and "pressure the federal government into providing vast new subsidies to families living as parasites on the taxpayers."[14] Similarly, an article headlined "Blacks on Relief Shun Work; Jamaicans Take Jobs" that appeared in November 1977 suggested that welfare payments and food stamps provided too many incentives for Americans not to work, forcing employers to turn to immigrant labor instead.[15]

The linkages that the Citizens' Councils made between African Americans and antipoverty programs were on the minds of other segregationists as well. In July 1964, Alabama congressman George Andrews called the proposed Economic Opportunity Act "nothing but another vehicle to be used to promote integration" and told constituents he would do everything he could to defeat it.[16] Mississippi representative Thomas Abernethy also believed that the War on Poverty aimed to use federal funds "for the purpose of financing and expanding the activities of civil rights [groups] in our state."[17] In April 1967, constituent Pearl Rodgers complained to a senator about Head Start programs in Mississippi where Black women got paid "just to sit" and white children were allowed to take naps with Black children. "If the Federal Government is going to help the poor, [why] don't they do it without integrating the babies!" she exclaimed.[18] Later that month, the annual report of a CAP that was struggling to gain acceptance from white people in the communities it served noted that local and state media consistently denigrated the War on Poverty in racial terms, with the result that "even now the people generally regard the antipoverty programs as efforts to force integration on them."[19]

Both rhetorical and real connections between the Civil Rights Movement and the War on Poverty inspired violent attacks on people who worked to ensure racial and economic justice in the South. In January 1966, for example, racist vigilantes bombed and burned down the home of local activist Vernon Dahmer in Hattiesburg, Mississippi. Although the family managed to escape from the fire, Dahmer later died from his burns and injuries. Dahmer had been an active member of the NAACP since 1946 and worked with newer organizations such as the Student Nonviolent Coordinating Committee and the Delta Ministry to encourage voter registration and the desegregation of stores and businesses in the 1960s. He had also supported antipoverty efforts, allowing the Delta Ministry to use buildings that he owned to operate a clothing distribution center and a Head Start program.[20]

Throughout the state, a campaign of harassment and intimidation against Head Start centers operated by the Child Development Group of Mississippi distressed employees and discouraged many local people from participating in the project. In its first grant year alone, opponents burned down two of its centers, ran one program director's car off the road at night, and fired shots into the vehicle of another director. Administrators of a center in Holmes County described how the violence interfered with efforts to create an interracial program that served all those who needed it: "Before we could really make any definite efforts to involve the white people in our center, we were harassed by many of the white citizens of our town," they stated. "They tried to burn our church down where we first started, until we had our center built. After the center was built, while having a staff meeting, some of them rode by and fired shots at us. We even had ads in the newspaper trying to involve them. Despite this, they burned crosses at our homes and threatened a great number of people. We were afraid most of the time and didn't know what to expect from them any of the time."[21]

Activists in other states also encountered violent resistance when they tried to initiate projects to help displaced workers. In June 1966, John Zippert of the Congress of Racial Equality wrote to the Department of Justice to report an incident of racial terror in Churchpoint, Louisiana, where Black farmers had recently formed a vegetable growers' cooperative in an effort to combat the political and economic forces that were pushing them off the land. A white man named Preston Savoy threatened the wife and children of co-op member Theogen Nero while he was not at home, firing three shots into the family's yard and forcing them to run for cover. Zippert complained that local police had done nothing to investigate or punish Savoy and warned that Black economic initiatives could be broken up by threats and intimidation unless something was done to stop the violence.[22] The same month, a school auditorium in St. Helena Parish that was slated to house a Head Start program was burned down. Civil rights worker Fred Lacey told reporters for the *Louisiana Weekly* that there had been "much opposition to Headstart from white segregationists in the parish."[23]

White supporters of antipoverty projects also came under attack. A white businessman in Lowndes County, Alabama, received threatening phone calls after renting a building to organizers of the local CAP, and opponents also poisoned some cattle belonging to a judge who helped to arrange the lease.[24] In April 1967, the Selma Inter-Religious Project reported on a spate of arsons directed at both white- and Black-owned properties that had been used for antipoverty projects in Alabama.[25] Later that year, a document summarizing the problems that beset an education program for seasonally employed agricultural workers in the state described similar forms of harassment that had occurred throughout the seven counties it served. A classroom had been burned down, a house bombed, and in every community teachers and participants encountered some kind of intimidation by opponents of the project. As was the case elsewhere, law enforcement agencies showed no interest in investigating these incidents or holding the perpetrators accountable. The report's authors concluded that local authorities were "not committed and they couldn't care less about the poor beyond the fact that it is good for them to remain poor."[26]

At the national level, federal officials displayed somewhat more concern. The Senate Committee on Labor and Public Welfare planned two hearings in Mississippi in 1967 aimed at exposing what one OEO staff member called the "growing menace" of violence against people who participated in the government's antipoverty programs.[27] President Lyndon B. Johnson was also aware that opponents of his policies were continuing to use lawless methods to hinder progress toward racial equality and economic justice. In a message to Congress in February 1967, he outlined the initiatives his administration had taken to end racial discrimination, then pointed out that "a right has little meaning unless it can be freely exercised." Johnson noted that African Americans seeking access to education, political power, and economic opportunities still risked violent reprisals. State and local officials were not meeting their obligations to enforce the law, and stronger federal deterrents were needed to discourage violent actions by private citizens who opposed Black equality. To address these problems, Johnson called on Congress to pass legislation that explicitly set out the rights that were protected under federal law, "including voting, purchasing a home, holding a job, attending a school, obtaining service in a restaurant or place of public accommodation," along with punishments for those who interfered with the exercise of those rights.[28]

Although Congress eventually incorporated these suggestions into Title I of the Civil Rights Act of 1968, civil rights and social justice activists continued to risk violent attacks.[29] Just two months after the legislation was passed, the Mississippi Freedom Democratic Party (MFDP) attributed a disappointingly low voter turnout in the Democratic primary election to Klan harassment that intimidated many newly registered voters, reporting that seven Black churches had been firebombed that spring.[30] Two years later, in the town of West Point, a white man shot and killed campaign worker John Thomas Jr., the day before a run-off election between Black mayoral candidate John Buffington and the white incumbent. An all-white jury later acquitted the murderer, Seth P. Stanley, whose initial explanation for shooting Thomas was because "he cussed me."[31] In July 1971, the director of a CAP in Louisiana asked the Justice Department to investigate a spate of incidents aimed at intimidating antipoverty workers in Caddo and Bossier Parishes. Staff at the Rodessa Neighborhood Service Center reported Klan literature being nailed to the door of the building, cross burnings, and Molotov cocktails being thrown into the center.[32] Five years later, vigilantes bombed the home of the director of an antipoverty agency in Montgomery, Alabama, and tried to burn down the building that housed the program.[33] Toward the end of the decade, the Mississippi Council on Human Relations observed that open Klan activity, including "marches, recruitment rallies, and ritual meetings complete with fiery crosses," had taken a toll on human rights organizations and threatened "the survival of the movement for economic and racial justice in our state."[34]

At the same time, the federal government was undermining antipoverty efforts by diverting hundreds of billions of dollars to its military intervention in Vietnam, a form of violence that critics decried as doubly immoral for its effects on people both within and outside the United States. Explaining his reasons for refusing to fight in Vietnam, civil rights activist John Sumrall stated: "*Women* and *children* are being *killed* and *crippled* for life with *liquid fire* (Napalm bombs). . . . We are spending *billions of dollars* in these jungles when right here *in Mississippi people are starving*. In addition *we* are *helping Vietnamese starve* by bombing huts and rice paddies."[35] The MFDP made a similar point in a pamphlet outlining its stance on political issues in 1968. Listing "peace in Vietnam" alongside land reform and economic rights as a top priority, the MFDP argued, "None of the programs necessary to remake America can begin in earnest so long as our nation is militarily, politically and economically ensnared in the war in Vietnam. The interests of the masses of the American people cannot be advanced while this war continues."[36] Sargent Shriver, who served as director of the OEO from its creation in 1964 until his resignation in April 1968, joined activists in expressing concern about the impact of the Vietnam War on antipoverty programs. Speaking in a television interview, Shriver asserted, "If we devote the kind of money to it, let's say half of what we're putting into Vietnam, we can eliminate poverty in this nation. . . . The question is not whether we can; the question is: will we, do we have the will power to do it, do we have the motivation to do it?"[37]

The Poor People's Campaign also criticized the government's prioritization of the war in Vietnam over the War on Poverty in scathing terms. In the same speech noting that poverty and neglect of human needs were forms of violence, Coretta Scott King castigated political leaders for expending vast amounts of resources on killing people overseas at the same time that they claimed not to have enough money to fully fund antipoverty programs. Calling the conflict in Vietnam "the most crucial and evil war in the history of mankind," Scott went on to suggest some ways in which the nation's energies could be redirected more productively: "We could create 400,000 new jobs with the money we would save if we stopped the war fourteen minutes sooner. If we stopped the war two months sooner, we could build 300,000 new housing units with the money. One hour of war could buy your community a new school, hospital, or cultural center. All of this is to say that a guaranteed income, a job for those who need a job, could be had if the war was stopped and the will created by our government to act on behalf of its deprived citizens."[38]

While social justice activists increasingly expressed antiwar sentiments, opponents of antipoverty initiatives added the need for military victory in Vietnam to their arsenal of arguments against government funding for social programs. Louisiana resident Ashton P. Roberthon wrote to Sen. Russell B. Long in August 1967 to express his view that communists and other subversives had infiltrated federally funded projects and were using taxpayers' money to incite riots and undermine private property rights in the United States. "I am for reducing or cutting out all programs shown to be of doubtful value, and using this money for an all out effort to win the Viet Nam war decisively," he stated.[39] Responding to a similar letter from a constituent who urged denying funds to the OEO and employment training programs, Thomas Abernethy pointed to his record of fiscal conservatism and agreed that the federal treasury could not "stand the drain from these costly programs and at the same time meet the vital and much more important tremendous expenditure required for the military struggle we are in."[40] Sen. John Stennis expressed identical concerns in an address to a joint session of the Mississippi legislature, stating that winning the Vietnam War was "the first order of business with me, and it should be the first order of business throughout Washington. This means that those Great Society programs with the billions that they are gulping down, should be relegated to the rear—far to the rear, I think."[41]

Siding with those who thought that bombing campaigns over Southeast Asia were a better way to ensure national strength than investing in the health and wellbeing of their fellow Americans, President Johnson and his successor Richard Nixon escalated the war, incurring costs that totaled $111 billion for direct military operations in Vietnam between 1965 and 1975 (not including financial aid to allies, veterans' benefits, or interest on debts incurred by war spending).[42] The Federation of Southern Cooperatives, an organization that fostered a variety of economic development efforts to help displaced agricultural workers in the South, noted that federal support for social justice projects evaporated as the Vietnam War "sapped the energy and resources of the War on Poverty and Nixon began his cutbacks and impoundment of funds for social programs."[43] Between 1973 and 1979 the federal government spent $648 billion on national defense compared with $137 billion on education, training, and employment programs.[44] During the presidency of Ronald Reagan, a staunch anticommunist and free-market proponent who saw most forms of government assistance for poor people as unnecessary, annual defense expenditures increased from $134 billion to $290 billion while funding for education, training, and employment programs remained static at around $30 billion per year between 1980 and 1988.[45]

Failure to invest in initiatives that could have helped displaced workers to learn new skills, find alternative employment, and earn higher incomes only cost the government more in the long run. In the 1960s, federal antipoverty efforts helped to bring the percentage of Americans living below poverty level down from 22 percent to 12 percent, but in the next two decades this number hardly moved at all, standing slightly higher at 13 percent in 1988. That left thirty-two million people unable to earn adequate incomes, necessitating expenditures of $113 billion that year on housing assistance, food and nutrition programs, income support, and health services for struggling families.[46] Reagan's attempts to stimulate economic growth by cutting taxes for individuals and corporations further decimated the federal treasury, contributing to an increase in the national debt from $909 billion to $2.6 trillion during his two terms in office.[47]

Critics of rising deficits in the late twentieth century attributed the problem to wasteful spending on social welfare programs rather than spending on military interventions or tax breaks, often playing on racist stereotypes that equated poverty with Blackness to undermine popular support for government initiatives that could insulate people from the vicissitudes of the market. Ronald Reagan reinforced the idea that lazy and dishonest Black people dominated public assistance rolls by repeatedly telling (and exaggerating) the story of "welfare queen" Linda Taylor, an African American woman who fraudulently claimed several thousand dollars in government benefits in the 1970s.[48] The *Citizen* also promoted this trope by regularly printing stories that portrayed the federal agencies charged with administering antipoverty programs as bloated, corrupt bureaucracies serving clients whose criminal behavior threatened to bankrupt the nation. An article focusing on the trial of another Black welfare recipient, Barbara Williams, claimed, "Untold millions of dollars worth of food stamps paid for by American taxpayers are being stolen or otherwise wasted because of inefficiency in the administration of the Health, Education and Welfare Department. . . . From Mississippi to Michigan and from Florida to Oregon have come reports of widespread cheating—not only by women receiving food stamps, rent subsidies and cash for aid to their illegitimate dependent children, but also by persons benefiting by all other forms of government handouts."[49] After Reagan's election to the presidency in 1980, the magazine celebrated his plans for reducing government spending and eliminating "waste, fraud and extravagance in welfare, subsidized housing and other programs."[50]

Racism remained a barrier to economic reforms that aimed to ensure a fairer distribution of the nation's wealth for the rest of the century. During Reagan's administration and those of his successors, working-class communities in the urban North and West were decimated by job losses caused by automation, deindustrialization, and global free trade agreements that sent factories and jobs overseas. The same hardships that beset displaced agricultural workers in the South in the 1960s affected millions of white Americans in the decades that followed, but the association of antipoverty programs with Black people caused many voters to reject proposals for expanding government assistance for unemployed people. As Chicago carpenter and self-described "working-class Democrat" Dan Donahue explained to researchers who wanted to know why he and others like him switched to supporting Republican candidates for political office in the 1980s, "We have four or five generations of welfare mothers. . . . Unfortunately, most of the people who need help in this situation are Black and most of the people who are doing the helping are white. . . . We [white voters] are tired of paying for the Chicago Housing Authority, and for public housing and public transportation that we don't use."[51]

Democratic politicians such as Arkansas governor (and later president) Bill Clinton took note. In a campaign speech delivered in 1991, Clinton promised to "repair the damaged bond between the people and their government" by listening to the "voices of forgotten middle-class Americans lamenting the fact that government no longer looks out for their interest or honors their values—values like individual responsibility, hard work, family and community."[52] Neither major political party was interested in reviving the War on Poverty, instead pursuing initiatives that curtailed the government's role in the economy and trusted in market forces to solve social problems. The results were disastrous not just for low-income families but for many middle-class Americans as well. Tax cuts and deregulation allowed wealth to accumulate in the form of private fortunes at the top of the income scale instead of being reinvested in education, job training, health care, infrastructure, and other activities that could benefit all the nation's people. Between 1978 and 2018, inflation-adjusted average pay for the nation's corporate executives increased by more than 940 percent while workers' wages rose by only 12 percent.[53] By 2017, three men (Jeff Bezos, Bill Gates, and Warren Buffett) together owned as much wealth ($249 billion) as the bottom 50 percent of Americans combined.[54]

As a small number of superrich Americans profited exponentially, millions of other people struggled to afford housing, health insurance, and college tuition or to fund retirement savings accounts. Thirty-nine percent of adults who responded to a survey designed to gather data about the economic wellbeing of American households in 2018 stated that they would have to borrow money, sell something, or simply be unable to cover a hypothetical unexpected expense in the amount of $400, and 17 percent reported not being able to pay all of their actual regular bills in the month they were surveyed.[55] The mental health toll of economic precarity was evident in the growing scourge of "diseases of despair"—drug addiction, alcoholism, and suicide—noted by researchers seeking to explain the rising death rate among middle-aged white Americans. Economists Anne Case and Angus Deaton first drew attention to this trend in a study that was published in 2015, following up with more analysis in 2017 that attributed the problem to "the collapse of the white, high school educated, working class after its heyday in the 1970s, and the pathologies that accompany that decline."[56] In white communities as well as Black, the violence of the market continued to undermine the health and wellbeing of large numbers of Americans mentally and physically.

Meanwhile, responses to the threat of global terrorism in the wake of al-Qaeda's attack on September 11, 2001, squandered trillions of dollars on overseas military interventions and left public services in the United States severely underfunded. Analyzing the lost opportunities represented by spending roughly $260 billion per year to fund major wars in Afghanistan, Iraq, Pakistan, and Syria as well as smaller operations in dozens of other countries between 2001 and 2019, researchers at Brown University's Costs of War Project raised the same questions about political leaders' priorities that earlier activists had expressed in their criticisms of the Vietnam War. Heidi Garrett-Peltier estimated that the same amount of money that created approximately 1.8 million defense-related jobs in these decades could have generated 2.5 million jobs in clean energy or infrastructure, or 3.7 million jobs in health care, or 4 million jobs in education.[57]

Fiscal hawks who were quick to decry instances of fraud or abuse in public assistance programs were less vocal about similar practices that pervaded the nation's defense apparatus. A government report on the war effort in Afghanistan found that billions of dollars that were supposed to help rebuild the nation's war-torn economy and society were instead used to enrich private contractors, drug dealers, warlords, and corrupt government officials. In contrast to the stingy funding levels, complex grant procedures, and bureaucratic surveillance that characterized economic development programs in the United States, agencies operating in Afghanistan were "under pressure to spend money quickly," leading to lax oversight and lucrative opportunities for graft. In one case, an agricultural program initiated by the United States Agency for International Development "expanded within a few weeks from $60 million to $360 million, resulting in rampant waste and fraud."[58] Similarly, forensic accountants who analyzed three thousand defense contracts worth $106 billion that were awarded between 2010 and 2012 concluded that "about 40 percent of the money ended up in the pockets of insurgents, criminal syndicates or corrupt Afghan officials."[59] The $42 billion lost on those contracts alone was more than double what the federal government spent in the same period on training and employment programs in the United States.[60]

The legacies of policy decisions that prioritized military interventions over social investments were evident in persistent racial and economic disparities in the twenty-first century. In 2018, 12 percent of the population of the United States (thirty-eight million people) still lived below the poverty line. Another ninety-four million lived in households with incomes that put them close to poverty level (less than two times their poverty thresholds), bringing the proportion who were struggling economically to 42 percent of the population. The poverty rate for African Americans was almost double the national rate, at 21 percent. Fourteen million households were classified as "food insecure" and suffering from inadequate nutrition. Hunger afflicted 21 percent of Black households compared to only 8 percent of white households. As always, residents of the southern states experienced higher rates of poverty and malnutrition than those in other regions.[61]

These problems were not the product of wasteful government spending on programs that encouraged loafing and dependence, as opponents of antipoverty efforts claimed. They were the combined result of market failure, massive resistance to racial equality, and militarism that undermined the economic justice initiatives of the 1960s. In that decade, activists and policy makers who believed that real freedom and equality depended on ensuring access to food, housing, education, employment, and health care for all people initiated a variety of innovative projects that provided displaced workers with the chance for a better life. Opponents responded by racializing and violently attacking the programs, portraying them as an illegitimate use of public funds that favored Black people over white people, subverted the nation's free enterprise system, and hindered its ability to defeat communism. Within a few years of pledging to wage an all-out war on poverty, the federal government reneged on its promise by cutting funding for antipoverty efforts and transferring resources to military interventions overseas. Half a century later, the consequences continue to affect all Americans, not just African Americans living in the Delta regions of Louisiana, Mississippi, and Arkansas, as they navigate the unpredictable violence of market forces that can upend the fortunes of anyone, any time.

Evil in the Delta

MICHAEL HONEY

Papa's out there on the front porch, the sun gone down
Old hound dog's howling, out on the edge of town.

CHORUS: *Elaine, Elaine, keep the children inside*
There's evil in the Delta, here on the Arkansas side.

Yeah, fetch me that shotgun off the cabin wall
It's night riders down near Hoop Spur, hear the night owl call . . .

Something burning there in the back woods, near the Johnson shack
There's demons riding those horses, burning up the tracks . . .

Something's floating in that river, washed up there last night
Looked like Junior Johnson's boy, face swolled up tight . . .

That river is deep and wide,
The devil's on the loose, here on the Arkansas side . . .

You better hide your eyes, there's evil here in the Delta
the Phillips County side . . .

Over in Memphis, they lynched Ell Parsons, only seventeen
Threw his head in the street, how could they be so mean?

Out in Chicago, they broke the packinghouse strike
They set the town on fire, using racial strife.

Later in Tulsa, they bombed out the town
They say 300 dead, all Black and brown.

CHORUS: *Elaine, Elaine, keep the children inside*
There's evil in the Delta, on the Arkansas side.

GREGG ANDREWS, SON OF a poor white working-class family, retired from teaching as a history professor at Texas State University in San Marcos and went back to his first loves: music and telling stories he remembered from his youth in Hannibal, Missouri. People think of this as Mark Twain country, but it is also a harsh environment where his father died due to dust in his lungs from working at a cement plant. Gregg's song, "Evil in the Delta," written about the murderous events of 1919 in Elaine, Arkansas, reconnects us to those horrific murders of Black sharecroppers and tenant farmers with a ghostly blues refrain. I added verses that remind us of the evil that took place elsewhere in that era in response to widespread Black resistance to white supremacy, vigilante and state repression, and labor exploitation.[1]

David F. Krugler, in 1919, the Year of Racial Violence: How African Americans Fought Back, chronicles Black resistance, which ruling classes and some white working people alike tried to crush. As the literature on Elaine makes clear, one of America's worst racial massacres aimed to stop a striving African American farming and laboring community from advancing economically and organizing a farmer's union. We remember the Red Summer of 1919 and the various racial holocausts of that time, from Chicago to DC and later to Tulsa in 1921, as turning points in the solidification of white supremacy. Racial terror and division also destroyed a national steelworker strike and other union efforts, as well as Black economic and union advancement and the American left for the next decade.[2]

A short summary reminds us of how that turning point of 1919 happened in Elaine on September 30. On that night, in a church at a country crossroads called Hoop Spur, about a hundred African Americans attended a meeting of the Progressive Farmers and Household Union of America. It was not a typical union, but it was a union nonetheless. Blacks far outnumbered whites in Phillips County, but whites had most of the guns. A carload of armed whites approached and exchanged fire with African Americans guarding the church. One white man was killed and another wounded, possibly by stray bullets from their own side. Numerous books and articles describe what happened next. Hundreds of white vigilantes from Arkansas and Mississippi, dozens of law enforcement officials, and, most deadly of all, five hundred U.S. soldiers mobilized by the governor of the state from nearby Camp Pike led hellish assaults for the next four days. According to eyewitness accounts of the victims and the perpetrators, mobs went from house to house killing

Black occupants. U.S. troops marched through forests where people went to hide, using machine guns to mow down every Black person in sight. One modest estimate is that between 100 and 237 Black people died. Other accounts suggest that hundreds more died but were never accounted for. The essays in this volume substantiate the horror as well as the generations of Black resistance to white supremacy.

This is a stunning story, but unfortunately it is only one of many of America's racial massacres. Each one had a purpose. The 1898 Wilmington, North Carolina, racial massacre, for example, capped a white supremacy movement that put an end to most Black voting in the South and destroyed a nascent reform coalition (called "fusion") between white Populists and Black and white Republicans. Racial terror had a double purpose: to suppress Black advancement and aspirations, and to destroy progressive reforms and union organization that benefitted Black and white workers alike. The 1917 riots in East St. Louis likewise helped to defeat labor organizing. The Red Summer of 1919 sought to crush Black assertiveness and destroy an upsurge in union organizing among steelworkers, packinghouse workers, and others. The Elaine Massacre destroyed a promising movement of Black farmers for a better living, while the Tulsa massacre of 1921 subsequently wiped out independent Black businesses and the hope for Black political power. Subsequent white supremacy uprisings throughout the twentieth century, in places like Chicago and Detroit, aimed to stop Black migrations into better housing, jobs, and schools, and to undermine unions.[3]

Hence, the white supremacy riots and insurrections and police violence during the era of President Donald Trump echoed these historic precedents. Martin Luther King Jr., warned in his last published article, in *Look* magazine on April 16, 1968, that racism potentially provides a pathway to an American form of fascism. That danger remains, making it all the more important that we understand and remember Elaine and other racist upheavals in American history. On the one-hundred-year anniversary of the Tulsa, Oklahoma, massacre, many commented that most Americans have known little to nothing about Tulsa or these other stories. That is why we must tell them, despite Republican efforts to whitewash or ban the telling of America's racial history inside and outside of the classroom.[4]

Why did the Elaine Massacre happen? That tells us a lot about why racial massacres happened in many other places. In Elaine, a landowning class had gained power by making fortunes based on labor conditions that were, in some respects, as brutal as slavery. With the support of other white social classes, white ruling elites had crushed Black freedom after the Civil War through lynching, rape, nightriding, disfranchisement, and segregation. In 1919, the plantation ruling class used oppressive laws, lynching, and vigilante violence to stop African Americans from getting ahead. The price of cotton shot sky high during the Great War. White landlords, merchants, and cotton factors controlled the market for sales and stood to gain millions if they could just keep the Black workers who planted, tended, and harvested the cotton from getting a fair share. Those farm workers meeting in the Hoop Spur church did so on the eve of the cotton harvest and planned on either getting higher prices for the cotton they picked from local white elites or going around them entirely to take their cotton to market somewhere else. Pure greed set the local white ruling class against them.

The context for this event, however, was national, even international. Widespread white paranoia and anger against Black progress raged in an America in the grip of an antilabor and anticommunist fervor sustained by the mass media, the military, and the federal government. The Russian Revolution and upheavals in Europe, the Seattle General Strike, and union unrest everywhere at the end of the World War I precipitated a massive propaganda campaign by the media and government against socialists, the left, unions, immigrants, Latino/as, and African Americans. Mass jailing and deportations by federal, state, and local governments largely crushed civil rights, civil liberties, and the American left during and beyond the war's end. On the West Coast, anti-Chinese and anti-immigrant racial violence helped to destroy organizing by Filipinos, Asian Americans, and Pacific Islanders.[5]

Black soldiers, workers, and farmers had made their way into the military, the cities, and industry, and were not about to abandon their progress, which the so-called race riots of 1919 aimed to stop. The riots, which we might more accurately call pogroms, set white workers and especially white immigrants against Black workers, who were sometimes brought in by employers to break strikes. As historians document, racial conflict killed off a national strike of 350,000 steelworkers, the interracial organizing of packinghouse workers in Chicago, Black union organizing, and the promising beginnings of an interracial labor movement. All of this set the stage for both the Elaine Massacre and continuing Black resistance.[6]

In Elaine and nearby Helena, Black soldiers returning from World War I had weapons and knew how to use them. It was the time of "the

New Negro," proletarianization, and the Black Great Migration to the North, and struggles for Black racial uplift everywhere. Organizing included the National Association for the Advancement of Colored People (NAACP) and also the Universal Negro Improvement Association led by Black nationalist Marcus Garvey (who the federal government later arrested and deported), which had numerous branches in Arkansas. African Americans in many communities fought fiercely against white racist attacks in the Red Summer. It required mass shootings by whites from Elaine to Chicago, Washington, DC, to Omaha, to suppress them. Incredibly, in 1921, another racist binge hit in Tulsa, Oklahoma, where whites raped, murdered, looted, and bombed from the air. They destroyed the thriving Black community of Greenwood, killing hundreds and burning the Black business district and hundreds of homes to the ground.[7] We remember Elaine as a turning point, but it remains important to understand it as only one of many.

Putting down Black and union power put white supremacy fully in command. It was most devastating when white workers joined mobs attacking Black communities. As W. E. B. Du Bois explained, after emancipation, racial division and white supremacist violence drove a stake through the heart of the nascent free labor movement in the South. Following the orgy of violence after World War I came the rebirth of the Ku Klux Klan as a mass movement and its takeover of parts of the political structure in the South and Midwest of the 1920s. White supremacy also froze union organizing in the Deep South. Many of the stories we remember are necessarily stories of defeat but they need to be told. Most Americans know nothing about Elaine, so it is one of those stories we should never forget to tell.[8]

Within defeats, however, we can also find kernels of hope and seeds of organizing for the future. Writer and organizer Ida B. Wells-Barnett, Black Arkansas attorney Scipio Jones, and the NAACP all fought tenaciously through a series of trials and publicity campaigns to save the Elaine Twelve, falsely convicted of murdering white supremacist attackers, from the electric chair. By 1925, they were all released from prison (and spirited quickly out of the state). Their case before the U.S. Supreme Court—1923's *Moore v. Dempsey*— strengthened the Court's interpretation of the due process clause of the Fourteenth Amendment to correct state criminal trials that blatantly ignored the rights of defendants.

The next generation of labor and civil rights organizers also learned something from these events. The United Packinghouse Union and labor's left made antiracism and interracial organizing the keys to success in the 1930s, when they helped to organize the Congress of Industrial Organizations and finally break down many of the color barriers to mass unionization.[9] The Communist Party and its related organizations made Black–white unity a fundamental part of organizing and laid the grounds for many of the era's labor and civil rights advances.[10] In that context, a history of Black resistance to racial and economic oppression broke through again even in the Arkansas Delta, and left behind a hopeful memory that, even amidst racism and repression, agricultural workers in the most difficult places can and will organize.

In 1985, I first met John Handcox, then in his eighties, through my friendship with musicologist and singer Pete Seeger. Sponsored by Ralph Rinzler of the Smithsonian Institution American Folklife project, I interviewed John at length, and we collaborated to write his oral history.[11] John never spoke of Elaine to me, and I didn't have the presence of mind to ask him about it. But he didn't need to reference that particular story, because his own story of growing up and living in eastern Arkansas reflected the white supremacy terrorism that led to murder and mayhem in Elaine and continued in its wake. John's story also built on the past to maintain a resistance story that went back to his family's story of slavery in Arkansas.

Born in 1904 outside Brinkley, about fifty miles north of Elaine, John could recall his grandfather's terrible stories of being a slave in Arkansas, such as when as a child he had to eat cornmeal with his hands out of a trough like a pig and later served as a stud for his owner to produce more enslaved offspring. But John's father told him that the Jim Crow era of the early twentieth century was "worse than slavery": before, whites had valued slaves as property, but now the white relationship to Black labor was "kill one, get another." It was also "open season" on Black people for any white person who wanted to shoot or lynch you. Now "we were everyone's slave," John told me. He recalled that whites would attack and sometimes kill any Black person who owned a farm, could afford a car or a decent home, tried to walk down the sidewalk, or sought to cast a vote. As a teenager, at the end of the Great War, he went into Forrest City, Arkansas, not far from his home, and bought some used military clothes from a Salvation Army store. But he found that wearing a uniform was likely to get him killed by whites, and he quickly shed his military jacket. John grew up experiencing the racist legacy of Elaine.

However, John also learned of the tradition of resistance through the Black church. He conveyed this tradition to me by singing a song that went back to the struggle for emancipation during the Civil War. In the Civil Rights Movement, we knew it as "Oh, Freedom." In John's version, it was "No More Mourning," and he changed the words to "No more sorrow, no more slavery, no more Jim Crow." His chorus became the refrain, "Oh, Freedom after 'While," an acknowledgment that freedom would not come soon, and he changed the ending of the chorus. Instead of "before I'll be a slave, I'll be buried in my grave, and go home to my Lord and be free," John's last line was "and take my place with those who loved and fought before." He understood the mix of spiritualism with the continuation of resistance.

John's family of eleven brothers and sisters had done better than most. His father rented and even owned some land, farm animals, and equipment, understood math, and would argue with cotton factors and merchants when they tried to cheat him by using fake figures in the annual balance sheet. In a one-room schoolhouse in Brinkley, John learned the poetic muse of Paul Lawrence Dunbar, which told of the "New Negro" sensibility of resistance but also the "old Negro" reminiscences about a supposedly better time. Poetry allowed John to tell the story of workers for the rest of his life. He was an optimistic man, but John's generation of strivers also knew they could lose everything if they went against the racial system. As Jeannie Whayne's essay in this volume recounts in horrifying detail, retaliation included six hundred whites in 1921 slowly burning Henry Lowery to death in Nodena, Arkansas. Some ten thousand attended a KKK rally in Helena in that period, and twenty-eight people were reportedly lynched in Arkansas in the 1920s.[12]

In 1923, John's father died suddenly when a runaway team of mules crashed his buckboard into a tree. John as the oldest son took over the family and tried to feed everyone. But in the 1920s, like almost everyone else who grew cotton, the Handcox family fell into deep indebtedness as the price of the crop crashed. They worked harder and harder for less and less. The family lost the small lands his grandfather had come to own in the aftermath of the Civil War. Rental lands in the upcountry got too expensive and too unproductive. John moved everyone down into the rich lands closer to the St. Francis River. But now his family members worked as sharecroppers rather than as tenants. Sharecroppers hoped to save up money in order to step up into land ownership but instead almost always stepped down into peonage.

By 1934, in the midst of the Great Depression, John Handcox, his wife, and their four children existed in a parallel universe with the Black sharecroppers of Elaine in 1919. Living not far from Elaine, the Handcox family barely survived by working someone else's land and buying food, seeds, and fertilizer at exorbitant rates of credit of up to 30 percent. John supplemented their meager income by fishing in the St. Francis River and selling the catch to people in the plantations. Then he heard about the Southern Tenant Farmers' Union (STFU). "That's what we need, a union!" he recalled thinking at the time. John's family had survived both slavery and lynch law in Arkansas. Now, as had workers in Phillips County, he saw the union as a way to demand a more just distribution of the profits from the sharecropping system. John also pointed out that many of the people oppressed by the landlords were poor whites and that they, too, needed to organize.

In the fall of 1935, secretly organized day laborers, tenants, and share-croppers went on strike at the moment when cotton had to be harvested. Blacks and whites both struck, sometimes in isolated local groups and sometimes working together. Landlords and employers gave in, virtually doubling the wages paid to agricultural workers. John used his practice of going door to door on the plantations selling fish to secretly recruit people to join the union. He championed the STFU's philosophy, which encompassed socialism—"land to the tiller"—and interracial union solidarity. At the founding meeting of the union in Poinsett County in 1934, people had debated whether they should form two unions, one for whites and one for Blacks. Isaac Shaw, a survivor of the Elaine Massacre, objected that racial separation was the trouble all along. "We colored can't organize without you . . . and you white folks can't organize without us," he reportedly told the meeting.[13]

The STFU created a policy of white members in the top elected positions and Black activists in secondary positions, fearing that a Black leader as a top or coleader would stand out and likely be killed. The union organized interracial conventions, joined white and Black workers in rallies and on picket lines, and required Black and white members to address each other respectfully as "mister" or "miss" or "missis." (Most whites would call a Black man twice their age "boy," a practice banned in the union). The union's formation as an interracial one raised the possibility of farm laborers once again fighting for their right to the land, or for a minimum of day labor wages and cash crop prices that would allow families to survive. Only this time, they vowed not to be divided by letting the cotton kings set whites against Blacks based on race.

Numerous historians have told the story of the union. Most recently, Matt Simmons has provided more nuanced views of how well the union did or did not do in organizing interracially, and has detailed the strong role of women in the union.[14] For my part, I would like to emphasize a few things that I learned from John Handcox. His storytelling and singing expands our understanding of racism and resistance after Elaine. In 2015, I visited the Southern Tenant Farmers Museum in Tyronza. The museum has a jukebox dedicated to Handcox's songs and poems that helped unionists to revere their past and to hope for a future based on union organizing and human rights.

His first responsibility, he felt, was to tell the truth about the conditions his people lived under in Arkansas. To the tune of "How Beautiful Heaven Must Be," he ironically twisted the song to the reality of the day:

> Raggedy, raggedy are we
> Just as raggedy as raggedy can be.
> We don't get nothin' for our labor,
> So raggedy, raggedy are we.

In his most stunning poem, published in the STFU's newspaper, *The Sharecropper's Voice*, Handcox stripped off the veneer of a planter class that claimed to provide a good life but actually impoverished workers like serfs and underfunded rural communities. If anyone wants the most succinct description of the inhumanity of the Delta sharecropping system, read John's two-page long poem, "The Planter and the Sharecropper." I quote its opening lines:

> The planter lives off the sweat of the sharecroppers' brow,
> How the sharecropper lives, the planter cares not how.
> The sharecropper raises all the planter can eat,
> And then gets tramped down under his feet.

In other poems and songs, John helped people in the plantation districts to identify the sources of their misery and poverty. In the planting season of 1936, the union tried to follow up its successful cotton-picking strike of the previous year. This time, the planters and the forces of the law and order were ready. Planters ejected union members from their homes and their land. Repression victimized hundreds of union members, both

Black and white, as police and vigilantes used beatings, jailing, kidnapping, and a few killings to break up union meetings, marches, and strike activities. John's songs of resistance, "Join the Union Tonight" and "Roll the Union On," among others, became labor movement hits. They were immortalized by Pete Seeger, Woody Guthrie, and Alan Lomax in their book, *Hard-Hitting Songs for Hard-Hit People.* "There Are Mean Things Happening in This Land" also became a signature John Handcox song:

> The planters throwed the people off the land without a bite to eat.
> They cursed them and kicked them and some with axe handles beat.
> There are mean things happening in this land.
> There are mean things happening in this land.
> But the union's going on and the union's going strong.
> There are mean things happening in this land.[15]

Despite impressive union solidarity, the majority of locals were either all Black or all white because that's the way the plantations were organized. Racism and violent attacks hurt the union, but ultimately the mechanization of cotton production destroyed it. By 1939, the STFU was a skeleton of what it had been in 1936. Nonetheless, John took great pride in what the union had done. He told me that the ability of working people to form a union of Blacks and whites in the heart of Ku Klux Klan country provided the most important thing to remember about this history. Unlike the tragedy in Elaine, the struggle of the STFU left behind a legend of interracial organizing that went on to the next generation. Carrie Dilworth, a Black woman who in 1936 surreptitiously scattered STFU leaflets while laying down on the floorboards from the back of a car so as not to be seen riding with white folks, played an important role in organizing Student Nonviolent Coordinating Committee (SNCC) in the 1960s. White SNCC activist Ed King recalled that memories of the STFU inspired him and other activists in the Mississippi Delta, who saw the STFU as the beginning of a grass-roots movement to challenge segregation, disfranchisement, and plantation rule.[16]

The mere fact that Black and white workers joined together in the heart of Klan country in the 1930s, called each other brother and sister, or mister and missus, and created a voice of protest against intolerable conditions, gave those SNCC people who knew about it hope that racial barriers could be broken down and that a poor people's movement could win.

My introduction to Elaine's continuing reverberations happened when I lived in Memphis. In September 1970, I drove in a caravan of cars across the Mississippi River to support Black families resisting police repression and school resegregation in Earle, Arkansas. Located in Crittenden County, where repression against the STFU had been intense, Earle remained one of those unreconstructed places the Civil Rights Movement had hardly touched. Black students had walked out of school protesting a fake desegregation plan that consolidated the schools by removing Black administrators, teachers, and coaches and placing Black students in the back of the classrooms. Police arrested the protesting students. When they and their parents held a rally in front of City Hall, state troopers, local police, and deputized white vigilantes fired over their heads and then beat and arrested many of them. Rev. Ezra Greer, who suffered a broken arm, fractured ribs, and twenty stitches across his face, was charged with inciting a riot. Writing in the *Southern Patriot*, the newspaper of the Southern Conference Educational Fund, I called it the Earle Massacre.[17]

As our caravan turned off the highway toward Earle, sheriff's deputies holding shotguns and wearing cynical smiles confronted us. We were in poverty-stricken majority-Black Crittenden County, surrounded by cotton fields being turned into soybean fields, and dotted with abandoned shacks of people who had lost their jobs to agricultural mechanization. We met the Greers and rallied with other Black residents who had the courage to come out. We felt thankful to get out of town without incident.

Only as a historian did I later come to understand this effort in the so-called post–civil rights era as but one part of a long history of resistance. As a doctoral student, I researched the 1930s and 1940s and learned that southern workers rebuilt the labor movement in various places and in many ways to overcome the legacy of white supremacy that became so entrenched following the Elaine Massacre and the Red Summer of 1919. I learned how Black workers fleeing from eastern Arkansas, west Tennessee, and northern Mississippi migrated to Memphis, where some of them built successful lives as unionized workers despite segregation. I also learned about the Black Memphis sanitation workers, many of them fleeing from the poverty of the Mississippi and Arkansas Deltas, who built a movement and won union rights with the help of Dr. Martin Luther King Jr.[18] More recently, Michael Pierce's story of Arkansas labor shows that labor organizing did not die as the result of the Elaine Massacre. No, unionism did not die among the workers. Rather, we have learned in recent years how deindustrialization, globalization, and government attacks killed off the hopes of economic security and rights on the job for so many working-class southerners, white and Black alike.[19]

As historians, when we tell the disaster of Elaine a hundred years later, will we include the resistance stories of those who went before, the generations of slaves and semi-slave laborers, as well as the organizers who followed? It's important to remember the legacy of both racism and resistance in Elaine. Social movements can rise and then suffer horrendous defeats under impossible conditions, as in Elaine and as in the case of the STFU in the 1930s. Yet another generation might pick up that prior struggle and triumph to some degree under new conditions. Working people continue doing it today. The most optimistic of organizers say that no struggle, no matter how badly it may be defeated, is entirely lost. Why? Because those who struggle prove that *it is possible to organize.* Even in Nazi Germany and the Holocaust, we have the stories of those who resisted and kept alive some hope that people would survive and, in the future, things could get better.

The Elaine story continues to reverberate through Delta communities. In Elaine and Helena, on the hundred-year anniversary of the massacre, both white and Black residents organized in different ways to acknowledge the hellish events that occurred on that last weekend of September in 1919. As scholars, we are also once more reevaluating what it all means. Noticeably, Elaine has not recovered from this horrendous event. Under the impact of agricultural mechanization, jobs are gone. A little more than five hundred people, about 40 percent of them African Americans, live in a place where median household income is estimated at between $16,000 and $19,000 and some 40 percent live in poverty. Traveling the back roads of eastern Arkansas, one can readily see that the plantation cotton economy has been replaced by mechanized soybean farming, leaving generations of people who used to do the work without work to do. And there is no closure on racism. When a local group dedicated a marker to the Elaine martyrs by planting a tree, someone cut the tree down. The ghosts of the evil Red Summer of 1919 still haunt the land.[20]

For us as historians, it remains extremely important that we remember, as well as what and how we remember. We should ensure that the next generation does not continue to believe the white supremacy myths, or the lies about what happened, created by those who carried out the murders. This situation also cries out for reparations. Racial terror undercut the fortunes of generations of Black farmers who might have become self-sufficient property owners but instead were cast into poverty. Many white and Black workers lost the opportunity to improve their lives through unionization as well. We should demand federal and state investigations to clarify what happened in Elaine and elsewhere, and to advocate for funds to repair Delta communities, as part of a larger reckoning with America's history of racial oppression and injustice.

We also need to remember that past in order to honor those who gave their lives and recognize the difficult conditions under which people have struggled. I want to shout out again to the legacy of people like John Handcox. He did not expect too much and remained mindful of the restraints imposed by his family's dreadful history of slavery and segregation in Arkansas. But he remained an optimist until his death in 1992. He would always sign off on his letters to me with, "Yours for a better world." To his dying day, he kept singing, "Oh no, we don't want Reagan anymore," and "We gonna roll the union on." Too bad he didn't get to see America's first Black president, and just as well he didn't experience America's first fascist president. Regardless, he would still be singing the STFU theme song, later picked up in a new version by SNCC as "Fighting for Our Freedom," that links the struggles of the past to the present and the future:

We're fighting for our union, we shall not be moved.
Just like a tree that's standing by the water, we shall not be moved.

The story of the farmers' and farm workers' union's struggles leave a trace in history that can be picked up, learned from, and built upon today, as we struggle anew against white supremacy terrorism. "Evil in the Delta" today is afoot all across the land, but so is the tradition of struggle to build cross-racial alliances and working-class unity. It is a different struggle than in 1919, but in some ways the same. I add these words to the Gregg Andrews song, "Evil in the Delta":

Out in Charlottesville, the Nazi flag unfurled,
White men beat and killed, to show they still rule the world.
Race haters and presidents, still on the loose
When will it end? Today's our time to choose.
Elaine, Elaine, hatred's deep and wide,
Evil's still on the loose, you've got to take a side.

NOTES

INTRODUCTION

1. The best monograph on the Elaine Massacre is Grif Stockley, Brian K. Mitchell, and Guy Lancaster, *Blood in Their Eyes: The Elaine Massacre of 1919*, rev. ed. (Fayetteville: University of Arkansas Press, 2020). Important works include Ida B. Wells-Barnett, "The Arkansas Race Riot" (Chicago: self-published, 1920); B. Boren McCool, *Union, Reaction, and Riot: The Biography of a Rural Race Riot* (Memphis, TN: Memphis State University Press, 1970); Richard Cortner, *A Mob with Intent on Death: The NAACP and the Arkansas Riot Cases* (Middletown: Wesleyan University Press, 1988); Cameron McWhirter, *Red Summer: The Summer of 1919 and the Awakening of Black America* (New York: St. Martin's, 2011); Robert Whitaker, *On the Laps of Gods: The Red Summer of 1919 and the Struggle that Remade a Nation* (New York: Crown, 2008); David F. Krugler, *1919, The Year of Racial Violence: How African Americans Fought Back* (New York: Cambridge University Press, 2015).
2. Joe Martin to William Woods, August 6, 1943, in the author's possession.

CHAPTER 1

1. William F. Holmes, "The Arkansas Cotton Pickers Strike of 1891 and the Demise of the Colored Farmers' Alliance," *Arkansas Historical Quarterly* 32 (Summer 1973): 107–19. See also Steven Hahn, *A Nation under Our Feet: Black Political Struggles in the Rural South from Slavery to the Great Migration* (Cambridge: Harvard University Press, 2003), 423–25; Gerald H. Gaither, *Blacks and the Populist Movement: Ballots and Bigotry in the New South*, rev. ed. (Tuscaloosa: University of Alabama Press, 2005), 16, 27–30; Omar H. Ali, *In the Lion's Mouth: Black Populism in the New South, 1886–1900* (Jackson: University Press of Mississippi, 2010), 62, 70–71, 75–76.
2. Holmes, "Arkansas Cotton Pickers Strike," 107–108, 111 (quotation). See also Hahn, *Nation under Our Feet*, 424.
3. M. Langley Biegert, "Legacy of Resistance: Uncovering the History of Collective Action by Black Agricultural Workers in Central East Arkansas from the 1860s to the 1930s," *Journal of Social History* 32 (Fall 1998): 78–79; Grif Stockley, *Ruled by Race: Black/White Relations in Arkansas from Slavery to the Present* (Fayetteville: University of Arkansas Press, 2009), 49–50 (quotation p. 49); "Henry Turner," in *Bearing Witness: Memories of Arkansas Slavery Narratives from the 1930s WPA Collections*, 2nd ed., ed. George E. Lankford (Fayetteville: University of Arkansas Press, 2006), 293–94.
4. Carl H. Moneyhon, *The Impact of the Civil War and Reconstruction on Arkansas: Persistence in the Midst of Ruin* (1994; reprint, Fayetteville: University of Arkansas Press, 2002), 246; Jeannie M. Whayne et al., *Arkansas: A Narrative*

History, 2nd ed. (Fayetteville: University of Arkansas Press, 2013), 237, 241–46; Eric Foner, *A Short History of Reconstruction, 1863–1877*, updated ed. (New York: Harper Perennial, 2015), 125–26; Randy Finley, "Arkansas," in *Encyclopedia of the Reconstruction Era*, ed. Richard Zuczek (Westport: Greenwood, 2006), 1: 51.

5. "Office of the Governor," CALS Encyclopedia of Arkansas, accessed July 13, 2019, https://encyclopediaofarkansas.net/entries/office-of-the-governor-5676/; Harry S. Ashmore, *Arkansas: A Bicentennial History* (New York: W. W. Norton, 1978), 132; Foner, *Short History of Reconstruction*, 226, 234–35, 247; Matthew Hild, *Arkansas's Gilded Age: The Rise, Decline, and Legacy of Populism and Working-Class Protest* (Columbia: University of Missouri Press, 2018), 7, 20; Carl H. Moneyhon, *Arkansas and the New South, 1874–1929* (Fayetteville: University of Arkansas Press, 1997), 18; *Gubernatorial Elections, 1787–1997* (Washington, DC: Congressional Quarterly Press, 1998), 41. The Civil Rights Act of 1875 was declared unconstitutional by the Supreme Court in 1883; *Civil Rights Cases*, 109 U.S. 3 (1883).

6. Matthew Hild, *Greenbackers, Knights of Labor, and Populists: Farmer-Labor Insurgency in the Late-Nineteenth-Century South* (Athens: University of Georgia Press, 2007), 20–23, 30–31 (quotation p. 30); *New York Times*, May 18, 1876; Moneyhon, *Arkansas and the New South*, 78–79.

7. Hild, *Arkansas's Gilded Age*, 15.

8. *Gubernatorial Elections*, 41; Hild, *Arkansas's Gilded Age*, 17.

9. Hild, *Arkansas's Gilded Age*, 8–12, 23–28 (quotation p. 27), 40, 125.

10. Reprinted in *The Industrial Revolution in America: A Primary Source History of America's Transformation into an Industrial Society*, ed. Corona Brezina (New York: Rosen Publishing Group, 2005), 55–56. General histories of the Knights of Labor include Norman J. Ware, *The Labor Movement in the United States, 1860–1895: A Study in Democracy* (New York: D. Appleton, 1929) and Craig Phelan, *Grand Master Workman: Terence Powderly and the Knights of Labor* (Westport: Greenwood Press, 2000).

11. Hild, *Arkansas's Gilded Age*, 29–31.

12. Hild, *Arkansas's Gilded Age*, 25, 27, 31–32; Hild, *Greenbackers, Knights of Labor, and Populists*, 88; Jonathan Garlock, comp., *Guide to the Local Assemblies of the Knights of Labor* (Westport: Greenwood Press, 1982), 11–21; Fon Louise Gordon, *Caste and Class: The Black Experience in Arkansas, 1880–1920* (Athens: University of Georgia Press, 1995), 15; Gaither, *Blacks and the Populist Movement*, 5.

13. John DeSantis, *The Thibodaux Massacre: Racial Violence and the 1887 Sugar Cane Labor Strike* (Charleston: The History Press, 2016). For a collection of primary sources about the sugar cane strike, see Philip S. Foner and Ronald L. Lewis, eds., *The Black Worker: A Documentary History from Colonial Times to the Present* (Philadelphia: Temple University Press, 1978), 3: 143–241. For examples of Knights of Labor activity among Black farmers and farm laborers elsewhere in the South, see Foner and Lewis, *Black Worker*, 3: 136–42; Robert C. McMath Jr., "Southern White Farmers and the Organization of Black Farm Workers: A North Carolina Document," *Labor History* 18 (Winter 1977): 115–19; Matthew Hild, "Organizing across the Color Line: The Knights of Labor and Black Recruitment Efforts in Small-Town Georgia," *Georgia Historical Quarterly* 81 (Summer 1997): 287–310.

14. *Journal of United Labor* (Philadelphia), June 25, 1884, October 10–25, 1886.

15. "War in Young," *Daily Arkansas Gazette* (Little Rock), July 6, 1886, 4 (first quotation); *Journal of United Labor*, October 10–25, 1886 (all other quotations); "Colored Knights of Labor," *New York Times*, July 7, 1886, 3; William Warren Rogers, "Negro Knights of Labor in Arkansas: A Case Study of the 'Miscellaneous' Strike," *Labor History* 10 (Summer 1969): 498–505; Theresa A. Case, *The Great Southwest Railroad Strike and Free Labor* (College Station: Texas A&M University Press, 2010), 214–15. Rogers says that the strike began on July 2, but the newspaper accounts cited earlier both reported that it began on July 1.

16. Case, *Great Southwest Railroad Strike*; Ralph V. Turner and William Warren Rogers, "Arkansas Labor in Revolt: Little Rock and the Great Southwestern Strike," *Arkansas Historical Quarterly* 24 (Spring 1965): 29–46; Hild, *Arkansas's Gilded Age*, 50–54.

17. Hild, *Arkansas's Gilded Age*, 54–57, 59–64; *Gubernatorial Elections*, 41.

18. Hild, *Arkansas's Gilded Age*, chap. 4; Kenneth C. Barnes, *Who Killed John Clayton? Political Violence and the Emergence of the New South, 1861–1893* (Durham: Duke University Press, 1998), 60–99.

19. For examples of this national attention, see the *Chicago Daily Tribune*, September 30, 1890; *San Francisco Chronicle*, October 2, 1890; *New York Times*, November 5, 1890; *Journal of the Knights of Labor* (Philadelphia), November 13 and December 11, 1890, January 15, 1891.

20. Barnes, *Who Killed John Clayton?*, 127 (quotation). On the "separate coach" law, see John William Graves, "The Arkansas Separate Coach Law of 1891," *Arkansas Historical Quarterly* 32 (Summer 1973): 148–65. On the disfranchisement laws of the early 1890s, see J. Morgan Kousser, *The Shaping of Southern Politics: Suffrage Restriction and the Establishment of the One-Party South, 1880–1910* (New Haven: Yale University Press, 1974), 123–30; John William Graves, *Town and Country: Race Relations in an Urban-Rural Context, Arkansas, 1865–1905* (Fayetteville: University of Arkansas Press, 1990), 164–74; Michael Perman, *Struggle for Mastery: Disfranchisement in the South, 1888–1908* (Chapel Hill: University of North Carolina Press, 2001), 61–64; Chris M. Branam, "Another Look at Disfranchisement in Arkansas, 1888–1894," *Arkansas Historical Quarterly* 69 (Autumn 2010): 245–62.

21. Robert C. McMath Jr., *Populist Vanguard: A History of the Southern Farmers' Alliance* (Chapel Hill: University of North Carolina Press, 1975), 15, 46, 58–60, 153; Ali, *In the Lion's Mouth*, 49.

22. Charles Postel, *Equality: An American Dilemma, 1866–1896* (New York: Farrar, Straus and Giroux, 2019), 308.

23. "Knights of Labor," *Arkansas Gazette*, August 20, 1890, 1; Garlock, *Guide to the Local Assemblies*, 11–21.

24. Hahn, *Nation under Our Feet*, 414–25; Melton Alonza McLaurin, *The Knights of Labor in the South* (Westport: Greenwood Press, 1978), 129, 138–42, 147–48; William F. Holmes, "The Leflore County Massacre and the Demise of the Colored Farmers' Alliance," *Phylon* 34 (September 1973): 267–74.

25. *Advocate* (Leavenworth, LA), September 28, 1889, reprinted in Foner and Lewis, *Black Worker*, 3: 347.

26. *Washington Bee*, September 27, 1889 (quotation), reprinted in Foner and Lewis, *Black Worker*, 3: 347–48; Holmes, "Leflore County Massacre," 267–74.

27. Holmes, "Leflore County Massacre," 267 (first quotation), 274 (second quotation).
28. Holmes, "Leflore County Massacre," 274; Robert C. McMath Jr., *American Populism: A Social History, 1877–1898* (New York: Hill and Wang, 1993), 93; Hahn, *Nation under Our Feet*, 443, 474; *Arkansas Democrat* (Little Rock), July 23, 1890, 1; Garlock, *Guide to the Local Assemblies*, xxi–xxii, 11–21; F. Clark Elkins, "The Agricultural Wheel in Arkansas, 1887," *Arkansas Historical Quarterly* 40 (Autumn 1981): 254; Willard B. Gatewood Jr., "Negro Legislators in Arkansas, 1891: A Document," *Arkansas Historical Quarterly* 31 (Autumn 1972): 224–25, 227–28.
29. Ware, *Labor Movement*, 66; *Proceedings of the General Assembly of the Knights of Labor of America, Eleventh Regular Session, Held at Minneapolis, Minnesota, October 4 to 19, 1887* (Madison: State Historical Society of Wisconsin, 1950), microfilm, 1850; *Arkansas Gazette*, August 20, 1890.
30. Holmes, "Arkansas Cotton Pickers Strike," 107; *American Citizen* (Kansas City, KS), September 11, 1891, reprinted in Foner and Lewis, *Black Worker*, 3: 331–332; *Southern Star* (Ozark, AL), September 16, 1891.
31. William F. Holmes, "The Demise of the Colored Farmers' Alliance," *Journal of Southern History* 41 (May 1975): 196–97.
32. Postel, *Equality*, 290.
33. *Compendium of the Eleventh Census: 1890* (Washington, DC: Government Printing Office, 1892), 477; *Journal of United Labor*, December 3, 1887.
34. *Atlanta Constitution*, September 8, 1891, reprinted in Foner and Lewis, *Black Worker*, 3: 332.
35. *Houston Daily Post*, September 8, 1891, reprinted in Foner and Lewis, *Black Worker*, 3: 332.
36. "A Cotton Picking Trust," *Arkansas Democrat*, September 9, 1891, 2.
37. Holmes, "Arkansas Cotton Pickers Strike," 113–14.
38. Hahn, *Nation under Our Feet*, 425; Biegert, "Legacy of Resistance," 82; Holmes, "Arkansas Cotton Pickers Strike," 114–15. Holmes does not identify Patterson as a Colored Allianceman but suggests that "he was either a [Cotton Pickers] League member or strongly influenced by Humphrey's call for a strike."
39. Biegert, "Legacy of Resistance," 82–83; Holmes, "Arkansas Cotton Pickers Strike," 115–16 (quotation p. 116); *Earth* (Brookville, KS), October 9, 1891.
40. Holmes, "Arkansas Cotton Pickers Strike," 116–17.
41. Holmes, "Demise of the Colored Farmers' Alliance," 200.
42. Holmes, "Arkansas Cotton Pickers Strike," 118; Hahn, *Nation under Our Feet*, 425; Postel, *Equality*, 304–5. For a more sanguine view of the relationship between the Knights' leadership and the Black poor in the South during the 1890s, see Deborah Beckel, "Southern Labor and the Lure of Populism: Workers and Power in North Carolina," in *Reconsidering Southern Labor History: Race, Class, and Power*, ed. Matthew Hild and Keri Leigh Merritt (Gainesville: University Press of Florida, 2018), 126–41.
43. *Arkansas Gazette*, June 8, 1892; Thomas S. Baskett Jr., "Miners Stay Away!: W. B. W. Heartsill and the Last Years of the Arkansas Knights of Labor, 1892–1896," *Arkansas Historical Quarterly* 42 (Summer 1983): 107–33; *Journal-Advance* (Gentry, AR), February 23, 1906.
44. Kenneth C. Barnes, *Journey of Hope: The Back-to-Africa Movement in Arkansas*

in the Late 1800s (Chapel Hill: University of North Carolina Press, 2004), 49–73; Holmes, "Arkansas Cotton Pickers Strike," 118.

45. Matthew Hild, "Labor, Third-Party Politics, and New South Democracy in Arkansas, 1884–1896," *Arkansas Historical Quarterly* 63 (Spring 2004): 39; Nancy Snell Griffith, " 'At the Hands of a Person or Persons Unknown': The Nature of Lynch Mobs in Arkansas," in *Bullets and Fire: Lynching and Authority in Arkansas, 1840–1950*, ed. Guy Lancaster (Fayetteville: University of Arkansas Press, 2018), 47 (quotations); Moneyhon, *Arkansas and the New South*, 90; Barnes, *Who Killed John Clayton?*, 110.

46. Hild, "Labor, Third-Party Politics," 38–39, 42.

47. Ashmore, *Arkansas*, 175.

48. Guy Lancaster, " 'Negroes Warned to Leave Town': The Bonanza Race War of 1904," *Journal of the Fort Smith Historical Society* 34 (April 2010): 24–29 (quotation p. 27).

49. Hild, *Arkansas's Gilded Age*, 130–32.

50. Hild, *Arkansas's Gilded Age*, 132–33.

51. G. Gregory Kiser, "The Socialist Party in Arkansas, 1900–1912," *Arkansas Historical Quarterly* 40 (Summer 1981): 136–37; Jeremy Brecher, *Strike!*, 3rd ed. (Oakland, CA: PM Press, 2014), 102; Ashmore, *Arkansas*, 175; Moneyhon, *Arkansas and the New South*, 107.

52. *Arkansas Gazette*, May 24, 1903, November 29, 1914; James R. Green, *Grass-Roots Socialism: Radical Movements in the Southwest, 1895–1943* (Baton Rouge: Louisiana State University Press, 1978), 302, 323–28; Nigel Anthony Sellars, *Oil, Wheat & Wobblies: The Industrial Workers of the World in Oklahoma, 1905–1930* (Norman: University of Oklahoma Press, 1998), 77, 84–86; Nigel Anthony Sellars, "Working Class Union," Encyclopedia of Oklahoma History and Culture, accessed September 6, 2019, https://www.okhistory.org/publications/enc/entry.php?entry=WO021; Covington Hall, *Labor Struggles in the Deep South and Other Writings*, ed. David R. Roediger (Chicago: Charles H. Kerr, 1999), 186–87.

53. Michael Pierce, "Great Women All, Serving a Glorious Cause: Freda Hogan Ameringer's Reminiscences of Socialism in Arkansas," *Arkansas Historical Quarterly* 69 (Winter 2010): 304–5, 324; J. Blake Perkins, *Hillbilly Hellraisers: Federal Power and Populist Defiance in the Ozarks* (Urbana: University of Illinois Press, 2017), 75; Brecher, *Strike!*, 102; Sellars, *Oil, Wheat & Wobblies*, 87–88, 91; Hall, *Labor Struggles*, 188–89; Nick Salvatore, *Eugene V. Debs: Citizen and Socialist* (Urbana: University of Illinois Press, 1982), 288–302, 326–28.

CHAPTER 2

1. "A Bad State of Affairs in a Portion of Lawrence County," *Arkansas Gazette* (Little Rock), October 14, 1887, 4.

2. Christopher Waldrep, *The Many Faces of Judge Lynch: Extralegal Violence and Punishment in America* (New York: Palgrave Macmillan, 2002), 182.

3. Amy Louise Wood, *Lynching and Spectacle: Witnessing Racial Violence in America, 1890–1940* (Chapel Hill: University of North Carolina Press, 2009), 5–6.

4. W. Fitzhugh Brundage, *Lynching in the New South: Georgia and Virginia, 1880–1930* (Urbana: University of Illinois Press, 1993), 19–28.

5. Kidada E. Williams, *They Left Great Marks on Me: African American Testimonies of Racial Violence from Emancipation to World War I* (New York: New York University Press, 2012), 40.

6. William F. Holmes, "Whitecapping: Agrarian Violence in Mississippi, 1902–1906," *Journal of Southern History* 35 (May 1969): 166.

7. Guy Lancaster, *Racial Cleansing in Arkansas, 1883–1924: Politics, Land, Labor, and Criminality* (Lanham, MD: Lexington Books, 2014), 45–82.

8. Claudia Card, *Confronting Evils: Terrorism, Torture, Genocide* (New York: Cambridge University Press, 2010), 166.

9. *Public and Private Acts and Joint and Concurrent Resolutions and Memorials of the General Assembly of the State of Arkansas, 1909* (Little Rock: Secretary of State, 1909), 778–80.

10. Jeannie M. Whayne, "What Is the Mississippi Delta? A Historian's Perspective," in *Defining the Delta: Multidisciplinary Perspectives on the Lower Mississippi River Delta*, ed. Janelle Collins (Fayetteville: University of Arkansas Press, 2015), 128.

11. "Jonesboro White-Caps," *Arkansas Gazette*, April 5, 1893, 2.

12. "Jonesboro Whitecaps," *Arkansas Gazette*, April 19, 1894, 8.

13. "A Whitecapper Killed," *Osceola (AR) Times*, May 5, 1894, 3. Brief though this newspaper report was, it offers some interesting contrasts with how accounts of Black transgression are typically understood. According to one accounting, in the 1890s in Arkansas, fifty-five African Americans were lynched for having allegedly committed murder and nineteen for sexual crimes, and so the killing of Colbert would seem to offer motive enough for the members of the band to lynch Louis White. Randy Finley, "A Lynching State: Arkansas in the 1890s," in *Bullets and Fire: Lynching and Authority in Arkansas, 1840–1950*, ed. Guy Lancaster (Fayetteville: University of Arkansas Press, 2018), 61–62. But this newspaper report also frames the interracial relationship as mutual—the white woman was visiting the Black man, and the band of vigilantes showed up at his place expecting to find her. This runs in stark contrast to accounts of how the discovery of interracial relationships were often framed as rape to justify the lynching of the Black transgressor. Ed Coy, lynched in Texarkana in 1892 for having allegedly raped a white woman, was, according to some accounts of the event, actually in a consensual relationship with the woman, who was compelled to make the accusation against him. Larry LeMasters, "Ed Coy (Lynching of)," CALS Encyclopedia of Arkansas, accessed March 19, 2020, https://encyclopediaofarkansas.net/entries/edward-coy-7035/.

14. "Whitecaps Threaten," *Helena (AR) Weekly World*, November 15, 1899, 3.

15. "Whitecappers at West Point," *Southern Standard* (Arkadelphia, AR), May 31, 1900, 1; untitled, *Arkansas Democrat* (Little Rock), May 26, 1900, 4; "State News," *Fort Smith Times*, May 28, 1900, 2.

16. "Arkansas News," *Arkansas Gazette*, March 25, 1894, 1.

17. "Excitement in St. Francis County," *Osceola Times*, April 7, 1894, 3.

18. "St. Francis County Whitecaps," *Arkansas Gazette*, October 24, 1894, 1.

19. Untitled, *Pine Bluff Daily Graphic*, October 30, 1894, 3; "Whitecaps Acquitted," *Arkansas Gazette*, November 7, 1894, 6.

20. Untitled, *Helena Weekly World*, September 1, 1897, 1; "Whitecaps," *Helena Weekly World*, September 1, 1897, 4.

21. "Notice!" *Helena Weekly World*, September 8, 1897, 4.

22. "Whitecaps," *Helena World*, February 23, 1898, 3.

23. "Arkansas State News," *Southern Standard*, April 22, 1898, 1.

24. "Whitecaps at Work," *Pine Bluff Daily Graphic*, January 20, 1902, 8.

25. "Brief Mention," *Osceola Times*, February 1, 1902, 3.

26. "Warned to Leave," *Arkansas Gazette*, January 29, 1898, 5. Other violence in the area around the same time included the murder of a schoolteacher and further attempts to drive off all African Americans from the area. See Nancy Snell Griffith, "Lonoke County Race War of 1897–1898," CALS Encyclopedia of Arkansas, accessed March 19, 2020, https://encyclopediaofarkansas.net/entries /lonoke-county-race-war-of-1897-1898-7459/.

27. "Negroes Much Alarmed," *Arkansas Gazette*, January 3, 1905, 2; "Negroes Will Be Protected," *Arkansas Democrat*, January 6, 1906, 1.

28. "Monroe Whitecaps," *Arkansas Democrat*, February 11, 1898, 4.

29. "Growers Are Threatened," *Arkansas Gazette*, September 15, 1908, 2; "Alleged Night Riders," *Batesville (AR) Guard*, September 18, 1908, 1.

30. Untitled, *Arkansas Democrat*, September 16, 1908, 4. Interestingly, the *Southern Standard* suggested on September 24 that recent reports of nightriding had been exposed as resulting from a practical joke played upon William Craddock of Lake City, who owned a horse that had allegedly created a disturbance in town, leading "some of the residents of that place to remark, in a joking manner, that they intended to have an ordinance passed in the city council prohibiting the animal from appearing on the streets." Shortly afterward, "switches," one of the symbols used by nightriders, "were found by Mr. Craddock pinned on the door of his barn in which the horse was kept." This, according to the newspaper, spurred reports of nightriding. However, as later events reveal, nightriders were active in the area. See "News of Arkansas," *Southern Standard*, September 24, 1908, 1.

31. "Night Riding Arouses Town," *Arkansas Democrat*, September 28, 1908, 1.

32. "Buying of Cotton Is to Be Resumed," *Arkansas Gazette*, October 1, 1908, 1.

33. "Merchants Reject the Union's Plan," *Arkansas Gazette*, October 2, 1908, 1, 10.

34. Charley Sandage, "Arkansas Farmers Union," CALS Encyclopedia of Arkansas, accessed March 20, 2020, https://encyclopediaofarkansas.net/entries/arkansas -farmers-union-6232/; Matthew Hild's essay in this volume.

35. "R. B. Snell May Leave the Union," *Arkansas Democrat*, October 1, 1908, 1.

36. "Night Riding Must Not Be Tolerated in Arkansas," *Arkansas Gazette*, October 9, 1908, 4. An editorial in *The Home Magazine* reprinted in the *Batesville Daily Guard* also used developments in Tennessee and Kentucky as a warning for Arkansans: "If the conditions which have prevailed in the twenty-odd counties of the dark tobacco district in Tennessee and Kentucky were to spread throughout the vast cotton country of the Carolinas, Georgia, Alabama, Mississippi, Louisiana, Arkansas and Texas, with all the attendant circumstances of midnight terror, arson, feud and murder, not only would fifteen million people have a little taste of hell on earth but the development of the entire south would be set back a good ten years before the time the flame could be got under control." "How the Trust Escapes the Night Riders," *Batesville Daily Guard*, February 17, 1909, 1.

37. "Night Riders Close 12 Cotton Gins," *Pine Bluff Daily Graphic*, October 8, 1908, 1.

38. "Night Riders Near This City," *Arkansas Gazette*, October 10, 1908, 1. The same

issue reported on a union meeting in Garland County, located just west of Saline County, which resulted in a resolution by county union members to condemn nightriding. "Unions Condemn Night Riding," *Arkansas Gazette*, October 10, 1908, 1.

39. "Sheriff Ready to Show Mailed Hand," *Arkansas Gazette*, October 11, 1908, 1.

40. "News from All over Arkansas," *Arkansas Gazette*, October 15, 1908, 3.

41. "Union Endorsed by Business Men," *Arkansas Gazette*, October 20, 1908, 1.

42. "Governor Pindall Willing," *The Monticellonian* (Monticello, AR), October 29, 1908, 1.

43. "Farmers' Union Offers Reward," *Arkansas Gazette*, November 8, 1908, 1.

44. "Stop Night Riders," *Fort Smith Times*, January 17, 1909, 1. Representative Little served in the Arkansas House of Representatives from 1909 to 1912; *Historical Report of the Secretary of State 2008* (Little Rock: Arkansas Secretary of State's Office, 2008), 685.

45. "Among the Law Makers," *Arkansas Democrat*, January 21, 1909, 6.

46. Christopher Waldrep, *Night Riders: Defending Community in the Black Patch, 1890–1915* (Durham: Duke University Press, 1993), 8.

47. Suzanne Marshall, *Violence in the Black Patch of Kentucky and Tennessee* (Columbia: University of Missouri Press, 1994), 98.

48. Holmes, "Whitecapping," 167.

49. According to sociologist Mattias Smångs, lynching, like the formal Jim Crow system, constituted a means of generating white racial identity across class boundaries after a Reconstruction period that "destroyed the institutionalized antebellum system of symbolic and social race boundaries, categories, and identities"; Mattias Smångs, *Doing Violence, Making Race: Lynching and White Racial Group Formation in the U.S. South, 1882–1930* (New York: Routledge, 2017), 9.

50. The Judiciary Committee reported favorably on the bill on January 26, 1909, and it passed the House on January 29. It was first read in the Senate on February 23, 1909 and was voted upon on March 16, 1909. "House Is Peer of Senate," *Arkansas Gazette*, January 27, 1909, 3; "In the House, Friday, January 29, 1909," *Arkansas Gazette*, January 30, 1909, 3; "House Wrangles over Farm Schools," *Arkansas Democrat*, January 30, 1909, 1; "In the Senate, Tuesday, February 23, 1909," *Arkansas Gazette*, February 24, 1909, 3; "The Senate," *Arkansas Democrat*, March 17, 1909, 2; "Tilt over Liquor Bill," *Arkansas Gazette*, March 17, 1909, 3; "Night Riding Bill a Law," *Arkansas Democrat*, April 7, 1909, 6.

51. *Acts of Arkansas of the General Assembly of the State of Arkansas, 1909* (Little Rock: General Assembly of the State of Arkansas, 1909), 315–17.

52. "Perils of the Night Riders," *Arkansas Gazette*, April 20, 1909, 4.

53. See, for example, "To Suppress Night-Riding," *Osceola Times*, January 28, 1909, 2.

54. "May Prosecute under New Act," *Arkansas Gazette*, May 16, 1909, 1.

55. "Continue 'Rider' Case at Lonoke," *Arkansas Gazette*, August 14, 1909, 2; "Circuit Court Is Over," *Lonoke (AR) Democrat*, August 19, 1909, 1.

56. "Alleged Night Riders," *Arkansas Democrat*, August 11, 1909, 10; "Twenty-Seven Indictments," *Lonoke Democrat*, August 12, 1909, 1.

57. "Continued to Suit Sen. Davis' Convenience," *Arkansas Democrat*, February 11, 1910, 7; "Many Criminal Cases," *Arkansas Democrat*, August 1, 1910, 5.

58. "News of the State," *Nashville (AR) News*, August 13, 1910, 3; "Circuit Court," *Lonoke Democrat*, August 4, 1910, 1.

59. "Bush Taken to the State Prison," *Pine Bluff Daily Graphic*, October 14, 1910, 6.
60. "Charged with Nightriding," *Arkansas Gazette*, October 10, 1911, 2; "Acquitted of Nightriding," *Arkansas Gazette*, October 17, 1911, 2.
61. "Forty-Eight Farmers Arrested," *Batesville Daily Guard*, May 31, 1912, 1; "Four Held for 'Night Riding,'" *Arkansas Gazette*, August 26, 1913, 1.
62. "Citizens Join to Protect Negroes," *Jonesboro (AR) Evening Sun*, April 18, 1912, 1; "Citizens Join to Protect Negroes," *Arkansas Gazette*, April 19, 1912, 2; "Whites Dynamite Home of Negro," *Arkansas Gazette*, April 21, 1912, 1, 3; "Walnut Ridge Negroes Ordered to Leave by Whites, Militia Called," *Jonesboro Evening Sun*, April 22, 1912, 1; "Militia in Camp at Walnut Ridge," *Arkansas Gazette*, April 22, 1912, 2; "Four More Held at Walnut Ridge," *Arkansas Gazette*, May 1, 1912, 1; "Alleged Night Rider Acquitted," *Arkansas Gazette*, May 2, 1912, 2.
63. "Four Held for 'Night Riding,'" *Arkansas Gazette*, August 26, 1913, 1.
64. "Night Riding Is Charge against Lonoke Men," *Arkansas Democrat*, March 3, 1914, 5.
65. "Held for Night Riding," *Arkansas Gazette*, March 8, 1915, 8.
66. "Night Riding Charged," *Batesville Daily Guard*, January 5, 1915, 3; "Seven Held for 'Night Riding," *Arkansas Gazette*, January 10, 1915, 17.
67. "Six Awarded Damages," *Arkansas Gazette*, September 24, 1916, 1.
68. "Accused of Night Riding," *Arkansas Gazette*, May 30, 1913, 2.
69. "100 Implicated in Nightrider Cases," *Arkansas Gazette*, March 16, 1915, 2; "Night Riders in Mississippi County," *Osceola Times*, March 19, 1915, 1; "Faces Term in Pen in Nightrider Case," *Arkansas Gazette*, March 24, 1915, 14; "Jury Says Guilty of Night Riding," *Osceola Times*, March 26, 1915, 1; "Captain of 'Riders' Gets 8-Year Term," *Arkansas Gazette*, March 26, 1915, 2; "Two Letters—A Contrast," *Osceola Times*, March 26, 1915, 4; "Rogers Given Seven Years and a Half," *Osceola Times*, April 2, 1915, 1; Mississippi County Circuit Court Criminal Record, Osceola District, Book 2, 258–59.
70. "Night Riding Charged," *Arkansas Gazette*, March 22, 1915, 2.
71. "More Night Riding Charge," *The Monticellonian*, April 29, 1915, 4.
72. "Indict Six Men for Night Riding," *Pine Bluff Daily Graphic*, May 27, 1915, 2; "Indictments Number 52," *Arkansas Gazette*, June 3, 1915, 1.
73. "Governors Take Hand in Checking Outrages," *Arkansas Democrat*, October 12, 1920, 1. Among the incidents cited by Brough was the murder "of a negro guard at a cotton gin in Arkansas" that occurred after the gin's owner received "warnings to discontinue operations until the staple reaches a price of 40 cents a pound." However, according to news reports, the murder had nothing to do with the warnings. Two African Americans were soon arrested—and one allegedly confessed—to carrying out the murder for the purpose of robbing the guard of cash he was known to carry. See "Two Negroes Are Held in Murder at Gin: One Denies Night Riding Was Cause," *Pine Bluff Daily Graphic*, October 12, 1920, 1.
74. "Farmers Justified in Holding Cotton, Gov. Brough Believes," *Arkansas Democrat*, October 16, 1920, 1.
75. "Night Riding Giving South 'Black Eye,' Says Mr. Ferguson," *Arkansas Democrat*, October 23, 1920, 1.
76. "Urge Decreased Cotton Acreage," *Arkansas Democrat*, October 25, 1920, 2. An editorial in the *Pine Bluff Daily Graphic* the following year applauded such efforts by farmers to decrease cotton acreage collectively, comparing such

cooperative efforts to labor unions and medical associations who work to protect their profession from "quacks"; "Night Riding," *Pine Bluff Daily Graphic*, February 9, 1921, 4.

77. "Fires May Cause Loss of Insurance," *Arkansas Gazette*, October 24, 1920, 29 (quotations); "Insurance Companies May Cancel Policies Where Night-Riding Does Not Keep to a Minimum." *Arkansas Democrat*, October 22, 1920, 1.

78. "Seven White County Farmers Confess to Night-Riding Charge," *Arkansas Democrat*, October 15, 1920, 1.

79. "Light Sentences for Night Riders," *Arkansas Gazette*, January 26, 1921, 5. The statute in question was likely Act 512 of 1919, a so-called criminal anarchy law passed during the Red Scare of 1919–20; Jamie Kern, "The Price of Dissent: Freedom of Speech and Arkansas Criminal Anarchy Arrests" (master's thesis, University of Arkansas, 2012).

80. "Jail Sentences for Terrorists," *Arkansas Gazette*, October 23, 1920, 1.

81. "More Night Riding Arrests Are Made," *Arkansas Democrat*, April 12, 1921, 1.

82. "19 Arrests Made in Night Riding Cases," *Arkansas Democrat*, April 13, 1921, 1; "Eight More Held for Night Riding," *Arkansas Gazette*, April 13, 1921, 1.

83. "20 Men Are Held as Night Riders," *Arkansas Gazette*, April 15, 1921, 10; "26 Are Now Held for Night Riding," *Arkansas Gazette*, April 16, 1921, 8.

84. "30 Men Indicted for Night Riding," *Arkansas Gazette*, April 19, 1921, 14.

85. "Saw Schoolhouse Fired, He Declares," *Arkansas Gazette*, April 23, 1921, 1; "Tell of Assisting in Burning House," *Arkansas Gazette*, April 24, 1921, 1.

86. "Indictment Flaw Holds up Hearing," *Arkansas Gazette*, April 22, 1921, 5; "Tells of Receiving Written Threats," *Arkansas Gazette*, April 26, 1921, 1. DeWitt Garrett was initially found not guilty on the basis of a faulty indictment that accused him of burning of H. H. McAdams's house, when, in fact, the house was jointly owned by N. A. Stroud and McAdams, but a new indictment was produced within thirty minutes. See "Indictment Flaw Holds up Hearing," *Arkansas Gazette*, April 22, 1921, 5. His attorneys later insisted that "the destroyed building was not a dwelling house as contemplated by the law," and thus the indictment continued to be faulty, but the court overruled the motion to instruct the jury to deliver a verdict of not guilty. See "Tells of Receiving Written Threats," *Arkansas Gazette*, April 26, 1921, 1.

87. "Accused Farmers Say Plead Guilty," *Arkansas Gazette*, April 27, 1921, 1; "20 To Plead Guilty to Night Riding," *Arkansas Gazette*, April 28, 1921, 1; "Nightriders Given Prison Sentences," *Arkansas Gazette*, August 2, 1921, 12; "Nightriders Reach Pen to Begin Terms," *Pine Bluff Daily Graphic*, August 11, 1921, 2. The stated number of indictments (thirty-one) does not equal the number of guilty pleas (twenty) plus the number of exonerations (ten). A follow-up article also strangely fails to do the proper math: "Thirty-one were arraigned in Circuit Court here last week, and 20 of them pleaded guilty, while 10 were discharged." "To Arrest Others for Night Riding," *Arkansas Gazette*, May 1, 1921, 11. Another report gave the number of guilty pleas for the main band as twenty-seven, adding that some three hundred "lesser offenders" also entered pleas of guilty, and that the incidents of arson carried out by this band smashed the national record. "Night Riders Working Hard for the State," *Little Rock Daily News*, May 5, 1921, 7.

88. "To Arrest Others for Night Riding," *Arkansas Gazette*, May 1, 1921, 11.

89. "Pardons Granted Two Night-Riders," *Little Rock Daily News*, August 5, 1922, 9. On Tom Slaughter, see Jerry D. Gibbens, "Tom Slaughter," CALS Encyclopedia of Arkansas, accessed March 20, 2020, https://encyclopediaofarkansas.net /entries/tom-slaughter-1765/.

90. "Hold Alleged Night Rider," *Arkansas Democrat*, August 25, 1921, 9.

91. "Farmer to Spend His Life in Pen," *Arkansas Gazette*, September 15, 1921, 8.

92. "Night Riding in Lonoke Leads to Arrest of Seven," *Pine Bluff Daily Graphic*, November 25, 1922, 1.

93. Jeannie M. Whayne, *A New Plantation South: Land, Labor, and Federal Favor in Twentieth-Century Arkansas* (Charlottesville: University of Virginia Press, 1996), 52. The case of striking workers to which Whayne refers is no doubt the charges of nightriding laid against workers along the Missouri and North Arkansas Railroad in 1923. See "M. & N. A. Strikers Indicted at Searcy," *Arkansas Democrat*, January 16, 1923, 1.

94. Grif Stockley, *Blood in Their Eyes: The Elaine Race Massacres of 1919* (Fayetteville: University of Arkansas Press, 2001), 109. Robert Whitaker, in a footnote, overgeneralizes regarding the motivation underlying anti-nightriding laws, claiming that "they had been enacted by Southern states to prevent whites from riding around at night and terrorizing Blacks in order to drive them from the land," thus ignoring the inter-class conflict among white Arkansans; *On the Laps of Gods: The Red Summer of 1919 and the Struggle for Justice That Remade a Nation* (New York: Crown, 2008), 168.

95. Brian K. Mitchell, "When the Depths Don't Give up Their Dead: A Discussion on New Primary Sources and How They Are Reshaping Debate on the Elaine Massacre," in *The Elaine Massacre and Arkansas: A Century of Atrocity and Resistance, 1819–1919*, ed. Guy Lancaster (Little Rock: Butler Center Books, 2018), 213. The list of indictments runs pp. 216–37 of Mitchell's chapter.

96. Wanda Gray, "Catcher Race Riot of 1923," CALS Encyclopedia of Arkansas, accessed March 20, 2020, https://encyclopediaofarkansas.net/entries/catcher -race-riot-of-1923-5885/.

97. *Johnson v. State*, 198 Ark. 871 (1939); Southern Tenant Farmers Union Records on Microfilm, Reel 9, Item 2, Kheel Center for Labor-Management Documentation and Archives, Cornell University Library, Ithaca, NY, accessed March 6, 2019, http://rmc.library.cornell.edu/EAD/htmldocs/KCL05204mf.html.

98. Michael G. Hanchard, *The Spectre of Race: How Discrimination Haunts Western Democracy* (Princeton: Princeton University Press, 2018), 6.

CHAPTER 3

1. *Hodges v. United States*, 203 U.S. 1 (1906); William H. Pruden III, "Hodges v. United States," CALS Encyclopedia of Arkansas, accessed August 12, 2020, https://encyclopediaofarkansas.net/entries/hodges-v-united-states-7404/; Jeannie Whayne, *A New Planation South: Land, Labor, and Federal Favor in Twentieth-Century Arkansas* (Charlottesville: University of Virginia Press, 1996), 49–50. On nightriding in Arkansas more generally, see Guy Lancaster's essay in this volume.

2. Whayne, *A New Planation South*, 50; *Hodges v. United States*; "White Cap Cases Now on Trial," *Arkansas Gazette* (Little Rock), March 17, 1904, x.

3. Pruden, "*Hodges v. United States.*"

4. *Lochner v. New York*, 198 U.S. 45 (1905).

5. Pamela S. Karlan, "Contracting the Thirteenth Amendment: Hodges v. United States," *Boston University Law Review* 85 (2005): 783–809.

6. Karlan, "Contracting the Thirteenth Amendment"; David Bernstein, "Thoughts on Hodges v. United States," *Boston University Law Review* 85 (2005): 811–12.

7. See, e.g., *Helena Weekly World*, September 1, 1897, 1.

8. *United States v. Morris*, 125 F. 322 (1903).

9. "White Cap Cases Now on Trial"; Carolyn Gray LeMaster, "Jacob Trieber," CALS Encyclopedia of Arkansas, accessed August 12, 2020, http://www .encyclopediaofarkansas.net/encyclopedia/entry-detail.aspx?entryID=26; Brent J. Aucoin, *A Rift in the Clouds: Race and the Southern Federal Judiciary, 1900–1910* (Fayetteville: University of Arkansas Press, 2007).

10. *United States v. Morris*, 325.

11. Karlan, "Contracting the Thirteenth Amendment," 786–87.

12. Martha R. Mahoney, "What's Left of Solidarity? Reflections on Law, Race, and Labor History," *Buffalo Law Review* 57 (2009), 1515, http://www.buffalolaw.org /past_issues/57_5/Mahoney%20Web%2057_5.pdf; Richard Niswonger, "James Paul Clark," accessed August 12, 2020, CALS Encyclopedia of Arkansas, https:// encyclopediaofarkansas.net/entries/james-paul-clarke-93/; Raymond Arsenault, *Wild Ass of the Ozarks: Jeff Davis and the Social Bases of Southern Politics* (Knoxville: University of Tennessee Press, 1988). Davis also represented nightriders accused of running off Black labor; see Guy Lancaster's essay in this volume.

13. Karlan, "Contracting the Thirteenth Amendment," 787.

14. "Statutes Will Be Put to Test," *Times* (Shreveport, LA), March 20, 1904, 1.

15. *United States v. Morris*.

16. *Civil Rights Cases*, 109 U.S. 3 (1883); *United States v. Cruikshank*, 92 U.S. 542 (1876); *Slaughter-House Cases*, 16 Wall (83 U.S.) 36 (1866).

17. *United States v. Rhodes*, F. Cas. 785, 794 (C.C. Ky. 1866).

18. *United States v. Rhodes*, 794.

19. *Slaughter-House Cases*.

20. *United States v. Cruikshank*, 25 F. Cas. 707, 711 (C.C. La. 1874).

21. *Blyew v. United States*, 80 U.S. 581, 601 (1871).

22. *Civil Rights Cases*, 24.

23. *Civil Rights Cases*, 22.

24. *Civil Rights Cases*, 25.

25. *United States v. Waddell, et. al.*, 112 U.S. 76 (1884); Guy Lancaster, "United States v. Waddell et al.," CALS Encyclopedia of Arkansas, accessed August 12, 2020, http://www.encyclopediaofarkansas.net/encyclopedia/entry-detail.aspx?entry ID=7387.

26. *Plessy v. Ferguson*, 163 U.S. 537 (1896), 542.

27. *Plessy v. Ferguson*, 543.

28. *Hodges v. United States*, 17.

29. *Hodges v. United States*, 18.

30. *Hodges v. United States*, 19.

31. *Hodges v. United States*, 20.

32. Pamela Brandwein, "Features of Conventional Scholarly Wisdom about the Thirteenth Amendment" (unpublished manuscript, https://digitalcommons.law

.umaryland.edu/cgi/viewcontent.cgi?article=1122&context=schmooze_papers), accessed August 15, 2020, Microsoft Word file.

33. *Hodges v. United States*, 17–18.

34. J. Gordon Hylton, "The Judge Who Abstained in *Plessy v. Ferguson*: Justice David Brewer and the Problem of Race," *Mississippi Law Journal* 61 (1991), 353.

35. *Hodges v. United States*, 17–18.

36. *Hodges v. United States*, 19.

37. *Hodges v. United States*, 17.

38. James Gray Pope, "Thirteenth Amendment Optimism and Its Critics: A Sesquicentennial Assessment" (unpublished manuscript, accessed August 15, 2020, http://law.seattleu.edu/Documents/13thamendment/Pope,%20James%20 Gray%20-%20Thirteenth%20Amendment%20Optimism%20and%20Its%20 Critics%20-%20Copy.pdf), PDF file.

39. Pope, "Thirteenth Amendment Optimism and its Critics," 23.

40. *Hodges v. United States*, 17.

41. *Hodges v. United States*, 18.

42. Frederick Douglass, "Reconstruction," *Atlantic Monthly* (December 1866), accessed August 12, 2020, https://www.theatlantic.com/magazine/archive /1866/12/reconstruction/304561/.

43. *Hodges v. United States*, 32.

44. *Hodges v. United States*, 33–34.

45. D. J. Brewer, "Protection to Private Property from Public Attack: An Address Delivered before the Graduating Classes at the Sixty-Seventh Anniversary of the Yale School of Law on June 23, 1891" (New Haven: Hoggson and Robinson, 1891), 4. See also Linda Przybyszewski, "Judicial Conservatism and Protestant Faith: The Case of Justice David J. Brewer," *Journal of American History* 91 (September 2004): 471–96.

46. *Lochner v. New York*, 53; Melvin Urofsky, *Dissent and the Supreme Court: Its Role in the Court's History and the Nation's Constitutional Dialogue* (New York: Pantheon Books, 2015), 141.

47. *Hodges v. United States*, 35.

48. *Lochner v. New York*, 75.

49. *Lochner v. New York*, 75.

50. Karlan, "Contracting the Thirteenth Amendment," 809.

51. *Boyett v. United States*, 207 U.S. 581 (1907).

52. Mahoney, "What's Left of Solidarity?" 1530.

53. *Hodges v. United States*, 20.

54. "Among the Lawmakers," *Arkansas Democrat*, January 21, 1909, 6; "The House," *Arkansas Democrat*, January 23, 1909, 1; "Pass Night Rider Bill," *Arkansas Democrat*, March 17, 1909, 2; "Stop Night Riders," *Fort Smith Times*, January 17, 1909, 1; Guy Lancaster, "Act 112 of 1909," CALS Encyclopedia of Arkansas, accessed August 12, 2020, https://encyclopediaofarkansas.net/entries/act-112-of -1909-14368/; *Acts of Arkansas of the General Assembly of the State of Arkansas, 1909* (Little Rock: General Assembly of the State of Arkansas, 1909), 315–17.

55. Michael J. Klarman, *From Jim Crow to Civil Rights: The Supreme Court and the Struggle for Racial Equality* (New York: Oxford University Press, 2004), 502n49.

56. *United States v. Carolene Products Company*, 304 U.S. 144 (1938), 153n4. The literature on the *Carolene Products* footnote is extensive, but Louis Lusky's

"Footnote Redux: A 'Carolene Products' Reminiscence," *Columbia University Law Review* 82 (October 1982): 1093–1109, is a good starting place.

CHAPTER 4

1. On the Elaine Massacre, see Grif Stockley, Brian K. Mitchell, and Guy Lancaster, *Blood in Their Eyes: The Elaine Massacre of 1919*, rev. ed. (Fayetteville: University of Arkansas, 2020); Jeannie M. Whayne, "Low Villains and Wickedness in High Places: Race and Class in the Elaine Riots," *Arkansas Historical Quarterly* 58 (Autumn 1999): 285–313.

2. While a substantial historiography on the Elaine Massacre exists, only a few scattered treatments of the Lowery lynching have been rendered by historians. Jeannie Whayne, *Delta Empire: Lee Wilson and the Transformation of Southern Agriculture* (Baton Rouge: Louisiana State University Press, 2011), 117–19, 127–34; Nan Elizabeth Woodruff, *American Congo: The African American Freedom Struggle in the Delta* (Cambridge: Harvard University Press, 2003), 110–14. The historiography on lynching is extensive. For some of the most important works, see W. Fitzhugh Brundage, *Lynching in the New South: Georgia and Virginia, 1880–1930* (Urbana: University of Illinois Press, 1993); Karlos K. Hill, *Beyond the Rope: The Impact of Lynching on Black Culture and Memory* (New York: Cambridge University Press, 2016); and Stewart E. Tolnay and E. M. Beck, *A Festival of Violence: An Analysis of Southern Lynchings, 1882–1930* (Urbana: University of Illinois Press, 1995).

3. "An American Lynching: Being the Burning at Stake of Henry Lowry [*sic*] at Nodena, Arkansas, January 26, 1921, as Told in American Newspapers" (New York: National Association for the Advancement of Colored People, n.d.); Hill, *Beyond the Rope*.

4. Walter F. White, "Massacring Whites in Arkansas," *The Nation*, December 13, 1919, 714–16.

5. William Pickens, "The American Congo—The Burning of Henry Lowery," *The Nation*, March 23, 1921, 426–28; For more information on Pickens, see his autobiographies: *The Heir of Slaves: An Autobiography* (Boston: Pilgrim Press, 1911), and *Bursting Bonds: An Autobiography of a "New Negro"* (1923; reprint, Bloomington: Indiana University Press, 1991).

6. Sven Beckert, *Empire of Cotton: A Global History* (New York: Knopf, 2015); Pickens, "American Congo."

7. Michaeline A. Crichlow, Patricia Northover, and Juan Giusti-Cordero, eds. *Race and Rurality in the Global Economy* (Albany: State University of New York Press, 2018); Frank Uekötter,, ed., *Comparing Apples, Oranges, and Cotton: Environmental Histories of the Global Plantation* (Frankfurt and New York: Campus Verlag, 2014).

8. Pickens, "American Congo," 426. The historiography on sharecropping, tenancy, and debt peonage is extensive. A good beginning would consist of the following: Pete Daniel, *Shadow of Slavery: Peonage in the South, 1901–1969* (Urbana: University of Illinois Press, 1972); Roger Ransom and Richard Sutch, *One Kind of Freedom: The Economic Consequences of Emancipation* (Cambridge, U.K.: Cambridge University Press, 1971); Leon Litwack, *Been in a Storm so Long: The Aftermath of Slavery* (New York: Knopf, 1979); and Harold Woodman, *New*

South, New Law: The Legal Foundations of Credit and Labor Relations in the Postbellum Agricultural South (Baton Rouge: Louisiana State University Press, 1995).

9. For the decrease in the Black population in Phillips County and the increase in the Black population in Mississippi County between 1920 and 1930, see Valerie J. Farris, "After the Storm: Race Relations in Phillips County Arkansas after 1919" (honors thesis, University of Arkansas, 2006), 29, in possession of author.

10. *Arkansas Democrat*, January 26, 1921, 9.

11. W. David Baird, "Thomas Chipman McRae, 1921–1925," in *The Governors of Arkansas: Essays in Political Biography*, Timothy P. Donovan, Willard B. Gatewood Jr., and Jeannie M. Whayne, eds. (Fayetteville: University of Arkansas Press, 1995), 157–64; Derek Allen Clements, "Thomas Chipman McRae," CALS Encyclopedia of Arkansas, accessed August 3, 2017, http://www.encyclopedia ofarkansas.net/encyclopedia/entry-detail.aspx?entryID=114. For correspondence involving Knollenberg, the NAACP, and the two governors, see Hill, *Beyond the Rope*. See also Papers of the NAACP, Part 7, The Anti-Lynching Campaign, 1912–1955, Series A: Anti-Lynching Investigative Files, 1912–1953 (University Publications of America, 1987), and for information specifically having to do with the Lowery Lynching, see Reel 2, Group I, Box C-338 cont., Subject File—Lynching, Mob Violence, and Race Riots cont., Frames 0791 to 0805; and Reel 8, Group 1, Box C-350, Subject File—Lynching—Arkansas cont., Frames 0523 to 0628.

12. Hill, *Beyond the Rope*, 60.

13. Pickens, "American Congo," 426; Nancy Snell Griffith, "William Pickens," CALS Encyclopedia of Arkansas, accessed August 3, 2017, http://www.encyclopedia ofarkansas.net/encyclopedia/entry-detail.aspx?entryID=5891; Pickens, *Bursting Bonds*.

14. *Memphis Press*, January 27, 1921, n.p., in "An American Lynching."

15. Pickens, "American Congo," 426–27.

16. Pickens, "American Congo," 420–21. For R. E. L. (Lee) Wilson, see Whayne, *Delta Empire*. For the reference to Magnolia, Mississippi, see *Memphis Press*, January 27, 1921. For cotton prices, see Alan M. Omstead and Paul W. Rhode, "Cotton, Cottonseed, Shorn Wool, Tobacco—Acreage Production, Price, and Cotton Stocks, 1790–1999," in *Historical Statistics of the United States, Earliest Times to the Present: Millennial Edition*, ed. Susan B. Carter et al. (New York: Cambridge University Press, 2006), table Da755–765, 4–11. Cotton would slightly recover but then sink to new lows at the end of the decade (9.6 cents in 1930, 5.7 cents in 1931, and 6.5 cents in 1932).

17. Pickens, "American Congo," 427.

18. *El Paso Herald*, January 26, 1921, 1.

19. *Memphis Press*, January 26, 1921, in "An American Lynching."

20. *El Paso Herald*, January 19, 1921, 4.

21. Will Guzman, *Civil Rights in the Texas Borderlands: Dr. Lawrence A. Nixon and Black Activism* (Urbana: University of Illinois Press, 2015); "Death Takes Well-Known Attorney," *El Paso Times*, June 21, 1951; "Dr. Lawrence A. Nixon, Biography," accessed September 29, 2021, https://web.archive.org/web/2015 0912155913/http://www.rootsweb.ancestry.com/~txharris/Bios/NixonDr LawrenceA.htm; and "Lawrence Nixon Advocated the Right to Vote," African

American Registry, accessed September 29, 2021, https://web.archive.org/web/20170212094647/http://www.aaregistry.org/historic_events/view/lawrence-nixon-advocated-right-vote.

22. For correspondence involving Knollenberg, the NAACP, and the two governors, see Hill, *Beyond the Rope*.

23. Karlos Hill describes a harried Governor McRae making frantic efforts to convey the orders to the Arkansas officers. Hill concludes that the governor's request was delivered. Hill, *Beyond the Rope*, 53–54.

24. Anitra Van Prooyen, "Henry Lowery (Lynching of)," CALS Encyclopedia of Arkansas, accessed September 4, 2019, https://encyclopediaofarkansas.net/entries/henry-lowery-7064/; *Memphis Press*, January 26, 1921, in "An American Lynching."

25. *Commercial Appeal* (Memphis), January 27, 1921, 92.

26. *Commercial Appeal*, January 28, 1921, 12.

27. For information on the governor's instructions and their delivery, see Hill, *Beyond the Rope*, 53–54.

28. *Memphis Press*, January 26, 1921, in "An American Lynching."

29. *New York Times*, January 27, 1921, 1.

30. *New York Times*, January 27, 1921, 1; *Commercial Appeal*, January 27, 1921, 2; *Memphis News-Scimitar*, January 26, 1921 (quotation), in "An American Lynching."

31. *Osceola Times* cited in *Chicago Defender*, February 5, 1921, 1.

32. *New York Times*, January 27, 1921, 1.

33. *Arkansas Gazette*, January 27, 1921, 1.

34. Hill argues that Black narratives of lynchings fall into two types: (1) Blacks as victims and (2) Blacks as "exemplars of heroic manhood." He sees the NAACP's pamphlet, "An American Lynching," as falling into the first category. But the facts can be read another way, and certainly Pickens's essay in *The Nation* suggested the latter. See Hill, *Beyond the Rope*, 5, 11; Pickens, "American Congo"; "An American Lynching."

35. *Chicago Defender*, February 5, 1921, 1.

36. *Arkansas Gazette*, January 27, 1921, 1.

37. *Osceola Times*, January 28, 1921, 1.

38. At one point, the governor complained that he did not send state troops to Mississippi County, because "I can't get in touch with Sheriff Blackwood of that county, so I wouldn't know who to send the troops to. I understand that Sheriff Blackwood is at the Peabody hotel in Memphis and I have tried to telephone him there, but they say he is not in his room. What's the sheriff doing in Memphis? Why isn't he on the job? It's the worst outrage in the world to put a man to death without giving him a trial, and the sheriff of that county should be getting busy. He hasn't called me for assistance." Blackwood responded, "Nearly every man woman and child in our county wanted the negro lynched. When public sentiment is that way, there isn't much chance left for the officers." *Memphis Press*, January 26, 1921, in "An American Lynching"; *New York Times*, January 27, 1921, 1.

39. Whayne, *Delta Empire*, 170–72. It might be supposed that no judge would have had the nerve to issue a warrant for Lee Wilson's arrest, but Circuit Court Judge

R. H. Dudley had stood shoulder to shoulder with Sheriff Blackwood in the hours after Lowery's lynching to protect the two prisoners held in Blytheville. Indeed, the next day, prior to beginning proceedings in his courtroom, he took the opportunity to address those in the court. He denounced the lynching of Lowery and called for those present to "to declare their position as being either for or against the sanctity and supremacy of law and constituted civil authority." The situation in the room was tense, "with every ear bent upon hearing the stirring statements of the convincing speaker." Upon closing his remarks, a local attorney "asked every person present who indorsed the courts stand to rise in approbation. A room-full of stalwart Mississippians arose with alacrity to attest their hearty response to the timely utterances of the gifted jurist"; *Commercial Appeal*, January 28, 1921, 12.

40. *Arkansas Democrat*, January 27, 1921, 1.

41. *Memphis Press*, January 26, 1921, in "An American Lynching."

42. *Commercial Appeal*, January 28, 1921, 12

43. Year: 1930; Census Place: Center, Sebastian, Arkansas; Page: 4A; Enumeration District: 0009; FHL microfilm: 2339829. As found in Ancestry.com, 1930 United States Federal Census (online database), Provo, UT, USA: Ancestry.com Operations Inc, 2002, accessed September 4, 2019, https://search.ancestry.com /cgi-bin/sse.dll?indiv=1&dbid=6224&h=85823686&tid=&pid=&usePUB=true &_phsrc=tc04&_phstart=successSource.

44. *Memphis Press*, January 26, 1921, in "An American Lynching."

45. *Memphis Press*, January 26, 1921, in "An American Lynching."

46. Whayne, *Delta Empire*, 134–35; Kenneth Barnes, "Inspiration from the East: Black Arkansans Look to Japan," *Arkansas Historical Quarterly* 69 (Autumn 2010): 203. See also Mary Rolinson, *Grassroots Garveyism: The Universal Negro Improvement Association in the Rural South, 1920–1927* (Chapel Hill: University of North Carolina Press, 2007).

47. Donald Holley, *The Second Great Emancipation: The Mechanical Cotton Picker, Black Migration, and How They Shaped the Modern South* (Fayetteville: University of Arkansas Press, 2000).

CHAPTER 5

1. "Mrs. Conner Replies to Recent Attack by Rotary Club Committee," *Arkansas Democrat* (Little Rock), July 9, 1922, 5.

2. Ryan Anthony Smith, "Gendered Confines: Women's Prison Reform in 1920s and 1930s Arkansas" (master's thesis, Arkansas State University, 2017), 13; Ryan Anthony Smith, "Laura Conner and the Limits of Prison Reform," *Arkansas Historical Quarterly* 77 (Spring 2018): 52–63; "Mrs. Conner Replies," 5.

3. "Horton Confident of Vindication, He Says," *Pine Bluff Daily Graphic*, October 5, 1921, 1.

4. Smith, "Gendered Confines," 18.

5. Interview with Toressia Dancler McDowell, October 8, 1921, Laura Cornelius Conner Papers Digital Content, Butler Center for Arkansas Studies, Central Arkansas Library System, Little Rock, accessed May 17, 2021, https://arstudies .contentdm.oclc.org/digital/collection/p15728coll3/id/13947/rec/1.

6. Sarah Haley, *No Mercy Here: Gender, Punishment, and the Making of Jim Crow Modernity* (Chapel Hill: University of North Carolina Press, 2016), 25.

7. Interview with Toressia Dancler McDowell.

8. Smith, "Gendered Confines," 18; "Mrs. Conner Replies," 5.

9. "Silence Greets Expose of Tucker Farm Conditions by Woman Board Member," *Arkansas Democrat*, August 8, 1921, 1; "Tucker Farm Visited by Grand Jury—All There Are Questioned," *Little Rock Daily News*, October 21, 1921, 1.

10. "Mrs. Conner Replies," 5; Smith, "Laura Conner and the Limits of Prison Reform," 61–62.

11. Talitha LeFlouria, *Chained in Silence: Black Women and Convict Labor in the New South* (Chapel Hill: University of North Carolina Press, 2015), 22.

12. LeFlouria, *Chained in Silence*, 22.

13. Haley, *No Mercy Here*, 33.

14. Mary Dewees, "The Training of the Delinquent Woman," in *Proceedings of the Annual Congress of the American Prison Association* (New York: American Prison Association, 1922), 90.

15. "Pen Population Gains," *Daily Arkansas Gazette* (Little Rock), May 8, 1919, 14.

16. Haley, *No Mercy Here*, 29.

17. Kali Nicole Gross, "Exploring Crime and Violence in Early-Twentieth-Century Black Women's History," in *Contesting the Archives: Finding Women in the Sources*, ed. Nupur Chadhuri, Shelly J. Katz, and Mary Elizabeth Perry (Urbana: University of Illinois Press, 2010), 56.

18. Deborah Gray White, "Mining the Forgotten: Manuscript Sources for Black Women's History," *Journal of American History* 74 (June 1987): 237.

19. Cherisse Jones-Branch, "Women and the 1919 Elaine Massacre," in *The Elaine Massacre and Arkansas: A Century of Atrocity and Resistance, 1819–1919*, ed. Guy Lancaster (Little Rock: Butler Center Books, 2018), 183, 184–85.

20. Cheryl Hicks, *Talk With You Like A Woman: Justice and Reform in New York, 1890–1935* (Chapel Hill: University of North Carolina Press, 2010), 126.

21. LeFlouria, *Chained in Silence*, 14.

22. "Pearline Moss," *Arkansas Democrat*, September 8, 1922, 4.

23. "Two Negro Women Break into the Holdup Game," *Daily Arkansas Gazette*, November 15, 1919, 9.

24. Evelyn Brooks Higginbotham, *Righteous Discontent: The Women's Movement in the Black Baptist Church, 1880–1920* (Cambridge: Harvard University Press, 1993), 213.

25. "Attempt to Burn Home Thwarted," *Daily Arkansas Gazette*, October 9, 1921, 1.

26. "Negro Women Attempt to Set Fire to Home," *Arkansas Democrat*, October 9, 1921, 8.

27. Mary Ellen Curtin, *Black Prisoners and Their World, Alabama 1865–1900* (Charlottesville: University Press of Virginia, 2000), 113.

28. "Negro Women Still at Large," *Arkansas Democrat*, March 31, 1919, 5.

29. Daina Ramey Berry and Kali Nicole Gross, *A Black Women's History of the United States* (Boston: Beacon Press, 2020), 132.

30. "Negro Woman Jailed," *Daily Arkansas Gazette*, March 6, 1920, 18.

31. "Negro Women Are Held on Charge of Transporting," *Pine Bluff Daily Graphic*, May 15, 1921, 3.

32. Sharon Harley, " 'Working for Nothing but for a Living': Black Women in the Underground Economy," in *Sister Circle: Black Women and Work*, ed. Sharon Harley (New Brunswick: Rutgers University Press, 2002), 50–51.

33. "Negro to Serve Year on Roads," *Arkansas Democrat*, December 6, 1922, 4.

34. "Alberta Forrest, Negro Girl Charged," *Arkansas Democrat*, November 12, 1922, 6.

35. Saidiya Hartman, *Wayward Lives, Beautiful Experiments: Intimate Histories of Riotous Black Girls, Troublesome Women, and Queer Radicals* (New York: W. W. Norton, 2019), 242–43.

36. "Vagrancy Is Charged," *Daily Arkansas Gazette*, February 9, 1921, 8.

37. "Fine Negro Women $50.00 and Costs," *Pine Bluff Daily Graphic*, May 14, 1919, 3.

38. "Seems Winner Was the Loser in This Battle," *Arkansas Gazette*, May 27, 1920, 2. For other arrests of Black women on charges of "disturbing the peace," see "Six Arrests Made," *Arkansas Gazette*, April 5, 1920, 10; "Many Arrests Made," *Arkansas Gazette*, May 7, 1920, 16.

39. "Negro Girl Held for Man's Death," *Arkansas Democrat*, June 22, 1920, 8.

40. LeFlouria, *Chained in Silence*, 41.

41. "Negro Women Fight," *Daily Arkansas Gazette*, November 2, 1920, 8.

42. "Arrests of Five Follow Robberies," *Daily Arkansas Gazette*, August 14, 1921, 5.

43. "Negro Women Administer Severe Beating to Negro Wife Deserter," *Pine Bluff Daily Graphic*, June 24, 1921, 3.

44. "Timber Worker Held on Negro Girl's Charge," *Arkansas Democrat*, June 7, 1922, 5.

45. "Around the City," *Arkansas Democrat*, December 1, 1922, 7.

46. Hartman, *Wayward Lives, Beautiful Experiments*, 28.

47. "Municipal Court Is Pervaded with Christmas Spirit," *Arkansas Democrat*, December 24, 1922, 1.

48. Hartman, *Wayward Lives, Beautiful Experiments*, 256.

49. "Soldiers Charged With Hold Ups Held," *Little Rock Daily News*, February 8, 1921, 8.

50. Berry and Gross, *Black Women's History of the United States*, 131.

51. "Around the City," *Arkansas Democrat*, June 3, 1920, 12.

52. "Around the City," *Arkansas Democrat*, January 31, 1921, 6.

53. "Walls May Be Made Venereal Hospital Now," *Little Rock Daily News*, February 16, 1921, 8; LeFlouria, *Chained in Silence*, 48–49.

54. Susan K. Cahn, *Sexual Reckonings: Southern Girls in a Troubling Age* (Cambridge: Harvard University Press, 2007), 46–47.

55. Cahn, *Sexual Reckonings*, 46.

56. "Around the City," *Arkansas Democrat*, December 8, 1922, 11; "Undertaker Is Sued for $5000 Damages," *Little Rock Daily News*, September 16, 1921, 8.

57. Cherisse Jones-Branch, "The Arkansas Association of Colored Women and Early Twentieth-Century Maternalist Political Activism," *Arkansas Historical Quarterly* 79 (Autumn 2020): 218–30.

58. "Farm Sentence for Negro Girl," *Arkansas Democrat*, June 22, 1922, 8.

59. "And the Chief Is Happy, His 'Pet Revolver" Returns Home," *Arkansas Democrat*, July 25, 1921, 10.

60. "Baptist Women Ask New Rights," *Daily Arkansas Gazette*, April 8, 1922, 4;

"Contract Let for New Building at Industrial School," *Pine Bluff Daily Graphic*, May 7, 1922, 1; "Senate Completes Warren Aid Bill: Budge Group Favors Raising Some Appropriations, *Hope Star*, January 21, 1949, 1.
61. Gross, "Exploring Crime and Violence," 67.

CHAPTER 6

1. "Flood, 1927 Mississippi River," *Mississippi Encyclopedia*, eds. Ted Ownby and Charles Reagan Wilson (Jackson: University Press of Mississippi, 2017), 438; Stephen Ambrose, "Man vs. Nature: The Great Mississippi Flood of 1927," *National Geographic Magazine*, May 2001, accessed April 2, 2020, https://www .nationalgeographic.com/culture/2001/05/mississippi-river-flood-culture/ (first quotation); John M. Barry, *Rising Tide: The Great Mississippi Flood of 1927 and How It Changed America* (New York: Simon & Schuster, 1997), 201 (second quotation).
2. Walter White to Herbert Hoover, June 14, 1927, box I, C-380, folder 17, 2, National Association for the Advancement of Colored People (NAACP) Records, Library of Congress, Washington, DC (hereafter "NAACP Records").
3. Roy Wilkins with Tom Mathews, *Standing Fast: The Autobiography of Roy Wilkins* (New York: Da Capo Press, 1994), 126. Wilkins assumed the executive secretary position upon Walter White's death in 1955. See Wilkins with Mathews, *Standing Fast*, 219–20.
4. Wilkins with Mathews, *Standing Fast*, 126–27.
5. Vincent Harding, *There Is a River: The Black Struggle for Freedom in America* (San Diego: Harcourt Brace Jovanovich, 1981).
6. Jim Barnett and H. Clark Burkett, "The Forks of the Road Slave Market at Natchez," accessed September 29, 2021, https://web.archive.org/web/2021091 4192809/http://mshistorynow.mdah.state.ms.us/articles/47/the-forks-of-the -road-slave-market-at-natchez (all quotations).
7. William Edward Burghardt Du Bois, *Black Reconstruction: An Essay toward a History of the Part Which Black Folk Played in the Attempt to Reconstruct Democracy in America, 1860–1880* (New York: Harcourt, Brace and Company, 1935), 30 (first quotation), 432 (second quotation), 449 (third quotation), 696 (fourth quotation).
8. *Daily Clarion-Ledger*, September 26, 1890, 2.
9. Neil McMillen, *Dark Journey: Black Mississippians in the Age of Jim Crow* (Champaign: University of Illinois Press, 1990), 123.
10. Robyn Spencer, "Contested Terrain: The Mississippi Flood of 1927 and the Struggle to Control Black Labor," *Journal of Negro History* 79 (Spring 1994): 170. See also Barry, *Rising Tide*; Richard M. Mizelle Jr., "Black Levee Camp Workers, the NAACP, and the Mississippi Flood Control Project, 1927–1933," *Journal of African American History* 98 (Fall 2013): 513–15.
11. "Death and Famine Grip Delta Section as Surging Rivers Take Frightful Toll," *Pittsburgh Courier*, May 7, 1927, 8.
12. Myles McMurchy, " 'The Red Cross Is Not All Right': Herbert Hoover's Concentration Camp Cover-Up in the 1927 Mississippi Flood," *Yale Historical Review* 5 (Fall 2015): 88.

13. "Conscript Labor Gangs Keep Flood Refugees in Legal Bondage, Claimed," *Pittsburgh Courier*, May 14, 1927, 1.

14. "Conscript Labor Gangs," 8 (all quotations). See also Walter White, "The Negro and the Flood," box I, C-380, folder 16, 6–8, NAACP Records.

15. White, "The Negro and the Flood," 11. For examples of the brutalities African Americans suffered, see Barry, *Rising Tide*, 315–16.

16. J. Winston Harrington, "Deny Food to Flood Victims in Mississippi," *Chicago Defender*, June 4, 1927, 1.

17. "Confidential Statement of Observations Made in Mississippi Delta: Conditions Affecting Laborers on Government Projects," Investigation # 1, December, 1932, box I, C-381, folder 3, 2–3, NAACP Records.

18. William Alexander Percy, *Lanterns on the Levee: Recollections of a Planter's Son* (Baton Rouge: Louisiana State University Press, 1941), 251 (first quotation); J. Winston Harrington, "Work or Go Hungry Edict Perils Race: Flood Victims Driven by Labor Bosses," *Chicago Defender*, June 11, 1927, 1 (second quotation).

19. Harrington, "Deny Food to Flood Victims in Mississippi," 1 (first through fifth quotations); Percy, *Lanterns on the Levee*, 253 (sixth and seventh quotations); Spencer, "Contested Terrain," 174.

20. J. Winston Harrington, "Deny Food and Clothing to Refugees in Mississippi," *Chicago Defender*, June 4, 1927, 2.

21. J. Winston Harrington, "Flood Refugee Shot to Death: 'Work or Die' Edict Again Perils Race," *Chicago Defender*, July 23, 1927, 1 (first, fourth, fifth, and sixth quotations); Barry, *Rising Tides*, 332 (second and third quotations). See also Percy, *Lanterns on the Levee*, 266–68.

22. Ida B. Wells-Barnett, "Flood Refugees Are Held as Slaves in Mississippi Camp," *Chicago Defender*, July 30, 1927, A11; "John Jones" was an alias Wells-Barnett used to protect his identity.

23. Wells-Barnett, "Flood Refugees Are Held."

24. Walter White to Herbert Hoover, June 14, 1927, 1, box I, C-380, folder 17, NAACP Records. See also Walter Wilson, "Storms and Floods Help Uncover Peonage: Writer Tells How Act of God Reveal Slavery in America's Dixieland," *Chicago Defender*, May 6, 1933, 10.

25. J. Winston Harrington, "Use Troops In Flood Area to Imprison Farm Hands: Refugees Herded Like Cattle to Stop Escape from Peonage," *Chicago Defender*, May 7, 1927, 1.

26. Spencer, "Contested Terrain," 171.

27. Harrington, "Use Troops In Flood Area," p. 2.

28. Barry, *Rising Tide*, 313–14. See also Nan Elizabeth Woodruff, "Mississippi Delta Planters and Debates over Mechanization, Labor, and Civil Rights in the 1940s," *Journal of Southern History* 60 (May 1994): 264.

29. White, "The Negro and the Flood," 5 (quotation); White to Hoover, 1–2. See also Wilson, "Storms and Floods Help Uncover Peonage."

30. John L. Spivak, "Shady Business in the Red Cross," *American Mercury* 33 (November 1934): 273. See also "Red Cross Exposed by Writer as Greatest Aide to Dixie Peonage," *Chicago Defender* (National Edition), November 24, 1934, 10.

31. White, "The Negro and the Flood," 5–6.

32. The Final Report of the Colored Advisory Commission, Mississippi Valley

Flood Disaster, 1927, NAACP Peonage, Labor, and New Deal Files: Mississippi Flood Control Folder, October 1, 1927–December 31, 1927, Papers of the NAACP, Part 10: Peonage, Labor and New Deal, 1913–1939, online folder number 001418-013-0611, Library of Congress, NAACP Records, 11 (all quotations); Spencer, "Contested Terrain," 171.

33. "Vicksburg: A Victory for the South," p. 7. (quotations), 3–4, box I, C-380, folder 18, NAACP Records, 7; White to Hoover, 1–2. See also White, "The Negro and the Flood," 9–10.

34. White to Hoover, 1 (quotation); "Vicksburg: A Victory for the South," 3–4.

35. Walter White, "In the Flood District," *Chicago Defender*, July 2, 1927, A1 (quotation).

36. Matthew T. Pearcy, "After the Flood: A History of the 1928 Flood Control Act," *Journal of the Illinois State Historical Society* 95 (Summer 2002): 176.

37. "Text of Coolidge's Message Giving His Views on the Needs of the Nation," *New York Times*, December 7, 1927, 24.

38. "Laud and Criticize Coolidge Message: Senators and Representatives from Mississippi Valley Caustic in Comment," *New York Times*, December 7, 1927, 25 (quotation); Karen M. O'Neill, *Rivers by Design: State Power and the Origins of U.S. Flood Control* (Durham: Duke University Press, 2006), 146. See also Pearcy, "After the Flood," 190.

39. Walter White to Bishop John Hurst, July 18, 1928, 1–2, NAACP Administrative File, January–July 22, 1928, Papers of the NAACP, Part 02: 1919–1939, Personal Correspondence of Selected NAACP Officials, July 25, 1928–August 3, 1928, online folder number 001469-011-0107, NAACP Records.

40. Walter White to Morefield Storey, July 22, 1928, 1, Papers of the NAACP, Part 02: 1919–1939, NAACP Records.

41. White to Storey, 1–2 (quotation). However, Smith did not sign the "pro-Negro statement," a decision he would later regret. See Robert A. Slayton, *Empire Statesman: The Rise and Redemption of Al Smith* (New York: Free Press, 2001), 286, and Walter White, *A Man Called White*, 99–101.

42. American Federation of Labor Report, December 5, 1931, 1, 3, box I, C-380-A, folder 1, NAACP Records.

43. Wilkins with Mathews, *Standing Fast*, 119; Roy Wilkins, "Mississippi Slavery in 1933," *The Crisis: A Record of the Darker Races* (April 1933): 82. For a timeline of events occurring as a result of Boardman's investigation, see "Investigation of Labor Camps in Federal Flood Control Operations," September 30, 1932, box I, C-380-A, folder 4, 1–4, NAACP Records.

44. NAACP, "Investigation of Labor Camps in Federal Flood Control Operations," August 1932, Helen Boardman Report, 1, 6, 8 (quotations), box I, C-380-A, folder 1, NAACP Records.

45. For examples of such letters, see box I, C-380-A, folders 1 and 2, NAACP Records. See also NAACP, "Investigation of Labor Camps Along the Mississippi Flood Control Project," box I, C-380-A, folder 4, NAACP Records.

46. Robert F. Wagner to Walter White (all quotations), September 10, 1932, box I, C-380-A, folder 4, NAACP Records. Wagner acknowledged in his letter that if the accounts were true, "every method of correction, whether legislative of administrative, must be employed." However, if what was described did not in fact exist, then the public was "entitled to receive that assurance" as well.

For newspaper accounts regarding Black labor exploitation and Sen. Robert F. Wagner's promise to put forth a resolution and call for an investigation, see box I, C-381, folder 5, NAACP Records. See also NAACP Press Release, "Wagner Promises Negroes Resolution for Senate Probe of Mississippi Project," box I, C-380-A, folder 4, NAACP Records.

47. Wilkins with Mathews, *Standing Fast*, 119 (quotations), 121. See also Mizelle, "Black Levee Camp Workers," 524.

48. Wilkins, "Mississippi Slavery in 1933," 82.

49. Wilkins, "Mississippi Slavery in 1933," 82.

50. Wilkins, "Mississippi Slavery in 1933," 82 (first and third quotations); "Confidential Statement of Observations Made in Mississippi Delta: Conditions Affecting Laborers on Government Projects," Investigation #2, December 1932, 1–2, box I, C-381, folder 3, NAACP Records (second quotation).

51. Newspaper clipping, *Denver Rocky Mountain News*, November 1, 1932, Mississippi Flood Control Project, NAACP Peonage, Labor, and New Deal Files: Mississippi Flood Control News Clippings, September 24–December 23, 1932, online folder number 001418-014-0535, Papers of the NAACP, Part 10: Peonage, Labor, and the New Deal, 1913–1939 (quotation).

52. General Brown sent a scathing letter to Walter White, then NAACP executive secretary, challenging the accuracy of the reports as well as the legitimacy of the investigator. In response, White defended the investigation and suggested Brown's willingness to overlook what was happening to Negroes may be linked to the fact that he was "a native of Nashville, Tennessee." Lytle Brown to Walter White, August 25, 1932, and White to Brown, August 29, 1932, 3, box I, C-380-A, folder 2, NAACP Records (quotation).

53. Wilkins, "Mississippi Slavery in 1933," 82 (quotation).

54. "Charge Gen. Pillsbury Misrepresents Testimony on Mississippi Peonage: Negro Aid Reports War Dept. Plan to Whitewash by Alleging 'Insufficient Details,'" undated press release, box I, C-380-A, folder 5, NAACP Records (quotation).

55. Wilkins, "Mississippi Slavery in 1933," 82 (all quotations).

56. "Levy Camp Workers Get More Pay: War Department Head Makes Announcement," *Chicago Defender*, October 14, 1933, 3.

57. For additional discussions of legislative economic changes and the continued financial issues levee workers faced afterward, see Mizelle, "Black Levee Camp Workers," 525–26.

58. Walter White, *A Man Called White*, 104 (quotation).

59. W. E. B. Du Bois, "Hoover: Du Bois Takes Pointed Issue with President: Here They Are—In Which One Do You Believe," *Pittsburgh Courier*, October 29, 1932, A1, 8 (quotation).

60. White, *A Man Called White*, 139 (quotation).

61. Franklin Roosevelt, "Presidential Nomination Address," July 2, 1932 (first and second quotations) and "Inaugural Address," March 4, 1933 (third quotation), Pepperdine School of Public Policy, accessed May 1, 2020, https://publicpolicy .pepperdine.edu/academics/research/faculty-research/new-deal/roosevelt -speeches/.

62. "Levee Camp Workers to Get Higher Pay, Shorter Hours: Payroll Rise of $75,000 Weekly," *Pittsburgh Courier*, October 14, 1933, A1.

63. Lewis Caldwell Jr., "What the NRA Is Doing to the Race! 'New Deal' Rapidly Becoming 'Raw Deal' for Dark Americans, Say Experts Who Have Checked on Recent Developments," *Chicago Defender*, May 26, 1934, 10.

64. Wilkins with Mathews, *Standing Fast*, 127–28.

65. "An Oral History with Mr. & Mrs. Charlie Smith," transcript of an oral history conducted in 1976 by Dr. Orley Caudill, USM Special Collections, University of Southern Mississippi, 1976, 51 (quotation).

CHAPTER 7

1. Ernest Valachovic, "New Subjects for King Cotton," *Arkansas Gazette Sunday Magazine*, July 14, 1957, 1.

2. Ethel Dawson to Don F. Pielstick, November 27, 1951, Pielstick to Dawson, December 4, 1951, record group 7, box 8, folder 9, National Council of Churches of Christ, Division of Home Missions Papers, 1950–1964 (hereafter "Division of Home Mission Papers"), Presbyterian Historical Society Archive, Philadelphia, PA. Lincoln County is just south of the city of Pine Bluff. Only part of Lincoln County—the area running along the Arkansas River—is in the Delta and home to large cotton operations. The rest of the county is in the Gulf Coast Plain and had mixed agricultural—mostly corn, soybeans, hogs, and cattle—in the 1950s. "Lincoln County Agricultural Program, 1954: A Report of the Lincoln County Agricultural Planning Committee" (pamphlet) in box 2, folder "Lincoln County," Arkansas Cooperative Extension Service Records, Special Collections, University of Arkansas Libraries, Fayetteville.

3. Between 1950 and 1960, Lincoln County's "non-white" population fell by 22.8 percent from 9,089 to 7,017, according to the U.S. Census Bureau. This led to Lincoln County having a white majority for the first time in the twentieth century. In 1950, 53.3 percent of Lincoln County was "non-white" and 46.7 percent white. Ten years later, whites constituted 51.4 percent of the population and "non-whites" 48.6 percent. Overall, the county's population dropped by 15.4 percent from 17,079 to 14,447. U.S. Census Bureau, *Census of Population and Housing, 1950*, accessed May 19, 2021, https://www.census.gov/prod/www /decennial.html; U.S. Census Bureau, *Census of Housing and Population, 1960*, accessed May 19, 2021, https://www.census.gov/prod/www/decennial.html.

4. This work is informed by Greta de Jong's *You Can't Eat Freedom: Southerners and Social Justice after the Civil Rights Movement* (Chapel Hill: University of North Carolina Press, 2016). de Jong details efforts in Mississippi and Louisiana during the 1960s and 1970s to push out Black laborers made jobless by mechanization and empowered by the legal successes of the Civil Rights Movement. Like those in Lincoln County, the white leaders in these areas undermined federal antipoverty programs that would have helped the Black workers remain on the land they considered to be home.

5. Mrs. D. A. Wooten to J. William Fulbright, July 8, 1956, BCN 18, folder 47, J. William Fulbright Papers, Special Collections, University of Arkansas Libraries, Fayetteville.

6. Julie M. Weise, "Braceros and Jim Crow in Arkansas," in *¿Que Fronteras? Mexican Braceros and a Re-examination of the Legacy of Migration*, ed. Paul

Lopez (Dubuque, IA: Kendall Hunt Publishing, 2010), 197–213 (republished as Julie M. Weise, "The Bracero Program: Mexican Workers in the Delta, 1948–1964," in *Race and Ethnicity in Arkansas: New Perspectives*, ed. John A. Kirk [Fayetteville: University of Arkansas Press, 2014], 125–40); Julie M. Weise, *Corazón de Dixie: Mexicanos in the U.S. South since 1910* (Chapel Hill: University of North Carolina Press, 2015), 83–117 (second quotation, 91–92; third quotation, 92). See also J. Justin Castro, "Mexican Braceros and Arkansas Cotton: Agricultural Labor and Civil Rights in the Post-War War II South," *Arkansas Historical Quarterly* 75 (Spring 2016): 27–46.

7. Weise, "Braceros and Jim Crow in Arkansas," 198 (first quotation); Weise, *Corazón de Dixie*, 91 (second quotation), 92 (third quotation). The unnamed Lincoln County resident whose testimony Weise dismisses is George Stith, a former Southern Tenant Farmers' Union activist then working for the National Farm Labor Union (AFL). It appears that Weise did not read Stith's entire testimony, though. The citation is to a secondary source—Jeannie Whayne's *A New Plantation South*—that actually contradicts Weise's larger point, with Whayne arguing that significant numbers of African Americans in the Arkansas Delta fought hard to remain on the land even in the face of Jim Crow, mechanization, and opportunities offered in urban areas. "Statement of George Stith, Gould, Ark., Agricultural Worker, Cotton Plantation," in *Migratory Labor, Hearings before the [Senate] Subcommittee on Labor and Labor-Management Relations, United States Senate, 82nd Congress* (Washington, DC: Government Printing Office, 1952), 226–29; Weise, *Corazón de Dixie*, 259n57; Jeannie M. Whayne, *A New Plantation South: Land, Labor, and Federal Favor in Twentieth-Century Arkansas* (Charlottesville: University of Virginia Press, 1996), 226. On Stith and his centrality to the struggles of workers in the Delta, see Bud Schultz and Ruth Schultz, *The Price of Dissent: Testimonies to Political Repression in America* (Berkeley: University of California Press, 2001), 25–33; "The Great Depression: Episode 5, Mean Things Happening," videorecording (Alexandria, VA: PBS Video, 1993).

8. "Church Leaders Discuss Basis For Making Brotherhood Work," *Pittsburgh Courier*, April 26, 1947, 12 (first quotation); Mrs. O. G. Dawson interview with Pine Bluff Women's Center, no date [1976], box 2, tape 6, Pine Bluff Women's Center Records, Special Collections, University of Central Arkansas Library, Conway (second quotation); "Fear Barrier to Brotherhood, Church Leaders Told," *Baltimore Afro-American*, April 26, 1947, 7. Dawson was born Ethel Bernice Ross in 1907. She married Oscar G. Dawson, who worked in Pine Bluff for the Missouri Pacific Railroad, in 1933. The couple did not have children. Cherisse Jones-Branch, *Better Living by Their Bootstraps: Black Women's Activism in Rural Arkansas, 1914–1965* (Fayetteville: University of Arkansas Press, 2021), 119–29. On the ability of Black women in Lincoln County to stand up to powerful planters in ways that would be dangerous to Black men, see Ozell Sutton interviewed by Alice Bernstein, November 15, 2005, *The Force of Ethics in Civil Rights Oral History Project*, accessed February 10, 2020, https://www.youtube.com/watch?v=9P97lXb1Mk4.

9. Valachovic, "New Subjects for King Cotton," p. 1; J. William Fulbright to Mrs. D. A. Wooten, July 13, 1956, BCN 18, folder 47, Fulbright Papers. On Fulbright's

dependence on Delta planters for votes, see Michael Pierce, "How to Win a Seat in the U.S. Senate: Carl Bailey to Bill Fulbright, October 20, 1943," *Arkansas Historical Quarterly* 76 (Winter 2017): 334–61.

10. Ethel Dawson to Don F. Pielstick, November 27, 1951 (first and third quotations), Ethel Dawson to Don F. Pielstick, December 3, 1951, Ethel Dawson to Pielstick, January 20, 1951, record group 7, box 8, folder 9, Division of Home Missions Papers; Dawson interview with Pine Bluff Women's Center (second quotation). For a first-person account of a Lincoln County sharecropper, see Vic Carter, *"From Yonder to Here": A Memoir of Dr. Ozell Sutton* (n.p.: Lee-Com Media, 2008), 9–30.

11. Ethel Dawson to Don F. Pielstick, November 27, 1951, Ethel Dawson to Don F. Pielstick, October 4, 1952, record group 7, box 8, folder 9, Division of Home Missions Papers.

12. Dawson, "Report of the Town and Country Church Rural Life Improvement Institute, Gould, Arkansas, May 7–8, 1954," pp. 8, 14 (quotation), record group 7, box 8, folder 9, Division of Home Missions Papers.

13. "Lincoln County Agricultural Program, 1954," 2, 3–4 (quotation); "From Mule to Machine . . . in Cotton," *Pine Bluff Commercial Farm Life* (monthly magazine), June 1955, 3; "Lincoln Farmers to Use Federal Classing Program," *Pine Bluff Commercial*, July 17, 1955, 15; "Cotton in Lincoln County Averaged High Grade in '54," *Pine Bluff Commercial*, January 16, 1955, 18. Some Lincoln County cotton operations were fully mechanized by 1950, and a state report concluded that the labor needs on such plantations were just 5 percent of non-mechanized operations: "One man in this type of operation does as much and accomplishes as much as twenty men could formerly accomplish"; Donald Holley, *The Second Great Emancipation: The Mechanical Cotton Picker, Black Migration, and How They Shaped the Modern South* (Fayetteville: University of Arkansas Press, 2000), 136–39; "Statement of the Arkansas State Department of Public Welfare of Substantiating Reasons for Surplus-Commodities-Only Program in Arkansas," December 20, 1956, series 9, subseries 1, box 334, folder 5, Orval Eugene Faubus Papers, Special Collections, University of Arkansas Libraries, Fayetteville.

14. "Lincoln County Agricultural Program, 1954," 15; "1955 Agricultural Statistics for Arkansas" (Little Rock: Agricultural Marketing Service USDA, 1956), 19. The federally enforced reduction in cotton acreage made it difficult for Lincoln County's African American workers to pick up extra money on the side. Before the reduction, it was a common practice for day laborers to cultivate cotton on vacant lots and fields and take it to the gin at the end of the season. But the new regulations prevented ginners from accepting such cotton, and domestic workers lost an important source of income. Dawson, "Report of the Town and Country Church Rural Life Improvement Institute, Gould, Arkansas, May 7–8, 1954," record group 7, box 8, folder 9, Division of Home Missions Papers.

15. "From Mule to Machine . . . in Cotton," 3; "Lincoln Farmers to Use Federal Classing Program"; "Lincoln County Agricultural Program, 1954."

16. Donald Holley, "Leaving the Land of Opportunity: Arkansas and the Great Migration," *Arkansas Historical Quarterly* 64 (Autumn 2005): 245–61.

17. C. A. Vines to Elveria Heard, February 8, 1957, box 8, folder 3, Arkansas Cooperative Extension Service Records.

18. Charles S. Aiken, *The Cotton Plantation South, since the Civil War* (Baltimore: Johns Hopkins University Press, 1998), 131; Richard H. Day, "The Economics of Technological Change and the Demise of the Sharecropper," *American Economic Review* 57 (June 1957): 427–49. Gavin Wright endorses Day's findings in *Old South, New South: Revolutions in the Southern Economy since the Civil War* (New York: Basic Books, 1986), 241–49.

19. "Statement of George Stith, Gould, Ark.," 226–29; Victor K. Ray, "The Hungry People II—Who's the Villain in Cotton Country? The Mexican, the Machine or Dirt," *Arkansas Gazette*, February 15, 1954, 1–2. See also Victor K. Ray, "The Hungry People I—It's Hard Times for Only a Few Folk but for Them It's Awfully Hard Times," *Arkansas Gazette*, February 14, 1954, 1–2.

20. Weise, *Corazón de Dixie*, 111; Ray, "The Hungry People II"; "Statement of the Arkansas State Department of Public Welfare."

21. Dawson interview with Pine Bluff Women's Center; "Statement of Farish R. Betton, St. Louis, Mo., First Vice President, National Farm Labor Union, AFL," in *Migratory Labor Hearings of the Subcommittee on Labor and Labor-Management Relations*, 231–33; Day, "The Economics of Technological Change." For an account of how Lincoln County's largest landowner controlled the daily lives of Black sharecroppers and how one Black family sought autonomy by becoming day laborers, see Ozell Sutton interviewed by Alice Bernstein, *The Force of Ethics in Civil Rights Oral History Project.*

22. Wiley A. Branton interviewed by James Mosby, January 16, 1967, Civil Rights Documentation Project, Ralph Bunche Oral History Collection, Howard University, Washington, DC, copy in box 9, folder 14, Southern Regional Council—"Will the Circle Be Unbroken" Program Files, Manuscript, Archives, and Rare Book Library, Emory University, Atlanta, GA. On planters "voting" their sharecroppers, see V. O. Key, *Southern Politics in State and Nation* (New York: Knopf, 1949), 196–97, 203. On Black voting in 1946 in Little Rock and Hot Springs, see "Nation Focuses Attention on Arkansas Voting: Labor Issue and Negro Balloting Closely Watched," *Arkansas Democrat*, July 28, 1946, 1–2.

23. Dawson interview with Pine Bluff Women's Center (first quotation), "The Progressive Women Voters Association of Lincoln County," flier, n.d. [1953], "News of Christianity at Work" (newsletter written by Dawson), April 6, 1955 (second quotation); Ethel Dawson to My Dear Friend (circular letter), May 11, 1955, record group 7, box 8, folder 9, Division of Home Missions Papers.

24. "Statement of George Stith, Gould, Ark.," 227. For 1954 wages for Lincoln County pickers, see *Mexican Farm Labor Program. Hearings before the Subcommittee on Equipment, Supplies, and Manpower of the Committee on Agriculture, House of Representatives, 1955,* 84th Cong., 1st sess., 19. For drop in wages paid during chopping season, see "Statement of H. L. Mitchell, President, National Agricultural Workers Union, AFL-CIO," *Farm Labor. Hearings before the Subcommittee on Equipment, Supplies, and Manpower of the Committee on Agriculture. 1958,* 85th Cong. 2nd sess. On Lincoln County's per capita income, see "Statement of the Arkansas State Department of Public Welfare." For national per capita income, see "Income of Persons in the United States," *Current Population Reports* series p-60, no. 16 (May 1955): 11, accessed February 14, 2020, https://www2.census.gov/library/publications/1955/demographics/p60-16.pdf.

25. "Human Interest Story" [December 2, 1953] (first quotation), record group 7, box 8, folder 9, National Council of Churches of Christ, Division of Home Missions Papers, 1950–1964; Glenn E. Garrett et al., *Mexican Labor Program Consultants Report* (Washington, DC: Department of Labor, 1959), 4 (second quotation).

26. Dawson, "Report of the Town and Country Church Rural Life Improvement Institute, Gould, Arkansas, May 7–8, 1954," 14; Ben F. Johnson III, *Arkansas in Modern America, since 1930* (Fayetteville: University of Arkansas Press, 2019), 111.

27. Louisa Shotwell to Don F. Pielstick and Dr. Nace, May 11, 1951, Don F. Pielstick to Ethel Dawson, November 19, 1951, record group 7, box 8, folder 9, Division of Home Missions Papers.

28. Ethel Dawson to Don Pielstick, November 24, 1951, record group 7, box 8, folder 9, Division of Home Missions Papers. For an analysis of how work to improve "race relations" undermines efforts to promote justice and equality, see Karen E. Fields and Barbara J. Fields, *Racecraft: The Soul of Inequality in American Life* (New York: Verso, 2012).

29. Don F. Pielstick to Ethel Dawson, November 19, 1951; Don F. Pielstick to Ethel Dawson, May 3, 1951, record group 7, box 8, folder 9, Division of Home Missions Papers.

30. Ethel Dawson to Don F. Pielstick, May 11, 1955, Don F. Pielstick to Ethel Dawson, November 19, 1951; Don F. Pielstick to Ethel Dawson, May 19, 1955, record group 7, box 8, folder 9, Division of Home Mission Papers; Ethel Dawson to Philip Weightman, March 3, 1955, box 1, folder 5, Philip Weightman Papers, Tamiment Library, New York University, New York. On Weightman's activities in Arkansas, see "CIO Maps Plans for 100,000 More Voters for Arkansas at Two-Day Meeting," *Arkansas State Press*, January 21, 1955, 1; Michael Pierce, "Odell Smith, Teamsters Local 878, and Civil Rights Unionism in Little Rock, 1943–1965," *Journal of Southern History* 84 (November 2018): 938. On Weightman, see Rick Halpern and Roger Horowitz, *Meatpackers: An Oral History of Black Packinghouse Workers and Their Struggle for Racial and Economic Equality* (Boston: Monthly Review Press, 1999), 30–41.

31. Philip Weightman to Ethel Dawson, June 3, 1955, Ethel Dawson to Philip Weightman, June 8, 1955, box 1, folder 5, Weightman Papers; Ethel Dawson to Don F. Pielstick, May 11, 1955, Ethel Dawson to My Dear Friend (circular letter), May 11, 1955, record group 7, box 8, folder 9, Division of Home Missions Papers.

32. "Paul F. Sifton, 74, Ex-Lobbyist, Reuther Aide and Writer, Dead," *New York Times*, April 7, 1972, 39; "Anna Douglas Rejoins Staff Nat'l CP FEPC," *Arkansas State Press*, October 17, 1947, 1.

33. "Statement of Paul Sifton, National Legislative Representative, UAW, CIO," in *Migratory Labor, Hearings before the [Senate] Subcommittee on Labor and Labor-Management Relations*, 408–9.

34. Paul Sifton to Roy L. Reuther, May 24, 1955, box 23, folder 20, United Automobile Workers Political Action Department, Roy L. Reuther Files (hereafter "Roy Reuther Files"), Walter Reuther Library, Wayne State University, Detroit, MI; Roy L. Reuther to Emil Mazey, June 10, 1955, box 7, folder 28, Roy Reuther Files; Roy L. Reuther to William Kimberling, June 24, 1955, box 1, folder 6, Weightman Papers.

35. Philip Weightman to Ethel Dawson, June 3, 1955, box 1, folder 5, Weightman

Papers; Mrs. D. A. Wooten to J. William Fulbright, July 8, 1956; J. William Fulbright to Mrs. D. A. Wooten, July 13, 1956.

36. Paul Sifton to Roy L. Reuther, May 24, 1955, Paul Sifton to Robert Oliver, June 14, 1955, box 23, folder 20, Roy Reuther Files; Paul Sifton to Ethel Dawson, June 20, 1955, box 23, folder 21, Roy Reuther Files; "Extension of Mexican Labor Act," *Congressional Record*, July 6, 1955, 84th Cong., 1st sess., vol. 101, part 8, 10006–24 (quotation p. 10015); Ellis Hawley, "The Politics of the Mexican Labor Issue," *Agricultural History* 40 (July 1966): 157–76, see esp. 161; Castro, "Mexican Labor and Arkansas Cotton," 41–42. Significant changes to the bracero program would not come until 1963, when a Democratic administration much more sympathetic to the labor movement negotiated with Congress the end of the program the following year.

37. Paul Sifton to Roy L. Reuther, June 20, 1955, box 23, folder 21, Roy Reuther Files; Reuther to Kimberling, June 24, 1955. On Faubus crediting the CIO for his victory, see "Governor Calls for Decent Wage," *Arkansas Democrat*, January 15, 1955, 1.

38. J. L. Bland to Orval E. Faubus, September 28, 1955 (quotation), Orval E. Faubus to J. L. Bland, October 7, 1955, Louie Hoffman to J. L. Bland, September 27, 1955, series 7, subseries 2, box 209, folder 1, Faubus Papers; "New Subjects for King Cotton."

39. Ethel Dawson to Paul Sifton, June 8, 1955 (quotation), folder 21, box 23, Roy Reuther Files; "$15,000 to Display Hogs; Naught to Feed Humans Reported from Lincoln County," *Arkansas State Press*, July 22, 1955, 1; Carl Adams to Orval E. Faubus, August 8, 1955, series 9, subseries 1, box 333, folder 8, Faubus Papers.

40. Philip Weightman to Ethel Dawson, June 3, 1955, box 1, folder 5, Weightman Papers.

41. Richard O. Comfort to Ethel Dawson, January 9, 1956, record group 7, box 8, folder 9, Division of Home Missions Papers; "Rev. Don Pielstick, Church Official, 48," *New York Times*, June 28, 1955, 27; Dawson interview with Pine Bluff Women's Center; Randy Finley, "Crossing the White Line: SNCC in Three Delta Towns," *Arkansas Historical Quarterly* 65 (Summer 2006): 127.

42. Olivia A. Draper to Louisa Shotwell, February 4, 1958, Olivia A. Draper to Mrs. Evans, November 29, 1956, record group 7, box 9, folder 5, Division of Home Missions Papers; Helen Kindt to Richard O. Comfort, January 23, 1956, record group 7, box 8, folder 9, Division of Home Missions Papers; "Ministry to Migrants," record group 7, box 7, folder 21, Division of Home Missions Papers. While the National Council of Churches took steps to make the bracero program operate more efficiently, a group of Catholic bishops demanded the program's immediate end and the resignation of the U.S. secretary of labor who oversaw it. The Bishops' Committee for the Spanish Speaking criticized the program for having "supplant[ed] colored workers" across the entire South and insisted the problem was most acute in Arkansas. "Catholic Bishops Urge Secretary of Labor to Resign: Southern Work Trend Criticized," *Baltimore Afro-American*, July 12, 1958, 3.

43. Roy Reed, "Amid Hoots, Jeers, Unionist Urges Bracero Wage Raise," *Arkansas Gazette*, March 3, 1962, 1–2; "Statement Made by J. Bill Becker before the United

States Department of Labor Committee Hearing at West Memphis, Arkansas, in Support of the Proposed Wage Increase for Mexican Nationals under PL78," in part 2, box 36, folder 36, National Sharecroppers Fund Papers, Reuther Library. Becker led the coalition of trade unionists, African Americans, and urban liberals that abolished the state's poll tax in 1964 and began to open places like Lincoln County to Black political participation. J. Bill Becker, interview with Jack Bass and Walter De Vries, June 13, 1974 (interview A-0025), 9–10, 13–4, Southern Oral History Project, Southern Historical Collection, Wilson Library, University of North Carolina, Chapel Hill.

44. Laura Foner, "82% Negro; 100% White," *Justice* (Brandeis University), October 26, 1965, clipping in box 1, folder 4, Arkansas SNCC Papers, Wisconsin State Historical Society, Madison; Laura Foner, "Arkansas SNCC Memories," in *Arsnick: The Student Nonviolent Coordinating Committee in Arkansas*, ed. Jennifer Jensen Wallach and John A. Kirk (Fayetteville: University of Arkansas Press, 2011), 148–54. See also "Excerpts from an Interview with Bob Cableton," in Wallach and Kirk, *Arsnick*, 128–31; Finley, "Crossing the White Line," 116–37.

CHAPTER 8

1. C. D. Wright, *One with Others [a little book of her days]* (Port Townsend, WA: Copper Canyon Press, 2010).
2. See James H. Meredith, *Three Years in Mississippi* (Bloomington: Indiana University Press, 1966); William Doyle, *An American Insurrection: The Battle of Oxford, Mississippi, 1962* (New York: Doubleday, 2001); Charles W. Eagles, *The Price of Defiance: James Meredith and the Integration of Ole Miss* (Chapel Hill: University of North Carolina Press, 2009); and Henry T. Gallagher, *James Meredith and the Ole Miss Riot: A Soldier's Story* (Jackson: University Press of Mississippi, 2012).
3. On Meredith's March against Fear, see Aram Goudsouzian, *Down to the Crossroads: Civil Rights, Black Power, and the Meredith March against Fear* (New York: Farrar, Straus and Giroux, 2014).
4. On the Elaine Massacre and its aftermath, see Richard C. Cortner, *A Mob Intent on Death: The NAACP and the Arkansas Riot Cases* (Middletown: Wesleyan University Press, 1988); Grif Stockley, *Blood in Their Eyes: The Elaine Race Massacres of 1919* (Fayetteville: University of Arkansas Press, 2001); and Robert Whitaker, *On the Laps of Gods: The Red Summer of 1919 and the Struggle for Justice that Remade a Nation* (New York: Crown, 2008).
5. Studies of lynching have proliferated. See, for example, Michael Pfeifer, *Rough Justice: Lynching and American Society, 1874–1947* (Champaign: University of Illinois Press, 2006); William D. Carrigan and Clive Webb, *Forgotten Dead: Mob Violence against Mexicans in the United States, 1848–1928* (New York: Oxford University Press, 2013); Amy Kate Bailey and Stewart E. Tolnay, *Lynched: The Victims of Southern Mob Violence* (Chapel Hill: University of North Carolina Press, 2015); Tameka Bradley Hobbs, *Democracy Abroad, Lynching at Home: Racial Violence in Florida* (Gainesville: University Press of Florida, 2015); Karlos K. Hill, *Beyond the Rope: The Impact of Lynching on Black Culture and Memory* (New York: Cambridge University Press, 2016); and Donald G.

Mathews, *At the Altar of Lynching: Burning Sam Hose in the American South* (New York: Cambridge University Press, 2018).

6. Herbert Shapiro, *White Violence and Black Response: From Reconstruction to Montgomery* (Amherst: University of Massachusetts Press, 1988).

7. Michael R. Belknap, *Federal Law and Southern Order: Racial Violence and Constitutional Conflict in the Post-Brown South* (Athens: University of Georgia Press, 1987), 229 (second quotation), 234 (third quotation), 250 (first quotation).

8. Gail Williams O'Brien, *The Color of the Law: Race, Violence, and Justice in the Post–World War II South* (Chapel Hill: University of North Carolina Press, 1999), 1 (quotation). O'Brien sketches out her arguments in the introduction and conclusion.

9. Jacquelyn Dowd Hall, "The Long Civil Rights Movement and the Political Uses of the Past," *Journal of American History* 91 (March 2005): 1233–63.

10. Bayard Rustin, "From Protest to Politics: The Future of the Civil Rights Movement," *Commentary* 39 (February 1965): 25–31.

11. On the "long" Civil Rights Movement in Arkansas, see John A. Kirk, *Redefining the Color Line: Black Activism in Little Rock, Arkansas, 1940–1970* (Gainesville: University Press of Florida, 2002).

12. Hall, "The Long Civil Rights Movement."

13. On the Red Summer, see, for example, Jan Voogd, *Race Riots and Resistance: The Red Summer of 1919* (New York: Peter Lang, 2008); Cameron McWhirter, *Red Summer: The Summer of 1919 and the Awakening of Black America* (New York: Henry Holt, 2011); and David F. Krugler, *1919, the Year of Racial Violence: How African Americans Fought Back* (New York: Cambridge University Press, 2015).

14. On the Ku Klux Klan nationwide in the 1920s, see Thomas R. Pegram, *One Hundred Percent American: The Rebirth and Decline of the Ku Klux Klan in the 1920s* (Chicago: Ivan R. Dee, 2011). In Arkansas, see Kenneth C. Barnes, *The Ku Klux Klan in 1920s Arkansas: How Protestant White Nationalism Came to Rule a State* (Fayetteville: University of Arkansas Press, 2021).

15. Useful starting points on the New Deal and civil rights include Ralph J. Bunche, *The Political Status of the Negro in the Age of FDR* (Chicago: University of Chicago Press, 1973); Harvard Sitkoff, *A New Deal for Blacks: The Emergence of Civil Rights as a National Issue: Volume 1: The Depression Decade* (New York: Oxford University Press, 1978); John B. Kirby, *Black Americans in the Roosevelt Era: Liberalism and·Race* (Knoxville: Tennessee University Press, 1980); Nancy J. Weiss, *Farewell to the Party of Lincoln: Black Politics in the Age of FDR* (Princeton: Princeton University Press, 1983); and Patricia Sullivan, *Days of Hope: Race and Democracy in the New Deal Era* (Chapel Hill: University of North Carolina Press, 1996).

16. Useful starting points on World War II and civil rights include Neil R. McMillen, ed., *Remaking Dixie: The Impact of World War II on the American South* (Jackson: University Press of Mississippi, 1997); Daniel Kryder, *Divided Arsenal: Race and the American State during World War II* (New York: Cambridge University Press, 2000); Charles D. Chamberlin, *Victory at Home: Manpower and Race in the American South during World War II* (Athens: University of Georgia Press, 2003); Kevin M. Kruse and Stephen Tuck, eds.,

Fog of War: The Second World War and the Civil Rights Movement (New York: Oxford University Press, 2012); Kimberley L. Phillips, *War! What Is It Good For? Black Freedom Struggles and the U.S. Military from World War II to Iraq* (Chapel Hill: University of North Carolina Press, 2012); Paul Alkebulan, *The African American Press in World War II: Toward Victory at Home and Abroad* (Lanham: Lexington Books, 2014); and Christine Knauer, *Let Us Fight as Free Men: Black Soldiers and Civil Rights* (Philadelphia: University of Pennsylvania Press, 2014).

17. Useful starting points on the intersections of the Cold War, international relations, foreign policy, and civil rights include Brenda Gayle Plummer, *Rising Wind: Black Americans and US Foreign Affairs, 1935–1960* (Chapel Hill: University of North Carolina Press, 1996); Penny Von Eschen, *Race against Empire: Black Americans and Anti-Colonialism, 1937–1957* (Ithaca: Cornell University Press, 1997); Mary L. Dudziak, *Cold War Civil Rights: Race and the Image of American Democracy* (Princeton: Princeton University Press, 2000); Thomas Borstelmann, *The Cold War and the Color Line: American Race Relations in the Global Arena* (Cambridge: Harvard University Press, 2002); Carol Anderson, *Eyes Off the Prize: The United Nations and the African American Struggle for Human Rights, 1944–1955* (New York: Cambridge University Press, 2003); and John Munro, *The Anticolonial Front: The African American Freedom Struggle and Global Decolonization, 1945–1960* (New York: Cambridge University Press, 2017).

18. For a discussion on this point, see Grif Stockley and Jeannie M. Whayne, "Federal Troops and the Elaine Massacres: A Colloquy," *Arkansas Historical Quarterly* 61 (Autumn 2002): 272–83.

19. Belknap, *Federal Law and Southern Order*, chapter 10.

20. On the events surrounding the 1957 desegregation of Central High School, see, for example, Tony A. Freyer, *Little Rock on Trial: Cooper v. Aaron and School Desegregation* (Lawrence: University Press of Kansas, 2007); Elizabeth Jacoway, *Turn away Thy Son: Little Rock, the Crisis that Shocked a Nation* (New York: Free Press, 2007); and Karen Anderson, *Little Rock: Race and Resistance at Central High School* (Princeton: Princeton University Press, 2010).

21. "WR in Arkansas: The Story of Win Rockefeller's Campaign for Governor 1966," 105, in record group IV, box 115, folder 2, Winthrop Rockefeller Collection, Center for Arkansas History and Culture, Bobby L. Roberts Library of History and Art, Little Rock, Arkansas.

22. Winthrop Rockefeller, "Rebel with a Cause," 1970, 3, unpublished book manuscript, record group IV, box 54, folder 4c, Winthrop Rockefeller Collection.

23. On Winthrop Rockefeller and civil rights see John A. Kirk, "A Southern Road Less Travelled: The 1966 Arkansas Gubernatorial Election and (Winthrop) Rockefeller Republicanism in Dixie," in *Painting Dixie Red: When, Where, Why, and How the South Became Republican*, ed. Glenn Feldman (Gainesville: University Press of Florida, 2011), 172–97.

24. Minister Sukhara A. Yahweh (formerly known as Lance Watson) interview with John A. Kirk, January 16, 2019, Forrest City, Arkansas. Interview in author's possession. See also Memphis Police Department, "Lance Watson, Criminal Arrest Record," in record group IV, box 128, folder 9, Winthrop Rockefeller Collection.

25. Yahweh interview. On the Poor People's Campaign, see Ronald L. Freeman, *The

Mule Train: A Journey of Hope Remembered (Nashville: Rutledge Hill Press, 1998); Hilliard Lawrence Lackey, *Marks, Martin and the Mule Train* (Jackson: Town Square Books, 1998); and Gerald D. McKnight, *The Last Crusade: Martin Luther King Jr., the FBI, and the Poor People's Campaign* (Denver: Westview Press, 1998). On King in Memphis, see Michael K. Honey, *Going Down Jericho Road: The Memphis Strike, Martin Luther King's Last Campaign* (New York: W. W. Norton, 2007).

26. On the background to civil rights struggles in Forrest City, see Michael R. Deaderick, "Racial Conflict in Forrest City: The Trial and Triumph of Moderation in an Arkansas Delta Town," *Arkansas Historical Quarterly* 69 (Spring 2010): 1–27.

27. Wayne Jordan, "Police, Reporters Outnumber Blacks as March Begins," *Arkansas Gazette* (Little Rock), August 21, 1969, 1B; Maurice Moore, "Negroes Step Out on Hike," *Arkansas Democrat* (Little Rock), August 20, 1969, 1A, 2A.

28. John Bennett, " 'Fear' March Is Due Today; Brooks Delays Trek by Poor," *Commercial Appeal* (Memphis), August 20, 1969, 3A; Moore, "Negroes Step Out on Hike," 2A; Jordan, "Police, Reporters Outnumber Blacks as March Begins."

29. Jordan, "Police, Reporters Outnumber Blacks as March Begins"; Moore, "Negroes Step Out on Hike," 2A.

30. Moore, "Negroes Step Out on Hike," 2A.

31. Jordan, "Police, Reporters Outnumber Blacks as March Begins."

32. Moore, "Negroes Step Out on Hike," 2A; Jordan, "Police, Reporters Outnumber Blacks as March Begins" (quotations).

33. Jordan, "Police, Reporters Outnumber Blacks As March Begins."

34. The role of the media in the Civil Rights Movement remains a relatively understudied topic. Useful starting points include Allison Graham, *Framing the South: Hollywood, Television, and Race during the Civil Rights Struggle* (Baltimore: Johns Hopkins University Press, 2001); Brian Ward, ed., *Media, Culture, and the Modern African American Freedom Struggle* (Gainesville: University of Florida Press, 2001); Brian Ward, *Radio and the Struggle for Civil Rights in the South* (Gainesville: University Press of Florida, 2004); Alan Nadel, *Television in Black-and-White America: Race and National Identity* (Lawrence: University Press of Kansas, 2005); Aniko Bodroghkozy, *Equal Time: Television and the Civil Rights Movement* (Urbana: University of Illinois Press, 2012); Darryl Mace, *In Remembrance of Emmett Till: Regional Stories and Media Responses to the Black Freedom Struggle* (Lexington: University Press of Kentucky, 2014); and Gayle Wald, *It's Been Beautiful: Soul! and Black Power Television* (Durham: Duke University Press, 2015).

35. Jordan, "Police, Reporters Outnumber Blacks as March Begins."

36. Moore, "Negroes Step Out on Hike," 2A.

37. Maurice Moore, "Tight Security for Walkers," *Arkansas Democrat*, August 21, 1969, 1A, 2A.

38. Jordan, "Police, Reporters Outnumber Blacks as March Begins."

39. Jordan, "Police, Reporters Outnumber Blacks as March Begins."

40. Maurice Moore, "She Backs Negroes, Loses White Friends," *Arkansas Democrat*, August 24, 1969, 1A.

41. Jordan, "Police, Reporters Outnumber Blacks as March Begins."

42. Jordan, "Police, Reporters Outnumber Blacks as March Begins."
43. Jordan, "Police, Reporters Outnumber Blacks as March Begins."
44. Jordan, "Police, Reporters Outnumber Blacks as March Begins."
45. George Douthit, "Rockefeller Says He Vetoed Plan to Jail Leaders of Walkers," *Arkansas Democrat*, August 21, 1969, 1A.
46. Matilda Tuohey, "Hazen Shuts Down; Armed Citizens Block Entry, Mayor Mobilizes, Waits for Watson, 4 Others," *Arkansas Gazette*, August 21, 1969, 1B. See also John Bennett, "Arkansas Town Arms, Barricades in Path of 'March Against Fear,'" *Commercial Appeal*, August 21, 1969, 3A.
47. Matilda Tuohey, "Hazen Shuts Down."
48. Wayne Jordan, "Watson, Group Reach Brinkley on 'Fear Walk,'" *Arkansas Gazette*, August 22, 1969, 1B (quotations); Moore, "Tight Security for Walkers," 2A.
49. Moore, "Tight Security for Walkers," 2A.
50. Jordan, "Watson, Group Reach Brinkley on 'Fear Walk.'"
51. Moore, "Tight Security for Walkers," 2A.
52. Jordan, "Watson, Group Reach Brinkley on 'Fear Walk.'"
53. Jordan, "Watson, Group Reach Brinkley on 'Fear Walk.'"
54. Jordan, "Watson, Group Reach Brinkley on 'Fear Walk.'"
55. Maurice Moore, "'Walk against Fear' Starts at Brinkley about an Hour Late," *Arkansas Democrat*, August 22, 1969, 6A.
56. Wayne Jordan, "White Teen-agers at Hazen Flash 'V' as Watson Passes," *Arkansas Gazette*, August 23, 1969, 3A.
57. John Bennett, "Hazen Mayor Removes Barricades and Guards," *Commercial Appeal*, August 22, 1969, 3A; Jordan, "Watson, Group Reach Brinkley on 'Fear Walk,'" (quotations); "Blacks in Arkansas Conclude 140-mile 'Walk against Fear,'" *New York Times*, August 25, 1969, 25A.
58. Maurice Moore, "Watson Says He'd Boycott Hazen Stores," *Arkansas Democrat*, August 23, 1969, 2A.
59. Jordan, "White Teen-agers at Hazen Flash 'V' as Watson Passes."
60. John Bennett, "Marchers Find Hazen Relaxed," *Commercial Appeal*, August 23, 1969, 3A; Yahweh interview.
61. Jordan, "White Teen-agers at Hazen Flash 'V' as Watson Passes"; "Four March in Arkansas; Town Police Threat Ends," *New York Times*, August 23, 1969, 33A.
62. John Woodruff, "'Beautiful,' Says Wine as Walkers Reach NLR Edge," *Arkansas Gazette*, August 24, 1969, 2A.
63. Woodruff, "'Beautiful,' Says Wine as Walkers Reach NLR Edge"; George Douthit, "'March against Fear' Ends," *Arkansas Democrat*, August 25, 1969, 1A.
64. Woodruff, "'Beautiful,' Says Wine as Walkers Reach NLR Edge," 2A.
65. "Secret Force Reportedly Keeping Marchers under Constant Watch," *Commercial Appeal*, August 24, 3A.
66. Woodruff, "'Beautiful,' Says Wine as Walkers Reach NLR Edge," 2A; "Bobby Brown Joins Sweet Willie Wine's 'Walk against Fear,'" *Arkansas Democrat*, August 24, 1A.
67. Woodruff, "'Beautiful,' Says Wine as Walkers Reach NLR Edge," 2A.
68. Bob Sallee, "Walk's Last Leg Draws Onlookers," *Arkansas Democrat*, August 25, 1969, 2A.
69. Douthit, "'March against Fear' Ends."

70. Mike Trimble and Ernest Dumas, "Capitol Rally Ends 'Walk'; Brooks, Cooley Criticized," *Arkansas Gazette*, August 25, 1A, 2A.

71. Trimble and Dumas, "Capitol Rally Ends 'Walk,'" 1A; "Blacks in Arkansas Conclude 140-mile 'Walk against Fear.'"

72. Deaderick, "Racial Conflict in Forrest City," 16.

73. "Watson, 2 Whites Attacked by Crowd at Forrest City," *Arkansas Gazette*, August 27, 1969, 1A; "Beaten Watson Retraces His Steps," *Commercial Appeal*, August 28, 1969, 23C.

74. "Guard Seals Off Forrest City Area," *Arkansas Gazette*, August 28, 1A; John Bennett, "Guard, State Policemen Clear Downtown Area in Tense Forrest City," *Commercial Appeal*, August 28, 1A; Martin Waldron, "Troops Disperse Arkansas Whites," *New York Times*, August 28, 1969, 26A.

75. Editorial, "When Patience Snaps," *Arkansas Democrat*, August 28, 4A.

76. Martin Waldron, "Whites in Arkansas Town Cry for 'Law and Order,'" *New York Times*, August 29, 14A.

77. "Forrest City Crowd Beats Negro Leader," *Arkansas Democrat*, August 27, 1A.

78. "Watson Plans Freedom Rally September 14," *Arkansas Gazette*, August 31, 1969, 2A.

79. "Watson Agrees to Arrest; Forrest City Rally Quiet," *Arkansas Gazette*, September 15, 1969, 1A.

80. Deaderick, "Racial Conflict in Forrest City," 21–27.

81. Yahweh interview.

CHAPTER 9

1. Freedom Information Service, "Notes on the Condition of the Mississippi Negro—1966," pp. 1, 3, folder 5, box 1, Freedom Information Service Records, Wisconsin Historical Society, Madison.

2. Robert Conn, "MD Finds Children Starving," *Charlotte Observer*, June 16, 1967, 1A, 2A.

3. Alex Waites and Rollie Eubanks, "Mississippi: Poverty, Despair—A Way of Life," Report Prepared for 58th Annual Convention [of the NAACP], July 13, 1967, pp. 4–5, folder "NAACP National Convention, Boston, Mass., July 10–15 [1967]," box 5, Program Records of the Assistant Director for Civil Rights, 1965–68, Office of Civil Rights, Office of Economic Opportunity, Record Group 381, National Archives, College Park, MD.

4. [Mississippi Freedom Democratic Party], "A Statement," n.d. [ca. 1966], p. 1, item 2, reel 2, Mississippi Freedom Democratic Party Records, microfilm, Wisconsin Historical Society, Madison.

5. Kenneth G. Slocum, "Ballots and Jobs," *Wall Street Journal*, May 7, 1965, 1, 18, esp. 18.

6. Joseph Meissner and Steven R. Nelson, "The Mississippi Challenge: Some Questions and Answers," August 8, 1965, p. 4, item 2, reel 2, MFDP Records.

7. Joseph Brenner et al., "Children in Mississippi: A Report to the Field Foundation," June 1967, p. 7, encl. in William Ling to Jule Sugarman, memorandum, June 27, 1967, folder "Administrative—Mississippi—1967," box 16, State Files, 1965–68, Records of the Director, Community Action Program Office,

Office of Economic Opportunity, Record Group 381, National Archives, College Park, MD.

8. Testimony of Raymond Wheeler, Subcommittee on Employment, Manpower, and Poverty of the Senate Committee on Labor and Public Welfare, *Hunger and Malnutrition in America*, 90th Cong., 1st sess., July 11–12, 1967, p. 8.

9. Greta de Jong, *You Can't Eat Freedom: Southerners and Social Justice after the Civil Rights Movement* (Chapel Hill: University of North Carolina Press, 2016), 34–35, 41–43.

10. Stokely Carmichael and Charles V. Hamilton, *Black Power: The Politics of Liberation in America* (New York: Random House, 1967), 4.

11. Coretta Scott King, "Solidarity Day Address to the Poor People's Campaign," June 19, 1968, 15:50–16:42, accessed May 18, 2021, https://pastdaily.com/2013/06/19/solidarity-day-coretta-scott-king-june-19-1968/.

12. de Jong, *You Can't Eat Freedom*, 62–87.

13. Strom Thurmond, " 'Poor' Excuse for Revolution," *Citizen*, December 1967, 14. Copies of *Citizen* can be found at Archives and Special Collections, University of Mississippi, Oxford.

14. Anthony Harrigan, "Producers Dwindle as Drones Multiply," *Citizen*, June 1972, 19–21.

15. George W. Shannon, "U.S. Blacks on Relief Shun Work; Jamaicans Take Jobs," *Citizen*, November 1977, 11–4.

16. George Andrews to G. P. Brock, July 28, 1964, p. 1, folder "Correspondence, July 28, 1964," box 27, George W. Andrews Papers, Special Collections and Archives Department, Draughon Library, Auburn University, Alabama.

17. Thomas G. Abernethy to C. B. Curlee, July 29, 1965, p. 1, cons. w/ Abernethy to Curlee, August 2, 1965, folder "Office of Economic Opportunity, General, 1965–1966," box 161, Thomas G. Abernethy Papers, Archives and Special Collections, University of Mississippi, Oxford.

18. Pearl Rodgers to John C. Stennis, April 14, 1967, p. 1, folder "Economic Opportunity, General Correspondence," box 2, ser. 25, John C. Stennis Collection, Congressional and Political Research Center, Mississippi State University Libraries, Starkville.

19. Walter D. Smith, Executive Director, "Overall Summary Statement," in Mississippi Action for Progress, Comprehensive Narrative Report, October 31, 1966–April 28, 1967, p. 2, unfoldered, box 1, 1998 Addition, Hodding Carter III Papers, Special Collections Department, Mississippi State University Libraries, Starkville.

20. Gloster B. Current, "Death in Mississippi," *Crisis*, February 1966, 103–6; "Another Murder in Mississippi," *Delta Ministry*, January 1966, 2, folder 6, box 2A, Allen Eugene Cox Collection, Special Collections Department, Mississippi State University Libraries, Starkville.

21. Citizens' Board of Inquiry, Citizens' Crusade Against Poverty, "Final Report on the Child Development Group of Mississippi," n.d. [October 1966], p. 15, folder 18, box 23, Papers of the Scholarship, Education and Defense Fund for Racial Equality, Wisconsin Historical Society, Madison.

22. John Zippert to Robert Owen, June 15, 1966, pp. 1–2, folder 11, box 42, Records of the Federation of Southern Cooperatives, Amistad Research Center, Tulane University, New Orleans, LA.

23. "St. Helena School Aud. Burned Down," *Louisiana Weekly*, June 11, 1966, sect. 1, p. 7.

24. Noel H. Klores to Theodore Berry, memorandum, March 13, 1967, p. 1, folder "Lowndes Co. Christ. Mvmt.," box 6, Grant Files, 1966–71, Migrant Division, Office of Operations, Office of Economic Opportunity, Record Group 381, National Archives, College Park, MD.

25. Selma Inter-Religious Project, *Newsletter*, April 12, 1967, p. 2, folder "Southwest Ala. Farmers Co-op (Shirley Mesher)," box 12, ser. 81-4, William F. Nichols Papers, Special Collections and Archives Department, Draughon Library, Auburn University, AL.

26. Theo James Pinnock and G. W. Taylor, "Tuskegee Institute–OEO Seasonally Employed Agricultural Workers Educational Project, Summary of Accomplishments and Disappointments, November 1, 1966–October 31, 1967," pp. 20–21, folder "Miscellaneous Alabama 8539," box 3, Migrant Division, Office of Operations.

27. Grady Poulard to Maurice A. Dawkins, memorandum, April 4, 1967, p. 1, folder "CVR: Poulard (in-office memos)," box 7, Program Records of the Assistant Director for Civil Rights.

28. "Text of President's Civil Rights Message to Congress Asking Open Housing Law," *New York Times*, February 16, 1967, 28–29.

29. Civil Rights Act of 1968, Pub. L. No. 90–284, 82 Stat. 73, accessed May 18, 2021, https://www.govinfo.gov/content/pkg/STATUTE-82/pdf/STATUTE-82-Pg73 .pdf.

30. "Freedom Candidates," *MFDP News Letter*, June 22, 1968, p. 2, item 11, reel 3, MFDP Records.

31. "West Point Mayoral Runoff," *Delta Ministry Reports*, August/September 1970, 2; "Self-Defense?" *Delta Ministry Reports*, November 1971, p. 2, both in folder 19, box 1, 1972 Addendum, Cox Collection.

32. Donald T. Moss to John Mitchell, July 23, 1971, p. 1, folder "Community Action Program of Caddo and Bossier Parishes," box 2, Inspection and Investigation Files, 1969–74, General Counsel, Office of Economic Opportunity, Record Group 381, National Archives, College Park, MD.

33. P. G. Tunde Balogun to Edward Levi, June 28, 1976, p. 3, folder "7 Department of Justice (General)," box 5, ser. 82-1, Nichols Papers.

34. "A Letter from the Director," *The Council Newsletter*, November 1978, p. 1, folder 13, box 14, Marjorie Baroni Collection, Archives and Special Collections, University of Mississippi, Oxford.

35. "Sumrall Convicted," *Hinds County FDP News Letter*, July 21, 1967, p. 1, item 12, reel 3, MFDP Records.

36. Mississippi Freedom Democratic Party, "Issues in 1968 for Mississippi," p. 1, pamphlet, item 2, reel 2, MFDP Records.

37. Sargent Shriver quoted in Leon Howell, *Freedom City: The Substance of Things Hoped For* (Richmond: John Knox Press, 1969), 121.

38. King, "Solidarity Day Address," 22:06–23:53.

39. Ashton P. Roberthon to Russell B. Long, August 10, 1967, p. 5, folder 5, box 103, Russell B. Long Papers, Hill Memorial Library, Louisiana State University, Baton Rouge.

40. Dorothy E. Fanyo to Thomas Abernethy, March 18, 1966, p. 1 and Abernethy to

Fanyo, March 22, 1966, p. 1, folder "Office of Economic Opportunity, General, 1965–1966," box 161, Abernethy Papers.

41. John Stennis, "Address to Joint Session of Mississippi Legislature," January 27, 1966, p. 8, folder 10, box 119, Paul B. Johnson Family Papers, McCain Library and Archives, University of Southern Mississippi, Hattiesburg.

42. Stephen Daggett, *Costs of Major U.S. Wars* (Washington, DC: Congressional Research Service, June 29, 2010), https://fas.org/sgp/crs/natsec/RS22926.pdf, 2.

43. "Federation/LAF History from the 25th Annual Report (1992)," Federation of Southern Cooperatives website, accessed October 3, 2021, https://web.archive .org/web/20121004004152/http://www.federationsoutherncoop.com/fschistory /FSC25hist.pdf.

44. U.S. Bureau of the Census, *Statistical Abstract of the United States: 1980* (Washington, DC: Government Printing Office, 1980), 261 (Table 436).

45. U.S. Bureau of the Census, *Statistical Abstract of the United States: 1990* (Washington, DC: Government Printing Office, 1990), 310–11 (Table 499).

46. U.S. Bureau of the Census, *Statistical Abstract of the United States: 1990* (Washington, DC: Government Printing Office, 1990), 458 (Table 743).

47. U.S. Bureau of the Census, *Statistical Abstract of the United States: 2012* (Washington, DC: Government Printing Office, 2011), 310 (Table 470), accessed May 18, 2021, https://www2.census.gov/library/publications/2011/compendiá /statab/131ed/tables/fedgov.pdf.

48. "'Welfare Queen' Becomes Issue in Reagan Campaign," *New York Times*, February 15, 1976, 51; "Negro 'Welfare Queen' Found Guilty of Fraud," *Citizen*, November 1977, 21.

49. George W. Shannon, "New Welfare Queen's Story Spotlights National Fraud," *Citizen*, May 1979, 4–5.

50. "New Hope for America," Editorial, *Citizen*, December 1980, 2.

51. Dan Donahue quoted in Thomas Byrne Edsall with Mary D. Edsall, *Chain Reaction: The Impact of Race, Rights, and Taxes on American Politics*, rev. ed. (New York: W. W. Norton, 1992), 6.

52. Bill Clinton, "The New Covenant: Responsibility in the American Community," speech at Georgetown University, October 23, 1991, 11:34–13:28, transcript, accessed May 18, 2021, https://www.c-span.org/video/?23518-1/clinton -campaign-speech.

53. Lawrence Mishel and Julia Wolfe, "CEO Compensation Has Grown 940% Since 1978," Economic Policy Institute, August 14, 2019, accessed May 18, 2021, https:// www.epi.org/files/pdf/171191.pdf, 1.

54. Chuck Collins and Josh Hoxie, *Billionaire Bonanza: The Forbes 400 and the Rest of Us*, Economic Policy Institute, November 2019, accessed May 18, 2021, https:// inequality.org/wp-content/uploads/2017/11/BILLIONAIRE-BONANZA-2017 -Embargoed.pdf, 2, 14, 16.

55. Governors of the Federal Reserve System, *Report on the Economic Well-Being of U.S. Households in 2018*, Executive Summary, May 2019, accessed May 18, 2021, https://www.federalreserve.gov/publications/2019-economic-well-being-of -us-households-in-2018-executive-summary.htm.

56. Anne Case and Angus Deaton, quoted in Jeff Guo, "The Disease Killing White Americans Goes Way Deeper than Opioids," *Washington Post*, March 24, 2017, accessed May 18, 2021, https://www.washingtonpost.com/news/wonk/wp/2017 /03/24/the-disease-killing-white-americans-goes-way-deeper-than-opioids/.

57. Neta C. Crawford, "United States Budgetary Costs and Obligations of Post–9/11 Wars through FY2020: $6.4 Trillion," November 13, 2019, Costs of War Project Website, Watson Institute of International & Public Affairs, Brown University, accessed May 18, 2021, https://watson.brown.edu/costsofwar/files/cow/imce /papers/2019/US%20Budgetary%20Costs%20of%20Wars%20November%20 2019.pdf, 1, 6; Heidi Garrett-Peltier, "War Spending and Lost Opportunities," March 2019, Costs of War Project Website, Watson Institute of International & Public Affairs, Brown University, accessed May 18, 2021, https://watson .brown.edu/costsofwar/files/cow/imce/papers/2019/March%202019%20Job %20Opportunity%20Cost%20of%20War.pdf, p. 2.

58. Special Inspector General for Afghanistan Reconstruction, *Corruption in Conflict: Lessons from the U.S. Experience in Afghanistan,* September 2016, accessed May 18, 2021, https://www.sigar.mil/pdf/lessonslearned/SIGAR-16 -58-LL-Executive-Summary.pdf, 8–12 (quotation p. 10).

59. Craig Whitlock, "Consumed by Corruption: Built to Fail," *Washington Post,* December 9, 2019, A1, accessed May 18, 2021, https://www.washingtonpost .com/graphics/2019/investigations/afghanistan-papers/afghanistan-war -corruption-government/.

60. Congressional Budget Office, *Federal Investment, 1962–2018,* June 2019, accessed May 18, 2021, https://www.cbo.gov/system/files/2019-06/55375 -Federal_Investment.pdf, 17 (Exhibit 9).

61. Jessica Semega et al., *Income and Poverty in the United States: 2018,* Current Population Reports, September 2019, accessed May 18, 2021, https://www .census.gov/content/dam/Census/library/publications/2019/demo/p60-266. pdf, pp. 50 (Table B-1), 52 (Table B-3); Alisha Coleman-Jensen et al., *Household Food Security in the United States in 2018,* U.S. Department of Agriculture, Economic Research Service, Report no. 270, September 2019, accessed May 18, 2021, https://www.ers.usda.gov/webdocs/publications/94849 /err-270.pdf?v=963.1, p. 15 (Table 2).

EPILOGUE

1. Lyrics used by permission from *My Daddy's Blues* CD, Doctor G and the Mudcats, Cheatham Street Records, San Marcos, TX. Gregg's most recent book is *My Daddy's Blues: A Childhood Memoir from the Land of Huck and Jim* (San Marcos: Mudcat Press, 2019). His other books include *Shoulder to Shoulder? The American Federation of Labor, the United States, and the Mexican Revolution, 1910–1924* (Berkeley: University of California Press, 1991); *City of Dust: A Cement Company Town in the Land of Tom Sawyer* (Columbia: University of Missouri Press, 1996); *Insane Sisters: Or, the Price Paid for Challenging a Company Town* (Columbia: University of Missouri Press, 1999); and *Thyra J. Edwards: Black Activist in the Global Freedom Struggle* (Columbia: University of Missouri Press, 2011).

2. David F. Kugler, *1919, The Year of Racial Violence: How African Americans Fought Back* (New York: Cambridge University Press, 2015).

3. Robert Whitaker, *On the Laps of Gods: The Red Summer of 1919 and the Struggle for Justice That Remade a Nation* (New York: Crown, 2008), tells the story in the most cinematic way. Other sources include Grif Stockley, *Blood in Their Eyes: The Elaine Race Massacre of 1919* (Fayetteville: University of Arkansas Press,

2001); Robert C. Cortner, *A Mob Intent on Death: The NAACP and the Arkansas Riot Cases* (Middletown: Wesleyan University Press, 1988); Guy Lancaster, ed., *The Elaine Massacre and Arkansas: A Century of Atrocity and Resistance, 1819–1919* (Little Rock: Butler Center Books, 2018), especially Cherisse Jones-Branch, "Women and the 1919 Elaine Massacre," 176–200. A treatment still worth reading is Kieran Taylor, " 'We Have Just Begun': Black Organizing and White Response in the Arkansas Delta, 1919," *Arkansas Historical Quarterly* 58 (Autumn 1999): 264–85. Michael Honey, "Class, Race, and Power in the New South: Racial Violence and the Delusions of White Supremacy," in *Democracy Betrayed: The Wilmington Race Riot of 1898 and Its Legacy*, ed. David Cecelski and Timothy Tyson, with a Foreword by John Hope Franklin (Chapel Hill: University of North Carolina Press, 1998), 163–84; David Zucchino, *Wilmington's Lie: The Murderous Coup of 1898 and the Rise of White Supremacy* (New York: Atlantic Monthly Press, 2020). The racial violence in Elaine is all too American, as Walter Johnson details in *The Broken Heart of America: St. Louis and the Violent History of the United States* (New York: Basic Books, 2020).

4. Martin Luther King Jr., "Showdown for Nonviolence," *Look*, April 16, 1968, 23–25; Tom Hanks, "You Should Learn the Truth about the Tulsa Greenwood Massacre," *New York Times*, June 4, 2021.

5. Moon Ho-Jung, ed., *The Rising Tide of Color: Race, State Violence, and Radical Movements across the Pacific* (Seattle: University of Washington Press, 2014); Beth Lew-Williams, *The Chinese Must Go: Violence, Exclusion, and the Making of the Alien in America* (Cambridge: Harvard University Press, 2018).

6. Joe William Trotter Jr., in *Workers on Arrival: Black Labor in the Making of America* (Berkeley: University of California Press, 2019), places American racial violence in the context of Black proletarianization and labor organizing.

7. Scott Elsworth, *The Ground Breaking: An American City and Its Search for Justice* (New York: Dutton, 2021); Tim Madigan, *The Burning: Massacre, Destruction, and the Tulsa Race Riot of 1927* (New York: St. Martin's Press, 2001).

8. W. E. B. Du Bois, *Black Reconstruction in America: An Essay toward a History of the Part Which Black Folk Played in the Attempt to Reconstruct Democracy in America, 1860–1880* (New York: Harcourt, Brace and Company, 1935).

9. Roger Horowitz, *Negro and White, Unite and Fight! A Social History of Industrial Unionism in Meatpacking, 1930–90* (Urbana: University of Illinois Press, 1997); Rick Halpern, *Down on the Killing Floor: Black and White Workers in Chicago's Packinghouses, 1905–54* (University of Illinois Press, 1997); Rick Halpern and Roger Horowitz, *Meatpackers: An Oral History of Black Packinghouse Workers and Their Struggle for Racial and Economic Equality* (New York: Monthly Review Press, 1999).

10. See, e.g., Robin D. G. Kelley, *Hammer and Hoe: Alabama Communists during the Great Depression* (Chapel Hill: University of North Carolina Press, 1990, 2015), and Michael K. Honey, *Southern Labor and Black Civil Rights: Organizing Memphis Workers* (Urbana: University of Illinois Press, 1993).

11. See Michael K. Honey, *Sharecropper's Troubadour: John L. Handcox, the Southern Tenant Farmers' Union, and the African American Song Tradition* (New York: Palgrave Macmillan, 2013), for song lyrics, poems and details that follow. See also the book's bibliography on the STFU and its history in the Arkansas Delta.

12. See Jeannie Whayne's "Henry Lowery Lynching: A Legacy of the Elaine Massacre?" in this volume, and Nan Woodruff, *American Congo: The African American Freedom Struggle in the Delta* (Cambridge: Harvard University Press, 2003), 92–105, 110–12, 132, 136.

13. Honey's notes in *Sharecroppers' Troubadour* provide a sampling of the literature on the Southern Farmers' Tenant Union, including Donald Grubbs, *Cry from the Cotton: The Southern Tenant Farmers' Union and the New Deal* (Chapel Hill: University of North Carolina Press, 1971); Woodruff, *American Congo*; Jeannie M. Whayne, *A New Plantation South: Land, Labor, and Federal Favor in Twentieth-Century Arkansas* (Charlottesville: University of Virginia Press, 1996); Jarod Roll, *A Spirit of Rebellion: Labor and Religion in the New Cotton South* (Urbana: University of Illinois Press, 2010); and James D. Ross, *The Rise and Fall of the Southern Tenant Farmers Union in Arkansas* (Knoxville: University of Tennessee Press, 2018).

14. Matt Simmons, "Revolt in the Fields: Building the Southern Tenant Farmers' Union in the Old Southwest" (PhD diss., University of Florida, 2019).

15. Alan Lomax, Pete Seeger, and Woody Guthrie, *Hard-Hitting Songs for Hard-Hit People* (New York: Oak Publications, 1967).

16. Ed King quoted in *Sharecroppers' Troubadour*, 154.

17. Michael Honey, "Earle Reacts to Desegregation," *Southern Patriot*, October 1970, 8.

18. Michael K. Honey, *Southern Labor and Black Civil Rights*; Honey, *Black Workers Remember: An Oral History of Segregation, Unionism, and the Freedom Struggle* (Berkeley: University of California Press, 1999); Honey, *Going Down Jericho Road: The Memphis Strike, Martin Luther King's Last Campaign* (New York: W. W. Norton, 2001); Honey, *To the Promised Land: Martin Luther King and the Fight for Economic Justice* (New York: W. W. Norton: 2018).

19. Michael Pierce, "Odell Smith, Teamsters Local 878, and Civil Rights Unionism in Little Rock," *Journal of Southern History* 84 (November 2018): 925–58.

20. Elaine had a population as high as 1,200 as recently as 1970, but this number has dropped to about 500 people at the centennial of the massacre in 2019; U.S. Bureau of the Census, "2019 Gazetteer Files," accessed May 19, 2021, https://www2.census.gov/geo/docs/maps-data/data/gazetteer/2019_Gazetteer/2019_gaz_place_05.txt. Rev. Mary Olson, president of the Elaine Legacy Center, and others are trying to mark the racial disasters but struggling with collapsing buildings and fleeing people. "More Than Memorials in Elaine," *Arkansas Times*, August 4, 2019, accessed May 19, 2021, https://arktimes.com/news/cover-stories/2019/08/04/more-than-memorials-in-elaine. The Legacy Center was the group that, in August 2019, had planted the tree that got cut down. In the same period, vandals once again shot holes in the marker of the Emmett Till lynching in Mississippi. Lateshia Beachum, "A Massacre of Blacks Haunted This Arkansas City. Then a Memorial Tree Was Cut Down," *Washington Post*, August 30, 2019, accessed May 19, 2021, https://www.washingtonpost.com/history/2019/08/30/massacre-blacks-haunted-this-arkansas-city-then-someone-cut-down-memorial-tree/.

GRETA DE JONG is a Foundation Professor of History at the University of Nevada, Reno. Her research focuses on the connections between race and class and the ways that African Americans have fought for economic justice as well as political rights from the end of Reconstruction through the twenty-first century. She is the author of *A Different Day: African American Struggles for Justice in Rural Louisiana, 1900–1970* (University of North Carolina Press, 2002); *Invisible Enemy: The African American Freedom Struggle after 1965* (Wiley-Blackwell, 2010); and *You Can't Eat Freedom: Southerners and Social Justice after the Civil Rights Movement* (University of North Carolina Press, 2016).

MATTHEW HILD is a Lecturer in the School of History and Sociology at the Georgia Institute of Technology. His books include *Greenbackers, Knights of Labor, and Populists: Farmer-Labor Insurgency in the Late-Nineteenth-Century South* (University of Georgia Press, 2007) and *Arkansas's Gilded Age: The Rise, Decline, and Legacy of Populism and Working-Class Protest* (University of Missouri Press, 2018). More recently, he is co-editor, with Michael Gagnon, of *Gwinnett County, Georgia, and the Transformation of the American South, 1818–2018* (University of Georgia Press, 2022).

MICHAEL HONEY, Haley Professor of Humanities, University of Washington Tacoma, is a recent Radcliffe/Harvard Institute and Guggenheim fellow. His six books have won numerous awards from human rights and history organizations, including the Robert F. Kennedy Book Award. The most recent are *To the Promised Land: Martin Luther King and the Fight for Economic Justice* (W. W. Norton, 2018), *Sharecropper's Troubadour: John L. Handcox, the Southern Tenant Farmers' Union, and the African American Song Tradition* (Palgrave Macmillan, 2013), and *Going Down Jericho Road: The Memphis Strike, Martin Luther King's Last Campaign* (W. W. Norton, 2007). He is also producer and director of the film *Love and Solidarity: Rev. James Lawson and Nonviolence in the Search for Workers' Rights* (Bullfrog Films, 2016) and co-editor of

James M. Lawson Jr.'s *Revolutionary Nonviolence: Organizing for Freedom* (University of California Press, 2022).

CHERISSE JONES-BRANCH is the James and Wanda Lee Vaughn Professor of History and Dean of the Graduate School at Arkansas State University–Jonesboro. She received her BA and MA from the College of Charleston, South Carolina, and a doctorate in history from Ohio State University. Jones-Branch is the author of *Crossing the Line: Women and Interracial Activism in South Carolina during and after World War II* (University Press of Florida, 2014) and *Better Living by Their Own Bootstraps: Black Women's Activism in Rural Arkansas, 1913–1965* (University of Arkansas Press, 2021). She co-edited *Arkansas Women: Their Lives and Times* (University of Georgia Press, 2018).

JOHN A. KIRK is the George W. Donaghey Distinguished Professor of History at the University of Arkansas at Little Rock. He taught at the University of Wales and the University of London in the United Kingdom before moving to UA Little Rock in the summer of 2010. Kirk served for five years as chair of the History Department and for four years as director of the Anderson Institute on Race and Ethnicity. His research focuses primarily on the history of the Civil Rights Movement. Kirk has published ten books including the award-winning *Redefining the Color Line: Black Activism in Little Rock, Arkansas, 1940–1970* (University Press of Florida, 2002), *The Civil Rights Movement: A Documentary Reader* (Wiley-Blackwell, 2020), and *Winthrop Rockefeller: From New Yorker to Arkansawyer, 1912–1956* (University of Arkansas Press, 2022).

GUY LANCASTER is the editor of the online Encyclopedia of Arkansas, a project of the Central Arkansas Library System, and the author, co-author, or editor of several books on racial violence, including *Racial Cleansing in Arkansas, 1883–1924: Politics, Land, Labor, and Criminality* (Lexington Books, 2014), *Bullets and Fire: Lynching and Authority in Arkansas, 1840–1950* (University of Arkansas Press, 2018), *The Elaine Massacre and Arkansas: A Century of Atrocity and Resistance, 1819–1919* (Butler Center Books, 2018), the revised edition of *Blood in Their Eyes: The Elaine Massacre of 1919* (University of Arkansas Press, 2020), and *American Atrocity: The Types of Violence in Lynching* (University of Arkansas Press, 2021).

WILLIAM H. PRUDEN III is the director of civic engagement and an instructor in history and social studies at Ravenscroft School in Raleigh, North Carolina. He earned an AB in history from Princeton University, a JD from Case Western Reserve University, and master's degrees from Wesleyan University and Indiana University. He has done stints as a legislative assistant to both a state senator and a member of the U.S. House of Representatives. He has written widely on U.S. history and politics, contributing chapters to several books as well writing op-eds and hundreds of articles for historical encyclopedias and reference works.

JEANNIE WHAYNE, University Professor of History at the University of Arkansas, is author of *Delta Empire: Lee Wilson and the Transformation of Southern Agriculture* (Louisiana State University Press, 2011) as well as author, co-author, or editor of nine other books. She has published more than a dozen articles and book chapters, including "Low Villains and Wickedness in High Places: Race and Class in the Elaine Race Riot," and, with Grif Stockley, "Federal Troops and the Elaine Massacres: A Colloquy." She is distinguished lecturer with the Organization of American Historians and recipient of several research and teaching awards, including the Charles and Nadine Baum Award for Excellence in Teaching in 2020.

MICHAEL VINSON WILLIAMS is the director of the African American Studies Program and Professor of History at the University of Texas at El Paso. He earned his BA in history and sociology and his MA and PhD in history from the University of Mississippi. His research and teaching interests include social and political resistance movements, grassroots activism, Civil Rights struggle and conflict, Black intellectuals and radicalism, and various aspects of African history. He has spoken extensively on the Civil Rights movement and has received numerous awards and recognition for his scholarship, teaching, and community service. Williams is the author of *Medgar Evers: Mississippi Martyr* (University of Arkansas Press, 2011) and has publications in *The Griot: The Journal of African American Studies*; *International Journal of Africana Studies*; *Journal of Mississippi History*; a co-authored work in the *Journal of Borderlands Studies*; and a contributing essay in the anthology *The Civil Rights Movement in Mississippi* (University Press of Mississippi, 2013).

Index

Abernethy, Thomas, 157, 161
Act 112 of 1909, 6, 31, 39–41, 47–48, 62
Act 258 of 1909, 31
Adkins, Homer, 5
African American fraternal organizations, 78–79. *See also* Garvey clubs; African American Odd Fellows; Knights of Pythias
African American Odd Fellows, 66, 71, 72, 77
African American soldiers, 10, 170
African Americans, expulsion of, 5, 25, 30, 35–36, 42, 43
Agricultural Wheel, 16–17, 19–20, 22, 24, 26–27. *See also* Colored State Wheel
Aid to Dependent Children, 115–16, 128
Aiken, Charles, 122
American Congo, 67, 68
American Federation of Labor, 25, 131, 106, 108
American Friends Service Committee, 154
"American Lynching, An" (NAACP), 66, 76
Anderson, Dorothy, 92
Andrews, George, 156–57, 168
anti-poverty programs, 10, 160, 162–66. *See also* Aid to Dependent Children; Community Action Programs (CAPs); Head Start; War on Poverty; welfare
Arkansas AFL-CIO, 131
Arkansas Civil Rights Act of 1873, 15
Arkansas Cooperative Extension Service, 121
Arkansas Council of Church Women (ACCW), 125–26, 131
Arkansas Council of Churches, 125
Arkansas County, AR, 43
Arkansas Democrat (Little Rock), 22–23, 36, 45, 82, 90, 148; on nightriders, 37, 39, 41, 44
Arkansas Department of Public Welfare, 123
Arkansas Employment Security Division, 125
Arkansas Farmers' Union, 37–38
Arkansas Gazette (Little Rock), 84, 88, 122, 142–44; on nightriders, 32, 34, 35, 37, 38, 40
Arkansas General Assembly, 6, 15, 31, 39, 40
Arkansas National Guard, 47, 138, 142, 148
Arkansas State Capitol, 146–47
Arkansas State Farm for Women, 84
Arkansas State Federation of Labor, 25
Arkansas State Police, 140, 143–45, 147
Arkansas Supreme Court, 47
Arkansas Valley Cotton Oil Company, 38
arson, 49, 157–58, 160; of houses, 34, 45–46, 49, 86
Associated Negro Press, 99
Association of Colored Women (AACW), 92–93
Atlanta Constitution, 22

back-to-Africa movement, 25, 78–79
Baker, H. L., 35
Baker, Kenny, 140, 143
Banks, Henry, 34
Barnes, Kenneth C., 19, 25, 79
Barnett, J. W., 46
Barnhart, Ralph, 139–40
Bateman, Tom, 35
Beavers, Henry, 41
Beavers, John, 42
Becker, J. Bill, 131–32
Beckert, Sven, 67

Beittel, A. D., 154
Belknap, Michael R., 134, 135, 138, 149
Bell, Jim, 34
Benton, AR, 140
Berry, Daina Ramey, 87
Birmingham (AL) church bombing, 155
"Black codes," 69
Black Patch War, 39
Black power, 133, 139, 141, 145
Black Power (Carmichael and
    Hamilton), 155
Black United Youth (BUY), 146
Black, Artie, 88
Black, George, 32
Blackwood, Dwight, 73–74, 76–77
Blytheville, AR, 77–78, 131
Boardman, Helen, 106–7, 108
boll weevils, 71, 92
Bonanza Race War, 25
Boone, Wide, 141
bootlegging, 7, 87, 93
Bossier Parish, LA, 159
Bowman, E., 45–46
Bowman, Heeke, 45–46
Boy Scouts of America, 99
Boyett v. United States (1907), 61–62
bracero program, 9, 118–19, 122–23, 125,
    131. See also Mexican Labor Bill
Bradley, Joseph, 54–55
Brandywine Island, AR, 32–33
Branton, Wiley, 123–24
Breckinridge, Clifton R., 19
Brewer, David, 57–58, 59–60, 62
Brinkley, AR, 144
Broadway, George, 42
Brooks, Cato, Jr., 139–40, 147, 148
Brotherhood of Sleeping Car
    Porters, 96
Brothers of Freedom, 16. See also
    Agricultural Wheel
Brough, Charles Hillman, 43–44, 138
Brown, Bobby, 146, 147
Brown, J. H., 49
Brown, Joe, 35
Brown, Lyle, 109
Brown, Mareva, 145
Brundage, W. Fitzhugh, 30
Buffington, John, 159

Burke, R. C., 34
Bush, J. R., 41
Byrd, Bertha, 90

Caddo Parish, LA, 159
Caldwell, Lewis, Jr., 112
Calhoun, Joe, 140, 143
Calhoun County, AR, 5
Camp Pike, AR, 87, 91
Card, Claudia, 31
Carmichael, Stokely, 133, 155
Carolene Products (1938), 63
Carter, Mary, 89
Case, Anne, 164
Cat Island, AR, 13, 24, 25
Catcher Race Riot of 1923, 47
Chained in Silence (LeFlouria), 83
Chicago, IL, 163
Chicago Defender, 76, 96, 102, 109–10,
    112
Chicago Housing Authority, 163
Child Development Group of
    Mississippi, 157
Chisenhall, J. P., 33–34
Churchpoint, LA, 158
Citizen, 156, 162–63
Citizens' Councils of America, 156
Citizens Opposed to Starvation
    Taxes, 146
Civil Rights Act of 1866, 7, 50, 58
Civil Rights Cases (1883), 54–55, 59
Civil Rights Movement, 10–11, 135–37,
    141, 177
Clampit, William, 53, 56
Clark, Henry, 86
Clark County, AR, 90. See also Gurdon,
    AR
Clarke, James P., 52
Clayton, John M., 19
Clover Bend, AR, 29
coal miners, 16, 25
Cogbill, Tebo, 119, 124
Colbert, Hess, 32–33
Cold War, 137. See also Vietnam War
Collier, J. M., 90–91
Collins, Salina, 86–87
Color of the Law (O'Brien), 134–35

Colored Advisory Commission, 103
Colored Farmers' Alliance, 13–14, 20–25
Colored Farmers' Union, 26
Colored State Wheel, 21, 25. *See also*
　Agricultural Wheel
Commercial Appeal (Memphis, TN), 95
Community Action Programs (CAPs),
　155–56, 158, 159
Community Civic Club, 124
Congress of Industrial Organiza-
　tions, 127, 129; Political Action
　Committee (CIO PAC), 116–17,
　126–27, 130, 172
Congress of Racial Equality
　(CORE), 158
Congress Opposing Belligerent
　Revolutionary Action
　(COBRA), 146
Conner, Laura, 81, 82
conscription of Black labor, 99–101
Cook, Jess, 42
Cooley, James F., 139–40, 147, 148
Coolidge, Calvin, 104
Cooper, Peter, 16
Corbin, Henry, 77–78
Costs of War Project, 164–65
cotton agriculture, 7, 67–68, 79, 178.
　See also plantation agriculture;
　mechanization of agriculture
Cotton Pickers' Strike of 1891, 5–6,
　13, 14, 22–25
Cotton Planters' Association, 23
cotton prices, 45, 69, 71, 92
Cotton-Pickers' League, 22
Counce, A. L., 36–37
Coward, John, 46
Cox, J. S., 36
Craig, Hugh, 72, 75
Craig, Oscar, 65, 69, 72
Craig, Richard "Dick," 71–72, 75
Craighead County, AR, 36–37, 38, 41,
　42, 45–46. *See also* Lake City, AR;
　Jonesboro, AR
Crawford County, AR, 47
Crenshaw, Cornelia, 146–147
criminality, 34, 38, 76; allegations cast
　upon African Americans, 30, 81,
　83–93. *See also* prisons

Crisis, The, 96, 107–9
Crittenden, Joseph, 146
Crittenden County, AR, 24, 45, 78, 177.
　See also Brandywine Island, AR;
　Cat Island, AR; Earle, AR; Marion,
　AR; West Memphis, AR
Crittenden County jail, 77
Cromwell, Oliver, 20–21
Cross County, AR, 6, 46, 49. *See also*
　Hickory Ridge, AR
Cummins Prison Farm, AR, 81, 119
Cunningham, Charles F., 19

Dahmer, Vernon, 157
*Daily Arkansas Gazette. See Arkansas
　Gazette*
Daily Clarion-Ledger (Jackson, MS), 98
Davis, Jim, 6, 50
Dawson, Ethel, 9, 125–26, 129, 132; early
　life, 117–18; voter mobilization,
　124, 127
day labor, 22, 123, 130, 174–75. *See also*
　sharecropping
Day, Richard, 122
Deaton, Angus, 164
debt, and foreclosure, 33–34, 173.
　See also peonage
Deeson, MS, 103
Delta and Pine Land Company, 102–3
Delta Ministry, 157
Democratic Party, 9, 14, 124, 138–39,
　163; election of 1928, 105–6, 111; as
　one-party system, 5, 29–30; voter
　harassment by, 15, 19, 159
Dern, George H., 109–10, 111
Dewees, Mary, 84
Dickson, D. H., 73–74
Dilworth, Carrie, 176
disfranchisement, 60, 111, 137, 154,
　176; in Arkansas, 19, 25; in
　Mississippi, 98
disturbing the peace, 88, 89
domestic service, 7–8, 81, 85–86, 87
Donaghey, George Washington, 40, 42
Donahue, Dan, 163
Douglas, Beatrice, 89, 91
Douglass, Frederick, 58–59

Draper, Olivia, 125–26, 131
Driver, J. W., 43
Du Bois, W. E. B., 97–98, 110–11, 171
Dubisson brothers, 92
Dudley, R. H., 77
Dudley Lake Township, AR, 36
Dunbar, Paul Lawrence, 173
Durant, MS, 20–21
Durham (of West Point, AR), 33

Earle, AR, 177
Eastland, James O., 154
Economic Opportunity Act, 156–57
El Paso, TX, 72–73
Elaine, AR, 178
Elaine Massacre (1919), 3, 85, 168–69,
    169–70; in court, 47, 62, 70; com-
    pared to Henry Lowery lynching,
    65–66, 77
Empire of Cotton (Beckert), 67–66
Employment Security Division, 129
Estes, Jim, 90
Eubanks, Rollie, 153
"Evil in the Delta" (Andrews with
    Honey), 167, 179

F. W. Tucker & Co., 29
Fallis, R. R., 49
Farm Security Administration, 119
Farmers' Alliance. See Colored Farmers'
    Alliance; National Farmers'
    Alliance; Southern Farmers'
    Alliance
Farmers' Union, 26, 36–39, 44, 127.
    See also Arkansas Farmers'
    Union; Colored Farmers' Union;
    Jackson County Farmers' Union;
    Marmaduke Farmers' Union;
    Randolph County Farmers' Union
Faubus, Orval, 129, 138
Federal Law and Southern Order
    (Belknap), 134
Federation of Southern Cooperatives,
    161–62
Ferguson, Jim, 44
Fiddyment, J. C., 36

Field Foundation, 154
Fifteenth Amendment, 57, 60. See also
    Reconstruction Amendments
Finch, AR, 43
Fisher, C. F., 34
Flood Control Act of 1928, 104, 106.
    See also levee construction
Flood of 1927, 8–9, 95–96, 98
Flood Relief Committee. See Red Cross
Flower, Christopher, 145
Flower, Clare, 145
Flower, Tom, 145
Foner, Laura, 131–32
Forrest, Alberta, 87
Forrest City, AR, 131, 139–40, 147–48, 172
Fort Smith Times, 39
Fourteenth Amendment, 55, 56–57,
    60. See also Reconstruction
    Amendments
Frank, J. F., 23–24
Freedom Information Service (FIS),
    152–53
Freedom Summer of 1964, 134
Freeman, Chester, 45–46
Fulbright, J. William, 116, 118–19, 128
Fuller, J. W., 44

Gaines, Donnell, 141
Gaines, Roy, 141
Galloway, Dwight, 143–44
gambling, 88, 89
Garrett, DeWitt, 45–46
Garrett-Peltier, Heidi, 163
Garvey, Marcus, 171. See also Universal
    Negro Improvement Association
Garvey clubs, 78–79. See also Universal
    Negro Improvement Association
Gathings, E. C. "Took," 129
George, Milton, 17
Gerow, Rice, 33–34
Gill, Hugh, 18
Gillam, Isaac T., 16
Gillespie, J. T., 86
Gillett, AR, 43
Glenwood, AR, 35
Going, J. C., 52
Gooden, James, 100–101

Goodwin, AR, 143
Gordon, H. Y., 124–25
Gore, T. P., 98
Gould, James, 36
Gould Citizens' Association, 124
Grady, AR, 127
Grady, F. E., 144
Granberry, George, Jr., 41
Grange. *See* National Grange of the
    Order of the Patrons of Husbandry
Gray, Sam, 33
Great Depression, 10–11, 96, 110, 113, 174
Great Migration, 121, 125, 137, 171
Great Society, 10, 161. *See also* War on
    Poverty
Green, Curtis, 102, 103
Greenback Party, 15–16
Greene County, AR, 37, 43. *See also*
    Finch, AR; Paragould, AR
Greenville, MS, 8, 99–101, 106
Greenwood, MS, 102
Greer, Ezra, 177
Greer, Jesse, 71, 73–74, 76
Grenada County, MS, 20. *See also*
    Leflore, MS
Griffin, Hattie, 88
Gross, Kali Nicole, 87, 93
gubernatorial election of 1966,
    Arkansas, 138–39
Gurdon, AR, 90

Hackney's Landing, AR, 24
Haley, Sarah, 82
Hall, Jacquelyn Dowd, 135–36
Hamilton, Charles, 155
Hampton, Ida Mae, 145, 147
Hanchard, Michael G., 48
Handcox, John, 10–11, 172–79
Hard-Hitting Songs for Hard-Hit People
    (Lomax, Seeger, and Guthrie), 175
Harding, Vincent, 97
Harlan, John Marshall, 59, 60
Harrigan, Anthony, 156
Harris, Josephine. *See* Anderson,
    Dorothy
Harrison, Byron, 104
Harrison, Cora, 87

Hartman, Saidiya, 88, 90
Hattiesburg, MS, 157
Haynes, Willie, 88–89
Hazen, AR, 142–43, 144–45
Head Start, 156, 157, 158
Helena, AR, 14, 33, 85, 131
Helena Weekly World, 34–35
Henderson, Ernestine, 125–26
Hickory Ridge, AR, 46
Hill, Dorsey Melvin, II, 140
Hill, Karlos K., 66, 70, 76
Hodges, Reuben, 52–53, 56, 62–63
Hodges v. United States (1906), 6–7, 32,
    47, 55–56
Holley, Don, 79
Holmes, Oliver Wendell, Jr., 60–61
Holmes, William F., 21, 23–24, 30, 39–40
Holmes County, MS, 157. *See also*
    Durant, MS
Hoover, Herbert, 8, 95–96, 105–6, 110–11
Horton, Dee, 81–82
Hot Springs, AR, 17
Houston Daily Post, 22
Hudspeth, Bob, 33–34
Hughes, Simon, 18, 19, 29
Humphrey, Richard M., 13, 20–23
Hunter, AR, 35

incarceration, 77; of Black women,
    83–89. *See also* prisons
Industrial Workers of the World, 26
Invaders, 133, 139–40

J. W. Noble Contractor, 107
Jackson, Ben, 146
Jackson County Farmers' Union,
    38–39, 44
James, Wilber T. C., 140
Jefferson County, AR, 35–36, 41, 81–82
Jenkins, Alice, 86
Jenkins, Jenny, 77–78
Jenkins, Morris, 77–78
Jenkins, S. A., 33
Jett, Babe, 33
Jett, Will, 32–33
Jewish people, 52, 153

Jim Crow, 9, 14, 19, 61, 83, 93, 112, 131
Johnson, Cleveland, 140
Johnson, James D., 138–39
Johnson, James Weldon, 105–6
Johnson, Lyndon B., 159, 161
Johnson, R. E. L., 45–46
Johnson, Walter, 45–46, 77–78
Johnson, Willie Lee, 90
Johnson County, AR, 16
Johnston, Oscar, 102–3
Jones, Daniel Webster, 36
Jones, Early, 24
Jones, John, 101
Jones, Mit, 24
Jones, Scipio, 171

Karlan, Pamela, 50
Kavanaugh, John, 33–34
Kentucky, 39
Kincade, Everett, 46
Kindle, James, 90
King, Coretta Scott, 155, 160–61
King, Ed, 176
King, Martin Luther, Jr., 139, 169
Kingston, V. S., 42
Kit Karson and Band, 42
Knights of Labor, 17–19, 20–22,
    24–25, 26–27
Knights of Pythias, 71
Knollenberg, Fred C., 70, 73
Knox, Philander C., 50
Krugler, David F., 168
Ku Klux Klan: first iteration of
    (1860s–1870s), 15; second iteration
    of (1910s–1930s), 136, 171, 176; third
    iteration of (1950s–1970s) 152,
    159–60

Lacey, Fred, 158
LaFargue, E. B., 43
LaGrange, AR, 21
laissez-faire constitutionalism, 7, 50–51,
    59–61, 63
Lake City, AR, 36–37
Lancaster, Guy, 25

Laster, Garra A., 85
Lawrence County, AR, 29. See also
    Clover Bend, AR; Walnut Ridge, AR
Lee, John, 95
Lee County, AR, 6, 13–14, 21, 23–24,
    36. See also LaGrange, AR;
    Marianna, AR
Leflore, MS, 20–21
Leflore County (MS) Massacre, 21
LeFlouria, Talitha, 83, 84, 89
Leggett, Verbon, 41
levee construction, 104, 106-110
Lincoln County, AR, 9, 115–32
Lincoln County Agricultural Planning
    Board, 120
Lincoln County Civic Association, 124
Little, A. G., 39–40, 62
Little Rock, AR, 16, 24–25, 91, 147, 148;
    crime in, 85, 86, 88, 89, 92; prisoner
    transportation to, 70, 73–74, 78
Little Rock Central High School,
    desegregation of, 138
Little Rock Police, 147
Lochner v. New York (1905), 50–51,
    60–61
"long" Civil Rights Movement, 135–36
Lonoke, AR, 35–36
Lonoke County, AR, 35–36, 41, 42, 46.
    See also Lonoke, AR
Lonoke County Club, 35–36
Louisiana, 17, 106, 158, 159
Louisiana Weekly, 158
Lowe, G. W., 21
Lowery, Henry, 70–71; lynching of, 7,
    65–66, 71–75, 173
Lowndes County, AL, 158
Lowry, Robert, 21
lumber mills, 6, 41, 42, 49–50, 51, 53,
    60–61, 62–63
lynching, 6–7, 13, 19, 29, 30, 31–32, 40,
    65–66, 71–75, 151, 170, 173. See also
    Lowery, Henry
Lyons, Hard, 42

Magnolia, MS, 70–71
Malone, W. R., 46

Marianna, AR, 23–24
Marion, AR, 77
Marmaduke Farmers' Union, 37
Marshall, Suzanne, 39
Martin, H. A., 34
Matthews, G. I., 129–30
Mayersville, MS, 106–7
McCall, Robert, 42
McClure, Nannie, 43
McDowell, Torressia Dancler,
    81–82
McGraw, Mable, 88–89
McKinney, Wash, 53, 56
McMillen, Neil, 98
McRae, Thomas, 45–46, 70, 73–75,
    75–76, 81
mechanization of agriculture, 10, 79,
    120–21, 125, 137, 151–52, 178
Memphis, TN, 104, 148, 177
Memphis Press, 77–78
Meredith, James, 133
Merriman, G. W., 18
Mexican labor, 115–32
Mexican Labor Bill, 127–29
military funding, 10, 152, 160–62, 164,
    165–66
Miller, Frank, 90
Miller, Tom, 23–24
Milling, A. W., 44
Millington, TN, 75
Mississippi Board of Health, 102
Mississippi Constitutional Convention
    of 1890, 98
Mississippi County, AR, 122–23; Henry
    Lowery lynching, 7, 65–66, 69–70,
    77, nightriding in, 43, 47–48, 62.
    See also Nodena Landing, AR;
    Blytheville, AR; Osceola, AR
Mississippi Freedom Democratic Party
    (MFDP), 159
Mississippi National Guard, 21, 102, 103
"Mississippi Slavery in 1933" (Wilkins),
    107–9
Mitchell, Brian K., 47
Moffatt, OK, 26
Monroe County, AR, 35, 36. *See also*
    Brinkley, AR

Montgomery, AL, 160
Monticellonian, 43
Moon, William, 45–46
Moore v. Dempsey (1923), 171
Morgan, W. Scott, 16–17
Mosley, James, 100–111
Moss, Pearline, 85
Myersville, MS. *See* Mayersville, MS

Nance, George, 42
Natchez Dailey Courier, 97
Nation, The, 66, 70
National Agricultural Workers
    Union, 96
National Association for the
    Advancement of Colored People
    (NAACP), 73, 147, 153, 157, 171;
    and Flood of 1927, 8–9, 95–97, 102,
    103–7, 109–10; and Henry Lowery
    lynching, 7, 66–67, 74, 76
National Association of Colored
    Women, 92
National Council of Churches (NCC),
    9, 115–18, 125–26, 130–31
National Farm Labor Union, 122
National Farmers' Alliance, 17
National Farmers' Union. *See* Farmers'
    Union
National Grange of the Order of the
    Patrons of Husbandry, 16
National Recovery Administration,
    111, 112–13
National Urban League, 96, 138
Neff, Pat Morris, 70
neoliberalism, 117, 132
Nero, Theogen, 158
New Deal, 8–9, 79, 109–13, 137; short-
    comings of, 96–97, 112–13
New York Herald, 44
New York Times, 148
Newport, AR, 89–90
1919, the Year of Racial Violence
    (Krugler), 168
Nixon, Lawrence, 73
Nixon, Richard, 161–62
Nodena Landing, AR, 66, 75, 173

North Little Rock, AR, 90, 145–47
North Little Rock Police, 147

O'Brien, Gail Williams, 134–35, 137, 149
O'Rourke, Joe, 145–46
Office of Economic Opportunity
    (OEO), 155–56, 160
Oklahoma, 25
*One with Others [a little book of her
    days]* (Wright), 133
Orr, Mott, 77–78
Osceola, AR, 43
Osceola Times, 33–34, 75

Palestine, TX, 23
Paragould, AR, 37
Patterson, Ben, 23–24
Patterson, Robert B., 156
Peckham, Rufus, 60
Pendleton, Millie, 87
peonage, 4, 98, 105, 152, 173–74.
    See also plantation agriculture
People's Party, 25, 38
Percy, William A., 100
Peters, Nannie Clark, 100
Phillips County, AR, 34–35, 47, 69, 138,
    168–69; labor organizing in, 14, 21,
    24. *See also* Elaine, AR; Helena, AR
Phillips, Mark, 42
Phillips County Circuit Court, 34
Philpot, C. Mason, 36
Pickens, William, 66–67, 70
Pickett, O. W., 146, 147
Pielstick, Don, 126, 127, 130
Pierce, Michael, 177
Pindall, Xenophon Overton, 39
Pine Bluff, AR, 36, 87, 88, 118, 123
Pine Bluff Daily Graphic, 46
Pinkston, Benny, 147
Pittsburgh Courier, 96, 98, 99
plantation agriculture, 3, 7, 65–71, 75–77,
    170, 176, 178; bracero program, 116,
    118–19, 122–24, 125–26; Flood of
    1927, 8, 98–99, 102–4; labor orga-
    nizing for, 14, 17–19, 23, 26. *See also*

cotton agriculture; mechanization
    of agriculture; peonage
"Planter and the Sharecropper, The"
    (Handcox), 175
Plessy v. Ferguson (1896), 53–54, 59
Plumerville, AR, 19
Poinsett County, AR, 116, 122, 174;
    nightriding in, 42, 49–50, 51, 62–63
policing, 36, 49, 73, 158–59, 168; and
    women, 85, 86, 88–92; and labor
    conscription, 100–101, 119; reliance
    on, 134, 135, 138, 149
poll tax, 25, 123–124, 127
Poor People's Campaign, 139, 155, 160
Pope, James Gray, 58
Populist Party. *See* People's Party
Postel, Charles, 20, 22, 24
Prairie County, AR, 16, 17. *See also*
    Hazen, AR
presidential election of 1928, 105–6,
    110–11
Price, Fannie, 87
prisons, 46, 78, 83–84, 86, 146, 171.
    See also Arkansas State Farm for
    Women; Cummins Prison Farm;
    Tucker Prison Farm; reformatories
Progressive Farmers and Household
    Union of American, 3, 27, 65–66,
    85, 168
Progressive Women Voters Association
    of Lincoln County, 124
prostitution, 90–91
public health, 91–92
Public Works Administration, 110, 112
Pulaski County, AR, 5, 17–18, 26–27, 38,
    90. *See also* Camp Pike, AR
Pulaski County jail, 86–87
Pulaski County sheriff, 147

R. T. Clark Company, 106–7
railroads: strike of 1886, 18; travel by,
    73–74, 75, 102
Randolph, A. Philip, 137
Randolph County Farmers' Union, 39
rape, 82, 90
Rast, Joe, 33

Rast, John, 33
Ratton, Sam S., 41
Reagan, Ronald, 10, 162–63
Reconstruction, 14–15, 29, 53, 59, 83, 97, 98. *See also* Third Recon-struction Act
Reconstruction Amendments, 53–54, 58–59
Red Cross, 95–96, 99–100, 103, 110–11
Red River, 15
Red Summer of 1919, 10, 136, 169, 178
Redditt, John, 77–78
reformatories, 92–93
Reidman, J., 41
religion, 108–9, 116, 173
Republican Party, 163, 169; African American support, 5, 13–14, 15, 138–39; and election of 1928, 105–6, 110–11
Rexer, Frank, 41
Rice, John, 41
Richardson, Pearl, 89
Ritchie, E. H., 18
Robertson, Ashton P., 161
Rockefeller, Winthrop, 138–39, 139–40, 142, 148, 149
Rodgers, Anna, 87
Rodgers, H. P., 23–24
Rogers, Mark, 43
Roosevelt, Franklin D., 106, 110–11, 112–13, 137
Rotenberry, Burl C., 85, 91, 92
Rustin, Bayard, 135

Saline County, AR, 38. *See also,* Benton, AR
Sardis, MS, 74
Savoy, Preston, 158
sawmills. *See* lumber mills
Schuyler, George, 107–9
Scott, Harold, 142
Screeton, Jerry J., 142–43, 144–45
Sebastian County, AR, 25
Selective Service Act of 1917, 26
Selma Inter-Religious Project, 158

Separate Coach Law of 1891, 19, 25
September 11, 2001, attack on, 164
Sessions, Laura, 86–87
sexually transmitted diseases, 91–92
Shapiro, Herbert, 134
sharecroppers, 65–69, 112–13, 115, 173–74; in labor unions, 22, 26–27, 29; intimidation by, 39, 45, 47–48; intimidation of, 6, 7, 32, 36–37, 51, 62, 119
Sharecropper's Voice, The, 175
sharecropping, demise of, 9, 79, 123–24, 130, 137, 151–52
Shaw, Isaac, 174
Shriver, Sargent, 160
Sifton, Paul, 127–29, 132
Simmons, Matt, 175
Simpson, Giles, 43
Singfield, Bryant, 14
Slaughter, Tom, 46
Slaughter-House Cases (1873), 54–55
slave resistance, 97
slavery, 54–56, 57–58, 63, 97
Smith, Al, 105–6
Smith, Estelle, 88
Smith, Frank, 38
Smith, John L., 36
Smith, Roşie, 113
Smith, Ryan Anthony, 82
Smith, W. F., 89
Smith v. Allwright (1944), 124
Snell, R. B., 38
Socialist Party of America, 26
soldiers, 10, 85, 90–91, 170
Sons of the Agricultural Star, 17
Southern Christian Leadership Conference (SCLC), 139
Southern Farmers' Alliance, 19–20, 24–25; merger with Agricultural Wheel, 21
Southern Tenant Farmers' Union, 47–48, 96, 174–76
Sparks, E. N., 85
Spencer, Robyn, 102
Spivak, John Louis, 103
St. Helena Parish, LA, 158
St. Frances County, AR, 21, 33–34. *See*

also Forrest City, AR; Goodwin, AR; Wheatley, AR
St. Francis River, 173–74
Stanley, Seth P., 159
Stennis, John, 161
Stith, George, 122, 124
Stockley, Grif, 47
Stone, Ed, 127–28, 129
Story, Bob, 46
Streeter, GA, 88
strikes, 13, 18–24, 26–27, 47–48, 147, 168, 170, 174, 175
Student Nonviolent Coordinating Committee (SNCC), 130, 131–32, 157, 176
Sumrall, John, 160
Sunflower County, MS, 153–54
surveillance, 102–3
Sutton, Ozell, 143
Swafford, Jesse, 43

Tate Plantation, 5, 18
Taylor, Linda, 162
Tennessee, 39, 40, 62
Tennyson, Mildred, 147
Terrorism, 31, 40
Texas, 20, 22, 23, 26, 72–73
Thibodaux (LA) Massacre, 17
Third Reconstruction Act of 1867, 15
Thirteenth Amendment. *See* Reconstruction Amendments
Thomas, Jennie, 92
Thomas, John, Jr., 159
Thomas, Matt, 42
Thompson, Sam. *See* Lowery, Henry
Thompson, William Hale, 104
Thurmond, Strom, 156
Tomson, Dan Fraser, 17–18, 27
Townsend, Frank, 146
Trieber, Jacob, 52
Trump, Donald, 169
Tucker, R. D., 38
Tucker Prison Farm, AR, 46, 81–82
Tudor, W. A., 140
Tulsa (OK) Massacre of 1921, 169, 171
Tuohey, Matilda, 142–43

Turner, Bart, 14
Tyronza, AR, 175

U.S. Highway 70, 140–47
Underwood, Felix J., 102
Union Labor Party, 19, 21, 25, 30
Union League, 15
United Mine Workers of America (UMWA), 25
United Automobile Workers (UAW), 116–17
United States Army, 14, 139, 169
United States Corps of Engineers, 95, 109
United States Department of Agriculture, 121
United States Department of Health, Education, and Welfare, 163
United States Department of Justice, 159
United States House of Representatives, 19, 129
United States Senate, 107, 122, 124; Committee on Labor and Public Welfare, 159; Subcommittee on Employment, Manpower, and Poverty, 154
United States Supreme Court, 7, 32, 50–56, 61–63, 66, 73, 124, 171
United States v. Cruikshank (1876) 54–55
United States v. Maples (1903), 51–53
United States v. Morris (1903), 6–7, 51–53
United States v. Waddell (1884), 55
United States War Department, 109, 111
Universal Negro Improvement Association, 171. *See also* Garvey clubs
Urban League. *See* National Urban League

vagrancy laws, 69, 88, 100
Vicksburg, MS, 98
Vietnam War, 152, 160–62

Vittitow, Peggy, 141, 143
voter mobilization, 14–16, 124, 127, 157

Wagner, Robert, 107
Waites, Alex, 153
Waldrep, Christopher, 29, 39
walk against fear, 9, 139–47
Walnut Ridge, AR, 42
War on Poverty, 152, 155–56, 157, 160–63, 163–64. *See also* Great Society; anti-poverty programs
Washington Human Rights Project, 154
Washington Bee, 20–21
Watson, Henry, 33–34
Watson, Lance, 9, 133, 139–40, 140–42, 144, 147–48
Weber, Del, 102
Weightman, Philip, 126–27, 129, 130, 132
Weise, Julie, 117, 131–32
welfare, 154, 156, 162–63
Wells-Barnett, Ida B., 101–2, 171
Weona Land Company, 42
West Memphis, AR, 140
West Point, AR, 33
West Point, MS, 159
Whayne, Jeannie M., 31, 47
Wheatley, AR, 144
Wheeler, Raymond, 153, 154
Whipple, John W., 41
Whipple, William G., 6–7, 50, 51, 61
White, Louis, 32–33
White, S. M., 39
White, Walter, 8–9, 66, 109, 111; election of 1928, 105–6; and Herbert Hoover, 95–96, 110
White Chapel, AR, 49
White Citizens' Councils, 152; in Arkansas, 138, 143

White County, AR, 33, 44. *See also* West Point, AR
White Violence and Black Response (Shapiro), 134
Whitehall, AR, 49–50, 51
Wilkins, Roy, 8–9, 96, 107–9
Williams, Barbara, 163
Williams, John, 77–78
Williams, Kidada E., 30
Williams, Lee, 140
Williams, Matilda, 141, 145
Williams, Minnie, 86
Williamson, C. O. "Maybelle," 72
Wilmington (NC) Massacre of 1898, 169
Wilson, R. E. Lee, 71–72, 76–77
Wilson, R. E. Lee, Jr., 76
Wine, "Sweet" Willie. *See* Watson, Lance
Winnifred, William, 37
Wood, Fenlon, 43
Woodruff, B. F., 42
Woodruff, George, 42
Woodruff County, AR, 22, 35, 67. *See also* Hunter, AR
Woods, William, 5
Working Class Union, 26–27
World War I, 10, 170, 172
World War II, 135, 137, 153
Worthen, Robert, 18
Wright, C. D., 133

Yahweh, Suhkara A. *See* Watson, Lance
Yell County, AR, 38
Young, Gene, 147
Young, Henry, 33–34

Zippert, John, 158